WarFair4: The Day The Markets stood *still...Into The Abyss... Global Citizen.*

M.Stow

ISBN 19: 9781087432526

2017 Copyright M.Stow

Tunisia 17th December 2010: According to friends and family, local police officers had allegedly targeted and mistreated Bouazizi for years, including during his childhood, regularly confiscating his small wheelbarrow of produce; but Bouazizi had no other way to make a living, so He continued to work as a street vendor.

Around 10 p.m. on 16 December 2010, Bouazizi had contracted approximately 450 dinar in debt to buy the produce to sell the following day. On the morning of 17 December, Bouazizi started his workday at 8 a.m. Just after 10:30 a.m., the police began harassing him again, ostensibly because He did not have a vendor's permit.

Bouazizi did not have the funds to bribe police officials to allow his street vending to continue. Bouazizi, angered by the confrontation, went to the governor's office to complain and to ask for his scales back.

The governor refused to see or listen to him. Bouazizi then acquired a can of gasoline from a nearby gas station and returned to the governor's office. While standing in the middle of traffic, he shouted,

"How do you expect me to make a living?"

Bouazizi then doused himself with the gasoline and set himself alight with a match at 11:30 a.m. local time, less than an hour after the altercation.

Part One: WarFair4: Rogue-Citizen: The Day The Market Stood Still…

1. **The Banker and the Clerk.**

The *I*-nvestment Merchant-Banker sat-back and glanced across at The *Admin.i-strative* Accounts-Clerk. They sat in opposite seats-a fixed-table between them, travelling on this same-train 2nd-Class carriage, same-time, same-carriage for The-Clerk the *same*-seat if that or any other was to be had amongst the everyday commuters seated *and a few standing today and as usually crammed-in each weekday early-morning* into The-Capital: *Financial*-City.

For The-Banker: *this* day too-early for the usual First Class re-servation today, with or *without* waiter or waitress-served breakfast, or a free-morning Newspaper *only those freely given-away* and piled-up in The Station Forecourt to be taken-away. That had to be paid-for, anyway, by publicising the latest events and product models and up-dated versions.

The most *reasonably*-priced, sold alongside copies of The Big Issue sold-on by homeless-people dis-advantaged and in Metropolis' around The World:

No such thing as a free-lunch the-Banker reasoned: i*n First-Class The Financial-Newspaper paid-for anyway by The Railway Company ticket-seated and breakfasted with The-Financial Newspaper at massively discounted Investment-Corporation. Market Business-Rate or Cost-Price freely as-Advertising as encouraging in-someway Paid-For and as all for: Financial Returns and the Power to* I*nfluence: Others' Economic and Political Campaign(s)…u*sing Political-Power to enrich and own People Family and Business-Associate(s):

The Financial Newspaper: could be easily afforded, anyway. From today's loss-leader, tomorrow's and everyday's winner paid-for upfront, from: The Station-Kiosk: The Newspapers' Corp-0-rate-In-vestment: borrowed on perma-credit: staff-costs and overhead(s) never paid-off entirely wealth effectively permanently in-debted bankrupted on- continuing steady-sales to be re-couped: shorted for the long-term in-*vestment short-term gains…achieved...everyday off-line…on-line.*

Shareholders and Company Corporation(s): Owner(s): *paid-back* to: in-vest *again* in-debted:

*Credit.*ed: next days' shop copy readied for repeat-status quoted confidence asking market-price bid-and-volume traded, as they were: before: The War.

2. The *Financial* Newspaper.

Today, The Newspaper: not given-away with the extortionately and exclusively permissive over-priced Rail-Pass this day into The City:

The Stock-Exchanges and Financial-Markets. The Annual-Executive Rail-Ticket: *paid-for*, whether used or-not. This day the first Train out and apparently only Standard-Class in sub-ordination available. A single First-Class carriage was filled-up quickly by anyone who had a ticket and *conceivably some who did-not:* there were no-tickets being checked *anyway* apparently the barriers left-open and *inviting all-comers.*

For The-Banker: for another-time that morning, something mildly, now-seconded and *markedly* unusual: the earlier, when: The Radio Alarm-Clock: had switched-on. Routinely with the early-morning fishing, farming, road, and rail, airline and shipping news, of arrivals and departures, delays and speculative *forecasts* as determined weather-reports local and global political-economic, media-news with the previous-nights' *closing…with The Stock*-Market(s) Prices from around The-World: *there had been developments, overnight, that needed attending-to…*

From the emptying platform: The-Banker and The-Clerk boarded The Train: together, more or less equal. The-Clerk with a free newspaper, and headphones plugged-in to a Mobile Media-Centre.

The-Banker for the first time in a long-while with a bought-copy of: The *Financial*-Newspaper from The Station-Kiosk and from The Trains' limited refreshments-trolley, a scalding boiling cup of tea from the hot water cauldron, paid-for, tapped, by card.

The-Banker: having taken the first seat-available in the nearest Standard-Class compartment available, coupled with a foul-stench reeking drain-leaking latrine *literally* retching between the brown and grey-green patterned seats.

Along the narrow aisleway The CEO-Banker waving The Government Newspaper ahead *as if to clear-the-air:* un-*wave*ring, when shunted across by the next-passenger inline to the only *vacant* window-seat, glanced across-to and sat sedentarily parked and leaned-forward: The-Table: between them, and asked of The-Clerk, already sat down-opposite:

'So what do you make of it all, then?'

'I don't know what to make of IT, but I expect I will find out soon enough, don't you?'

'So what do you make of IT all, then?' again, i*n the customary easy clear voice of one born with the interrogative confidence of swift appraisal…*

*A*s to The-Clerk as to The-Banker as to The First-Class ticket held-out, and The Newspaper Headline: shaken-out: as to: *the whole-carriage and The World beyond* to: The City, and the next.

And, the picture that could now be viewed, in print, and on-line, as to what was initially referred to, and the 'IT'?' that too, was soon made obvious. As if spoken to self then: that *sarcastic* thought, or was it sardonic?

Out-lined *out-loud, headline read:*

Markets in Turmoil!

photographed scene screen elsewhere de-picting:

'Market Closed.'

sounded all looked, sounded, differently.

As if someone-else had spoken the words instead. As a gauntlet thrown-down to be picked-up. Only as instantly-*realised* now, and as at the time-of-speaking, and that short-moment-later as-spoken now irritatingly *intimating* only-now at the-*gamble* seemingly already *commit*ted-to.

The *Uncertainty Factor in de-fence of, de-fiance of:*

<Project-*Fear*…resilience and stronger with Greater-Risk:

>N>nnn…*known:* un-*fearful: beyond*-Brave…*stupid.*

Now, as such a private yet communally and now seemingly *un*shared shared-venture: this *seemingly*-reasonable; or unreasonably as yet un-priced as yet only a projected proposal.

There would be a Price though and a *Cost-* too:

'Your Price?'

'Yours?'

'Costing(s)?'

'Debts. Credit in the Bank? Safe and Secure? De-Reg.(s) and increased slider on public-spending cut(s): Lower-Tax€(s):'

'If: The Price is Right...' *then as if both benevolence-educating and holding-back relevant secrets...*

'Purchase-price and re-sale onward that's all you need to know.'*...as yet, an un-bidden offer in-prospect. To follow-up the seemingly automatically-accepted challenge, as yet to be fully realised: prospecting-Approach?* Assessment-Presentation? The-Close?

Then:

'Where are you at there?' intimating at both newspaper and lap-top computer hand-held device: place and time that evening before, and now:

'Product?'

'WarFair4.'

'WarFare4?'

'Now?'

'Irrelevant.'

'O.K. Customer? Subscriber?' *regular: cash or bitcoin-payment rent for your basic (i)nformation: parked.*

3. They.

'It's like living in a rabbit hutch' She often said metaphorically and He replied with a shrug. *Nothing to say in reply. It was; and it would take long enough to pay for. Eight-floors up. Looking over the street below, now starting to become busy with traffic. They had lived with his parents for a time, and then after they were married in a small rented flat in The City, before they needed to afford somewhere to live together, and to bring-up their two small children. They had both saved, and with some financial help from a relative (deceased) they had managed to get this place. When the housing market was 'buoyant' and home loan Home-Buyer's Mort-Gages easy to get if you were in Work.*

The home was bought with a loan, a promissory note, deposited and co-lateraled together with the home itself. They were afloat, both worked to pay-off The Loan, which although it was supposed to reduce each year, did not seem ever to keep up with prices and pay. The loan would anyway be paid-off, many times over, if they were ever to pay off the debt. If this place was ever to become their own. If they managed to keep paying-off with interest for 'the shelter from the storm', as they called it, from everyday life.

A life or home that they did not now own, and may not ever actually own, if foreclosed to sell-back at Market Price the difference between the selling and originally bought price along with the interest paid, they would have lost to The Mortgage Company crediting Bank as landlord and financial overlord. No recourse, and be homeless.

On The Street. Refugees. Like wartime. Leave the home. Return to parents, and over-crowding as before or with friends similarly fixed. Their Home, such as it was theirs, re-possessed. Their home repossessed; their lives dis-possessed re-possessed...

Their-Home: a two-bedroom cabin apartment She thought of: *kitchen-lounge, bathroom and toilet, and tiny balcony between them, and the sky above, and onto the world below.*

Each day, each month, and each successive year into the unthinkable future; no-deposit but interest-only nearly two-thirds every month of what they both earned. She did the household accounts, and She knew. Of every week, every month, every year, every decade...two thirds of two lifetimes...the Loan would have been paid for several times over by the time and if ever it became theirs or The Children's; and perhaps even their Grandchildren's...paid-for with extortionate charges and zero-security...but that is the nature of the human animal, is it not?

To do over; and be done over again and again? She thought: *wanting more and more for less and less and prepared to do anything for it. Break the rules...even murder, in effect? A walking nightmare, as if a daydream* of violent retribution or suicidal; and in the quiet mind wandering moment of pillared door, a room, a table, *a bed let go and a bed sheet left behind ready to be buried with as they did in the olden times, shrouded* as now by window curtains *thinly* pulled-back.

Each worked to Pay-Off the loan on the house, and to pay for food and bills and extras, clothes, and nights out, occasionally. Maybe once a month, or not at all. Then He had been laid-off work at The Bakery: three-day-week, and three days' wages. The mortgage was renegotiated, and they continued struggling to pay-off the loan and other loans, credited and debited from what they both earned together for the basics of life. There was never an issue of who should earn more and be the main-breadwinner, and who would do the most caring of each other and the children: the unpaid responsibilities shared around The 'House'; and then: # *Civil-War: World of Work and Good-Times: with Other Friends and Family out-there in-here: Manly Madly Maidenly* made to-do.

They were equal, without even having to think about it or confront societies' and other's false expectations of gender and family. They were equal, and supported each other's frail and fragile egos with a natural equanimity.

Respectful, and loving, each contributing their best and differently according to their means, to make the whole: It's not all doom and gloom She did often think, and He tried not to think on it. *The homely claustrophobia only had to be relieved by going out.*

To the Cinema, to a Bar or Restaurant. But that was not very often. Now there were children as well.

Seldom did extras make their mark. Clothes bought carefully a piece at a time replacement rather than extravagance. The cupboards filled with groceries, and emptied by the time the next weeks shopping recipes for the week... mental-list...needed as wanted, and the next weeks earnings spent...

4. She.

She was awake first this morning, and She got up from the bed on which He still lay awake but not yet awake enough to leave its night-time warmth. She went through to the next room. The bedroom led across the narrow passage to the living room which led directly to the tiny gallery kitchen and balcony on one side and the door to the front room on the other. Except it wasn't the *front*-room, exactly; the 'front-room' of her childhood; *playing on the street and door directly to the matted rugged smell of cooking from the stone wall white-washed country kitchen upstairs one room on the gallery landing for the grand-parents to retire early in the evening, the loft room alongside the attic hay-store grain store. Foods prepared early next day for daily breads baked and dry-feed for the yard chicks and chickens and field stock, milk and meat and warm- clothing made and mended at home.*

Along The River Lands' fish. An outside closet-room to flush away into the ground to fertilise with a zinc-metal bucket of water into the slurry sump She thought *where you could hear it 'slurry' all the way down; and then to wash-out and replace from the outside tap pumped-up from the well re-filling the bucket and the decorated fired china clay bowl for washing, ready for the next use.*

At bedtime: The Children first, then: The Adults. Parents Aunts and Uncles and many cousins ...

Bagged bog-hare and rabid-rabbit rabid sickly and sick. Health problems and insecurity of work and market demands or with-work under-paid pay or under-staffed hard labour then without work only the rats and mice nested runs beetles and cockroach kept away by the epi-genetically domesticated cats and dogs that no-one owned, foxes and vixens. All fed and looked-after, ate, fed-on, and eaten like goat and chicken, for life, or not: as a last re-sort; and there were horses at the local stables, to ride at week-ends and holidays. Each month by cart, then by car or truck into The Market Town for food supplies and treats for The Children with whatever they had to sell, and buy.

Their Whole World: a living market place of work and play, and sell and pay like a circle, or cycle, or exciting un-predictable, circus, of never-ending life. Now great enclosed superstores and supermarkets and super-factory outlet superwarehouse parked.

Where goods are now transported She thought of: *to and from, by railway train and motor vehicle, by great tanker lorries and container freight ship and aircraft to and from The Docks at The City Harbour hub and Airport humming near distantly away, remotely yet directing everyday life everywhere.*

With Freight-Cargo for the Factory Workshops and Retail Markets and customers for: Business or mostly since this no longer required face-face contact anymore, or at least this now through the multiple screens established around workplaces and homes. Holiday-makers and Traveller-Tourist Hotel(s). With the affordable flight to get away from it all: necessary, a change, a necessary move, once in a while, not every year but to visit family here and there and elsewhere, or else you'd go stir-crazy; do a night-time flit, leave the rent, the mortgage, unpaid. Only to keep on fighting another day, for the bargain, cheapest within budget, to get through the next day; and the day after that.

*When debts and fines and fees could not be paid, the debt collector, bailiffs, the selling-off of the personal-possessions, and then the person...*the lap-top personal-computer on sleep and awakened placed on the table booted-up and She blogged instantaneously her thoughts:

'We all need a Roof over our heads and put Food on the Table! How?!'

Without any other word or contextual continuity that did not remain obvious or evitable to this early morning. *Everyone, and anyone in the same and similar circumstances...*getting the hastily tapped-out message twittering snap chatted briefly and her thought continued in the context of the mindful moment *and that which we all have to pay extortionately for over and again even when the food is eaten and the crap washed away there remains a nasty stain, a nasty taste. The original wages sweated over, wasted away and the loans ever in negative equity! To who? Them!*

Looking-up, and down again now, not in dejection, but circumspection against ever apparent possible failure, with optimism, with perfectibility warning, waning. Below the window, only mechanised traffic building-up, soon into a busy rush-hour congestion. Cars and buses, bicycles, motorbike and motorised delivery truck *from here, and there only another view of the same. From two-sides; and every all sides...*the bedrooms along the passage corridor, the sleeping Children slept.

Earlier peeked into *soundless in beautiful dream or dreamless seeming startling worrying death* of self, and other...checked for breathing. Crossing from night into daytime TV, remotely automatically turned on confirmation that *Life Goes On.*

The *Living*-Room: as She entered bore all the chatter and the silence of one who listens, still and safe, cosy and secure. The other rooms took over the emotions and needs: sleep and food, love, and arguments. The central room, the central chamber looked on and awaited eventual almost inevitable, but never certain, or taken for granted, reconciliation and rest. Indulged in social events, noisy chatter and quiet evenings indoors:

'*You have to Work at it Everyday...*' she heard her Mother saying, about marriage, children, and life in general. The furniture was adequate and filled the room. Table, chairs, television, a draw and shelved cabinet standing against a wall, displaying various icons. Family photographs in frames: a portrait of a famous film star, or a print of an oil painting, ornaments, statuettes, figures of worship and of novelty. The furniture the infrastructure, from the livelihoods, and eventually:

'The Roof 0*ver Our Heads...'*

'In over our heads...' heard as originally spoken.

There were opened envelopes and cajoling leaflet advertisement *Kill your debts! Die debts!* She saw and thought of the remarkable coincidence between her vision, and thoughts. Letters and bills for payment, propped up behind a ticking clock. There was a picture postcard from someone-else's holiday, forming a picturesque frontage to hide the stack of demands for reply and payment which lay beyond.

She drew back the curtains and looked out of the window across the balcony, with its un-flowering plants growing in flower-pots. It was still misty outside from the early morning warming; and She gazed over an area where many lived and it seemed to her, this morning, where they too lived out their lives *day to day, week to week. They too thought to themselves* as She looked-out onto the dawn of a gradually opening new day *that the world must have always been this way.*

Soon the television was blaring as usual in the morning, in the main room that was empty again for the moment, and beyond where She was now dressing hurriedly, and He was brushing his hair frantically. There was the noise of children getting washed and dressed, with incessant commentary and conversation to each other, and any other, or just to themselves. To each other as a one-way argument older to younger, incited over some triviality, shouted back in frustration. At that point the only-game-in-town and to be fought-out until one of them is crying, and the other shouting-the-odds; before calm brings e*ven loving fun again* at least while they all got ready for work, school and preschool-nursery. The sound of the kettle screaming on the kitchen cooker and television advertisements conveying to deaf ears, and blind eyes, but perhaps receptive memory:

'The Best in the World',

or:

'Longer-lasting',

or whatever the dubious selling point perhaps to be *unconsciously* recalled later that day at the supermarket. At present they seemed to be of no avail.

Both rushed to get the children to school, and themselves out to work. To earn the pay that would pay the prices at the supermarket later that day:

'Where is my shirt?' He called:

'Where you last put it!' She retorted. As She entered the living room She found Her shoes under a chair, and stopped in front of the television. The networked advertisements ended, and the programme-ramming returned to the main story of the day:

'Today there is no money to pay share dividends, or to buy shares with...'

She flicked up a channel and got texted:

'You? Safe?'

And on: The-Screen:

'Individual and group share prices have collapsed or become so high that they have become worthless. Confidence has collapsed. Debt undiminished price increases have been blamed, increases in pay and pensions have been blamed…'

Increases in interest-rates and profit-levels have all been blamed.

Each of these has pushed share prices ever upwards. As share

prices and shop prices overtake the customer's ability to pay, and

the ability to pay pushes prices-up profit margins re-captured by increases in interest rates on banking and other loans, these have pushed share prices up even further.

Her view passed across the TV screen: *to locked factory-gates, ports and land borders closed to traffic or trade. It did not seem too bad, or even unusual: the television experts and announcers liked to make a big deal out of anything*...She thought: *it was their jobs after all.*

The pictures shifted To-*City Office Buildings that only a few people were being allowed into and then closed-doors' Security* to *The-City Squares and Circus's around The-Town and village-hamlets. City-Centres all over The Globe all The-Streets and Roads and Highways leading there...*

*T*he TV reporter turned away from the camera, and let the scene somewhere else *could be anywhere* speak for itself.

On the kitchen-radio reports followed:

'From: The Stock-Market(s) around The World: London; New-York NASDAQ; Tokyo Nikkei and North Korea-Seoul Taiwan-Taipei; Sydney, Australian Securities Exchange. HSBC Shanghai Hong-Kong Shenzhen, Hang-Seng; Malay Singapore Indonesian. Bangkok, Delhi, Bombay and Saudi and Egyptian Stock Exchanges. RTS Moscow. Nairobi, SIX-Swiss; Euro-NXT: Frankfurt Deutsch-Borse, BME-Spanish French Bourse.'

'Cape Town to: The Kenyan and Nigerian Stock Exchanges…'

'…London OMX-Nordic and then TMX-Canada Stock Exchange: New York Wall Street and Rio, again; BM&F Bovespa Sao-Paulo Buenos Aires Lima. JSE Securities and Investment-Banks…'

'Savings Insurance and Pensions…'

'What-Savings? Insurance? Pension?' She *questioned-aloud...*

'Government-sponsored Private-Public Business and Industry…'

Secretive shared-information would reveal...

'Corporate.' Con-fid(i)dent(t)ial. Building and Nation-Builder(s): Urban-Land Institute(d). Real-Estate New-Century Accredited: *Un*-Prudential: uni-Presidential: Appraisal: Country-Wide: Quest:...

'Citi-Bank Northern-Rock Solid Accountants?'

'Not...' Freedom-Central:

*Options Nova-Star or E*Trade NetBank!* Mutual *Sun-Trust MortgageIT! The Rational-Equitable...*

Luminent-Aegis! Green-Deal Point: Velocity-Agency:

Commercial Indy-Mac Re-Mae re-sume...

'Horror-MIT's: Indian...Krugerand...'

'Shadow-Universe: Partisan-Mission Statement(s)...'

'HSBC Royal-Scot...Bank(s)...'

'Bearns to Wachovia...'

'LandsBanki- to: Ice-Land...all-over.' as, She went to look for tea-bags He got the cups out and put some bread under the grill to toast.

As the cups were emptied and The Front Balcony Door: was opened to go out. The Stock-Market Reports were interrupted by The TV/Radio-Announcer(s) in tandem that:

> 'We have heard in the last few minutes that The International Conference of the Leaders of Governments and World-Banks meeting in Geneva are to make statements at midday mean-time on the current state of financial affairs across the globe. The Financial Economic Crisis' around The-Globe...'

They stopped and looked at each other as they heard the announcement:

'What will they come up with this time I wonder?'

She asked aloud to Him, and to: The Radio Speaker as TV-off: *and as She went to the bathroom door*:

'Come on you two! ' to: The-Children, and-to: Him in the same *breath*:

'What time are you finishing?'

'On-Lates...'

'Again!'

His reply; with a shrug, noticed, as She said:

'I'll have to clock off early then', and She *thought*: *another opportunity to sack me for not doing overtime but if school finishes before work what are We supposed to do?*

'Then. I'm taking them in to: School anyway!' He called.

'I know!', She replied.

'... we will have to go to The Super-Market tonight' added knowingly *a reluctant imperative when it came to it*:

'Or tomorrow anyway...'

She kissed him on the lips, quickly, tantalisingly, knowingly *these weekly and often daily shopping trips for basics, food and water with a shelter over their heads is what they did all this for?*

Along with the mortgage-as-interest-only: rent and love of their family and children smiling:…

He went out of the door, and onto the communal balcony and hallway:

'Another Financial-Crisis!' He called out, to a neighbour, with more than a note of sarcasm, which did not need any reply, other than a disinterested:

'Is there?'

She went back inside: The Living-Room: and went to turn the television-on again. As the announcement of the impending declaration from Accountant Government-Leaders and World-Banks' Inter-National Monetary Fund World Trade Organisation deals, was being repeated:

'Won't make any *difference..!*' She shouted, over the noise of The-Television:

'...never does!'

She de-parted: The-Family-Home: soon-*afterwards...*

'Be careful, To-Day'

She speech to texted to Him:

'I love you' and He had replied:

'Ditto.'

She worked nights, evenings, day shifts. This week it was the late-day shift; or *the day late!* as some liked to call it. From: The Ambulance Station: She arrived at and clocked-on. From where She drove the ambulance, maintenance engineering and assisted at incidents as The *First Aider* third-responder to: first…but not yet as a so-called *SuperMedic* like some of the other Crews had and She was training now towards: *accident and emergency trained up in skills and procedures' assessment of injuries, life or death sometimes.*

Observing vital signs...moving patients safely, onto stretcher or aided walking, checking for any changes. To report to The Qualified Clinician and taking relevant-information from Carers and others at the scene administering First-Aid and supportive: (E)mergency Medical Procedures, transporting people to and from hospital, accident and emergency, the elderly and frail to The-Hospital: for check-ups and appointments.

It could be anything: Road-Accident mainly multiple severe injuries, or just a scratch.

Taking notes for: The Medics, and the (I)nsurance, and Police if there had been A Criminal Act. They would be on the scene-of-The-Crime. Alleged. Or The Fire-Service: if there had been a fire, or if someone needed cutting out of a car.

Rescuing from a roof. You name it. Anything, and everything could happen, and did. Never a dull moment. A good job, a great job, She enjoyed and was paid, well, reasonably well. Not poor. Definitely not rich! More poor it seemed daily recently, what with rising prices...could be a pedestrian, or housebound, head wound, heart attack, to a broken toe-bone.

A busy Shopping-Centre *or:L-earner: on: A Country Lane...*

Sick-baby and worried-parent. Or elderly infirm, worried well, or unconcerned brawler wanting to carry the wound back into the bar, to show-off, not realising how much blood was being lost.

That's when you needed back-up. Sometimes a suicide. Under a train, not much you could do them, bag them up and the undertakers take them away, to the morgue. Maybe later just find out the official-cause-of-death: 'crushed' or 'shattered body' and 'body parts...' in the jargon. May have been pushed? On the roof, threatening to jump...

'Go on then!' you always feel like saying:

'If you're going to! I've got children to collect from school!' Before thinking about the possibly seriously painful mess to clear up. For the public, family, not the suicide.

Maybe they would kill someone else rather than themselves. Make a public show turn the hurt on themselves, or to be carted off and made safe in prison and their own death eventually...

Once: The-Bouncy-Castle (The Safety-*Sack Suicide-Mattress) set up against the wall, and the Terrorist gets bored and tired and decides to walk the stairs.*

Could be someone fallen down stairs. Beaten-up in their own home. Domestic-violence, denying, screaming the odds. Unruly, intractable, recalcitrant, not well-behaved. Not well-mannered. Not biddable, broken-bones, not funny. It would all be reported, had to be. To the Social Care Agency, The Housing Project, The Police. They would press criminal-charges, if necessary. Must do, ought to. Some of the things you see....child-abuse...inflicted...We pitch-up and patch-up and tell their story as well as our own: witness.

Sometimes threatened as well. You had to stand your ground. Emergency blue-light, siren wailing. Steering in and out of that traffic, that never seemed to thin out, or even give way sometimes.

Still, that was: The-Job. Of: Work not-Home.

*Worth hanging onto. Going on to take the medic and paramedic exams in our own time; evenings and weekends, and bringing-up the children! Check out the vehicle, like it is a patient; stocked with bandages, medical and life-support equipment. Ventilator and de-fibrillator, stored properly and in good working order. Communication equipment, to the control-room...*where She had started-out.

Learning how to differentiate one emergency from another.

Over mobile radio-T.V. online in-line:

Video-link, inside and out the vehicle, and *The patients!*

They would joke...heckling themselves in their shared pain and need to overcome to relieve this agony of another, to help to heal.

Checking mileage, speed, safety, on the road, and in situ...clean. New documentation: date, time report charts, name... address if known, distinguishing features...

Check the fuel and oil and water, start up, at the start, and end of each shift...

The ID-Driving-Licence: of course, and passenger public service classification, different gross weights and bearing gear shifts and light and heavy goods for the larger vehicles used-in: Public-Event(s):* now, though, the regular chat, only if there was time…when She got in this morning-shift the morning newspaper, with the Lotto numbers and television and radio pages: this job you could make more than a TV drama any day of the week.

Fiction as Drama: She liked *a psycho murder thriller; or a biography. Not many of them write their own do they?* She *thought* to HerSelf.

What next? I know: Nothing! or The rest of my life I haven't lived yet! The accident and emergency department and hospital wings were as quiet as usual first thing in the morning: *there's always time for things to change...*

She thought...in my life: time: job: rest: enter-tain-ment: sleep: a-wakening(s):

'It always gets busy as soon as I think it's going to be a quiet day!' She called to a colleague, and thought to herself: *turn around and something happens, then it all starts happening! You hardly have time to think until the shift is ended, and no overtime-pay!:*

'When did I last finish on the dot, the bell?' She asked herself rhetorically out-loud to the others re-peat-(ed):

'When did I last finish on the dot, the bell!!?' answering herself in response with a thoughtful but blank thought:

'Never!' they all chanted as if they had does this routine before.

Waiting for the first call. That's when it always happened. Commuters driving from home, to work. A van, or lorry, at work, driven recklessly. Someone in a car crash. On the way to work, domestic, accident, or not. On their way to early-morning deliveries. Or to a job...not anyone's fault that they are late for but they blame everyone and put their own as well as everyone else's life at risk...

As if they are the only ones on the road:

'So. Who does not have an appointment to reach?!@ With fate, and a social duty ahead:

'Slow Down! You are not the only one! Think Safety!' The imperative to get –to and to-keep working too-ridiculous, ridiculous time(s0-set time-frames, shift(s)...

So. She could Feed Self and Family; and others could be fed, and keep: to: stay-alive...

Re-ferrals from All-Night Doctors; there was always work waiting anyway. No later than sooner, the first call of the day: the drunks and addicts and *Home more-or-less...*

Who slipped-in and slept-in with the waking-night-staff in the waiting-rooms during the night-shift and had to be moved-on; for the *EarlyDay shift* to start.

It was not any different today no day ever the-Same...although the last call out had been a disturbance. Some missiles thrown, and one person injured, the police were on the scene. When the ambulance crew arrived, the crowd had been moved away the nightshift…

Ambulance-crew told them all about it when they got back: #

#<u>The Bank</u> had not opened. A queue, a line had formed outside many metres long and wide, a crowd really. Of staff locked-out, and angry, upset, worried, scared, lackadaisical customers, with people trying to get wages and savings out The-Bank unlike the Hospital:

Closed until Further Notice.

There had been a *scuffle* between two of the waiting Bank customers over an unpaid unwritten loan, and eventually, after others had got embroiled, two or three lay injured.

Someone, bystander, onlooker, passer-by had called an ambulance. Several on-lookers came up to them, as they went to see to the injured customer, or patient-to-be; and the crowd, realising The Bank was not likely to open had dispersed to await the further news.

To see if The Bank might open that afternoon.

She was on next call but was not needed. The injuries were only slight, but the scene was ominous, an *omen it seemed for the day. If any real disaster did strike* She often thought *only enough bandages and fuel for the ambulance for a few days, and only if that is rationed from The Start.*

Only enough food at home, the same. The closer to the monthly Big Shop time, the less there was at home. Nothing-left-in-the house'(as they called it: the apartment really...nothing left, at home!) Not stocked up recently, and can hardly afford to go more than for a few days at a time. Sometimes, only one day at a time, for bread and milk, without replenishing need, and staple-goods…basics, nevermind the ordinary-Luxuries…as necessities…'

Everyone was talking about the crash of The Stock-Markets and the announcement expected at midday:

'We'll have to go to The Super-Market tonight!' She had called after him as He had left and left a voice-message and text; and *He collecting the children later or She? Her-Self??*

With certain familial protective panic immediate: after her first shift was done without-overtime…

She would be on second school-shift later in the day hand-over to the word second-day shift to the early evening-nightshift: split-shifts it was and would have to be:

'You going to Factory or The Rally, now?'

'Midday? Both. Finished-by:…'

'You collecting The Children?' She said, as a kind of premonition…

Suddenly, everything seemed more uncertain. And She really did start to wonder, what this day would bring:…

'Not Closed. Open for The Day' notice pinned on The School-Gate. He re-passed-on: The Way To Work: and now brought back to mind*: thank goodness*…had been His immediate response.

Although there were mutterings and mumblings about *whether: The Teachers and Nursery-Nurses would actually see their pay and pensions this month. How long The Parents would be able to keep on paying through taxation: for:*

*The Basic Free-Education: never mind the Ex-tra-i-ning-trips and activities equipment for this and that…*at least*:*

He texted her: The School was open and The Children did not need collecting until She finished her first-shift.

Would She be needed after that? He asked. Finished his late morning-shift at: The Bakery later that Day: after The Rally.

The deliveries would resume and the next days' batches made-up and put in the ovens for:

'Super-Baking' as it was called.

So that She could return to the Ambulance Station and start Her second split-shift:

'Don't forget: The After-School Club!' The Older-One had called after him:

'I Will Tell Your Mother!' He had called-back:

'OK!'

'Half-day today?' The-School-Teacher joked, and laughing together,

'No-Chance!' and He meeting a WorkMate on the way to work…

'Redundancy again?'

'Litigated-*Compensation…again…'*

'Quantitively-Easing…'

'Austerity!'

'Bail-Out! *Publicly-funded* ...' made from:

'Taxes!'

'Personal-Taxes: Building-Societ(y)ies:…'

For: Family: <u>Home</u>: *investment-in from* working-employment: from:…

'*Overseas:…* '

'Other-Oceans and rivers-running *clean...'*

Headline-Fact(s): *only* no-opinion…but that behind-closed-doors:

'Corporate-Tax: Crisis:…'

'CEO-Dictatorial *Democracy…*'

'Government: Investment-Bank…'

'Bollocks!'

'Ballot!'

'Tits-Up! Re-Presentative Re: Legion…'

'Democratic *un-doing...'*

'Of: Aged-Leaders and deputy-Sons' and Daughters' disputed right:...'

'Accused arrested im-prisoned dis-appeared…

'House-Arrest: Farm-Land: *taken without compensation...*'

'Fair-Enough! All has to be Taken at some Trading-Post!'

'Staging-Post For Government: …'

'Family-for: Trade-for-All:…' *'confessed' of New Peoples' Sports-Facility: kick-backs taken …*

'AirLine SpaceCraft: even: now:…'

'De-livering…*dealing...buying and selling...re-de-livering...*' as the accused *accusing...*'

'Blame(ing):…'

'Stronger-Forces…'

'...*weaker*-Variable(s)...'

5. IT.

The-Banker sat-back purposefully, purportedly and provocatively to-unfold and having unusually had to purchase: *The Financial-Newspaper* with the headline outer-most, upper-most:

WORLD MARKETS IN TURMOIL!

and *seen* again *that* photograph taking up the whole of The *grey*-top printed front-page remaindered and pictured in the *minds*' eye.

Now: turned inside-out and with a staring squeezed blink of the eyes, *fumbled* as if in a freak storm, a blown umbrella, folded quickly-away.

To: The-Clerk: hung-out to dry: having seen earlier the front-page photograph and one-liner, top headed re-referenced: re-conceived on-line and *connected...down-loading* and *updating*...milli-second minute-to-minute: cellular-mobile version *uploading*... freely with-advertising: counting-down optional: *free-view* choice or fee-paying subscription...*skipping*...as instantly as if *mysteriously-accusatory...*

As if with some felt need for *validation, valediction, justification, testimony, guilt? Even before any biased evidential fact-based fiction?* With a self and another-deceiving finality justifying, with instant-conviction...*but of who? By whom?* Despite the original opening-question, it seemed as if with no real right-of-reply. The initial conversational-question about what to make of *it* All?

Asked as if not-*intended* to be replied-to or any other-mindedly *mitigating* circumstances or any-answer-at–all particularly, or generally, listened-to or taken any notice-of. Yet. Or so the younger-Clerk, surprised to be spoken-to, then considered: *perhaps like a nurture-nature kind of thing?*

Possibly a-Plebeian enquiry? Selected-standard flagged with no-probation: The-Clerk decided: *more likely a command, to make something of IT, and to-be-taken-notice-*

of: mostly self-importantly: County-Country: E-*State: local-Fund(s) at study work life and death: democracy cannot flourish in-fear hate anger: only open-questioning: at any-Time and Space: constantly changing: Roots amongst seeming-Rage? Nnnn*-otice: given of anyway, dis-regarding of the possibly-paranoid maniacal rhetorical-answer awaited or not, by either, or Both. Regardless of The-Other*: On-Board: The Quickest to-the-Draw…or to: Withdraw?*

The Subtler –Inquisitor? Analyst? Strategist? adversaries all ready…

To: the initial-recipient *clerking* by-assumption: *looking*-up from a streaming mobile smart-phone camera and video-games-console: 4slotmachine...game...

downloading...

Personal Electronic Reader de-pocketed-*information*-recorded removing the ear-bud flex-plex: screen,-clip micro-phone socketed-lead off to on-line *searching*...for the source of the *mildly-irritating openly questive-words' spoken* as directly-to or so it seemed: Ground-Liaison: Kin-ex? wherever this may be The-Clerk: in almost immediate reply:

'*Senseless…*'

The-Clerk: *not*-looking-up, looking-down and into the same recently con-cealed picture and slowly re-storing from *browsing*-history as accurately *acutely*-historically as-depicted.

As verifiably veritably immediate and un-tampered-with: photo-scooped shopped mobile cell-phone worded and photographed: syndicated and: World-Wide-Web: *network*ed-scene as at the end of the previous-day:

The <u>City:</u> Stocks and Share-Bond *market(s)* as then as now: seen:

News-printed and pictured from the evening before: a *litter*-strewn like old ticker-tape looking across:

The Trading-Room Floor: *for-saken, soaking for-feit and un-forgivingly unforgiven: blankly awaiting-screens' strap-line seen*:

Market Closed.

For: The-Banker: The single-slogan as about to go up or down was not possible to tell.

For All to: *See...*

Diagonally, from one corner of the screen-page to the other, perhaps *tangentially-* to slip smoothly-across continuously shutter stuttering across, only-slightly *blurred* from the-top aloft, the-perfect: the-*normal* midway *ideally*-positioned, not at the-*extreme* outer-fielded or even ever truly-*centred:* but as *inside-out* and now, as stilled a-*flickering...*

As then, as now: as no-longer identically singularly signally existent: *or ever again: exactly-the-same.* Now: brought to-gether and as: Everywhere in: The World: and: *No-where* at-All. Except: everywhere, now, there, only as stop-framed as cinematographically stilled.

Grilled re-corded and re-peatedly time and again the same: stoop-looped any movement as any-moment of only *impendent* independent occurrence: of pixels printed and *glowing*-in: The-*Cloud*:

'Market. Closed.' *shimmering* grid-table mapping diagrammatic…a *flickering*…a coming-together:

'Re-tail: On-Line and Mobile…' *that bold bland statement flickering nonetheless-memorifically: monographically mnemonically stilled fuzzily held in-abeyance:* as a dawn held rising over The Worlds' Edge: Market. *Closed.* As a vertiginous horizontally remotely-geometrically sited Cityscape *skyline...diverting*...to:

<Banking- *details*...corporate-investment *scams perks of psychological-physical financial-bribery and seemingly accepted: Corruption and Fraud: Tax-evasion and avoidance: on-consultancy and management fees-only signatory contracts hostage-taking hi-jacking the richest and poorest: National E-Debt War($): spending and bribes out-running deficit federal-ransoming: working-deals projected un-founded optimism or pessimistically as life-threateningly:*

'Losses can exceed deposits…'

'As death exceeds Life…' *un-throated or keeping quiet: the-public purse: tax-dodging avoidance not open to everyone and evasion overseas…as if this would be enough to boost simple-confidence on: fixed multi-scalar fiddling jiggling violin-jigging burning words&figures in columns revealed above an open-dialogue boxed-in:*

>Options:…*with-structure and series arcade-style deviation from the normal…too complex-to-control, if at all…cutting-edge:* RE:booting…re-marking: perhaps, bringing The-City down? The-*Country*! Global! Being brought-down?! *tapped-into*:

<The-City: *Country-Global* News*: ethno-linguistically and-ability driven pluto-cracy(ies): strategically falsely declared other promoted-tactics shouted-out below a glass-ceiling silvery-mirror shattered in-difference to grotesque…*

'Over-Investment in Property: public-probity propriety-*privately*…'

'Over or *under*-valued Trade(s)! Un-Safe and un-Economical:…'

'*Risk…always…*Super-Boom and Bust!'

'New and emerging market(s): The-City?'

'Sin and Sexy!'

'Why not? Only *natural*…'

'Staples Basics?'

'Chemical Plastics Metals and Minerals…'

'Food and Fuels…'

'Home-Furniture *making… ' strongly in-vulnerable must-haves intuitive knowing certain flexible ups and downs: exag-ge-rated rises now* falls…

'Fraud?'

'Fined-only…a-few…there will be bribes…'

'In-surance? Pensions? Providential Vendor-Banking?'

'Industrial-Commercial: Credit-Crisis…'

'Domestic Home-Mort-gage…'

'Credit-Bubbles'

'Spiked! Burst! Sovereign-Debt!'

'How do you expect me to make a living?' *hold-the-nerve…*volatile…

'Called-in loans…'

'Market-Value…'

'*(I)ntrinsic-value…'*

'No-longer…'

Taken a-back:

'National Inter-National…'

'Market-Value! Gone!' dumped *dis-counting: The-past: Deals'…*

'Intrinsic-Value:…

'Selling-off fast!' Bundled packaged and parcelled:'

'Price(s) crashing:…'

'Future-Value for present…'

*'N*o-longer peforming…'

'Stopped! BRIC(K)BATS!' *out-numbering banquets' bouquet of plaudits…*

'De-Con-struction: Dot-Comm.s' and Spot-Purchase Puts and Stays…'

'Gauge Trade-Investment…'

'Oil and Coal-Gas' Money-*ness*…'

'Plastic-Banks.''

'ILL-liquid-Strike Price…'

'Burst!' *Balloon bubble into Space:*

'Banking-L*iquidity smashed*…'

'Insurance-and-Pensions…'

'Market Price-drops…'

'Everywhere!'

'Had to happen…'

'Peak: **Coal-Gas Oil**:…'

'Plastic and *E(*l)ect-rictus: Dot.Comm.s…'

'Banks. Only, *Money*…'

'Now.'

'*Aggressive*-Takeovers?'

'Going**…'**

'G*one…'*

'None too soon…Peak-Money!'

'Banking-Bubble… '

<Analysis: probing-probability(ies):…

>Standard Deviation(s)…

'Market-Algorithm(s)…'

'Machine-Memes…'

'Re-marketed-themselves…'

'Genetic-Genes…'

'Mimetic-Memes…'

'Marked-The-Cards…'

'Mined, *memed…*House(s)-of-Card(s)…' *publicly…pessimism: (i)nner-endless: Optimism…*

'In-House?'

'To: Each-Other…' *hidden and:*

'Home?' *Alternative(s): farmed for Solar-Wind and Lunar Tidal-Wave…*

*'Abroad: Ad-vertising: O*ver-Other(s): over-Optim-ism:'

'Get Rich Quick! How did you get so Rich?'

'Determination…and Luck!'

'Both? Of Birth and Single-Minded?'

'Focus: *interest-grouped*:…

'Earns The Money! Living-Laser!'

'Or Die!'

'*Cyborg*-Rat!'

'Caged! Digital-*Artifact*:…'

'Sting-Ray…'

'Puddle-Ducking…'

'Equity: Debt-Owner(ship) *gone*...(I)nterest(ed)?'

'In My Debt?'

'With Self and Others' Col-lateral?'

Online:

'Fraud-and-*Corruption*!'

'In-Life as in-Business:...'

'In-Business as in-Politics...'

'Politics as Business...as: Enter-tain-ment:'

'News: catering-to as travelling-with...'

'Meaning?'

'Provisions...'

'Victuals?'

'As Motivation...'

'Political-*purpose*...but...Closed?'

'Business-for-Sure...0nce at the top, stay there!'

'By *Foul means or Fair?'*

'Fear? Who said anything in The World, in Nature...*ever* was *intrinsically* Fair?'

'Or: Foul?'

'Or Good?' *Military/Civilian: Security: risk: Rebel-Plot? plotting: Global!: The-Government(s) loses: Control* : un-democratically done-away with...

'Split. The World...takes over:...'

‘To over-*throw*: The-Ex€cutive:…’

‘At the Ballot-Box:…’

‘Rigged:…’ *soft-coup…defending*-rights…*responsibly!*

‘From: Terrorist-Military?’

‘Absolutely-attacking Foreigners’ bodies attacking aggressive takeover:’ as-*defending*:

‘Criminals…’

‘Deferred-*prosecution…*’

‘Secret-pay-ment(s): made…’

‘Peace-Keepers…’

‘Bribery-*a-Broad…* ‘

‘Threats?’

‘De-nied Prostitution! Home? Foreign-Aid?’

‘Arms Sales? Minimal of-Course! Trading:…’

‘Friendly-Foe? Diplomatic-Spy? Espionage?’

‘Rape. Mis-placed…’

‘Mis-selling…’

‘Mis.-bought…

Politics? Politicians? Corporate?

‘Business. Land: re-claimation Island: The Richest! Most Populous in The World!’

‘Holiday-Haven!’

'Storm-Sea-Wall…'

'Crowded Cities everywhere…'

'Acidic: Aquifier Salt corrosion…'

'Solar-pollinated….'

'Nucleic-Polluted: noisy but organised not-chaotic…'

'Yet. Tumultuous!'

'Let The Atom be a Worker!'

'Worker: be A Soldier!'

'Artist; not a Soldier!'

'All. Too-much: GREEDY! For: Power!'

'Aren't we All?'

'Un-caring?'

'Want Some-thing for next-to-nothing! Take-It! All of Us! Bargains Galore!'

'Scamming…'

'Thieves! Robbers! Bandits! All of Us!'

'Some. Tricked! Held onto: ransoming *family health and care and ill-affording…*'

'Protect and Survive!'

'Protest and Survive!!!

A-*fraid as always of losing again-and-again:*

'Ever? Fear of losing?'

'Out! Un-fairly criminally and ill-egally…'

'Survive and Pro-Test!'

'Protect!'

'Fixing the-Rate:(s)…' *like(s) immoral immortal accidental-machine: God(s):* Magic

Be-lieved…

Re-lived: *fiddling* the-figure(s)…*juggling-in-favour…*

'As if they would not be found-out:'

'They? The-Fall€(n)0…no-one…else:…'

'Ig-*snore* the *true* picture?'

'*Made-up.*'

'*T*oo-much to too-few!'

'Over-valued commission-price and Bonus! Growth!' *recommended on a friend request: with out-collateral: to: back-up…*

'Stories: In the Real World:'

'Risk-*assessor(*s) down-grading…'

'A-voiding…hiding?'

'After-All they are in the same business…'

'Re-Gulator(s): Mis-Information-Age:'

'Money for *mere-information…*'

'Digital: Inter-changeable…'

'*Informative*: Money Ex-change…'

'Goods and Stocks and Services:'

'Food on The- Table…'

'Home.'

'Even or never-*near* enough outfield…'

'Enough…stop pitching?'

'Stopped.'

Dignified: Honorable…Re-spect: Qing TiMian Mu Pi Zi: Lian-Y(u)an: Ren Min Bi…

Gu-anzi and Gan-qing: In-tact: Energetic-Culture Centre(s)…' *controlled…with: The-Face…*

Slowed through an empty-station platform closed-too, close-to, before:

'If We don't Others will…' *continuing:*

'Trade-in: Truth.'

'False?'

'*Perfect*: Bru-tal Logic!'

'Un-believable!'

'Be-Live-Able. *False*-Trading!'

'What Col-lateral?'

'None!'

'Except jobs and Homes! People's Lives! Kill-Rates…'

'Police? Army sent-in…'

'Strategic-Fiscal: re-Colonialism…'

Camped-Psycho? I-n-camera: secret parallel-accounting: helper-Killer Cell(s):

False-Positive(s)… heard-headphoned:

'In-Corporate: Personal-Privatisation:…'

'Social-*Responsibilities…*'

Ha! Psycho-Social! Accidental-Default: en-*forced*-Rates' in-*crease(s):n/N…*On-ly! Limited-Liability: P*sycho-Path: in-Corporate: Personhood in Corporate-Government: man-i-pulative lacking-em-pathy: simply-focussed: confusing deliberately willing-winning formulae re-peated pre-judicial charge-sheet arrest:*

'Trade? Logistics?' *with or without collateral: geared-in: re-tainable…*

'Bank.'

'Inter-National Global-War!'

'Trade-War. Civil. The *Actual-Stock(s) and* Good(s) delivered to back *them-*up...'

'*United Trans-Mission Service(s):* Servicing: A-People(s) Logistics and Facilities: Re-Sources…'

'*Un-certain*-Lives…'

'Always!'

'Only: *false*-figures...'

'They are *all*-False! 'We' Are? You want: Certainty? From the moment we are born…from before birth! Credit-De-bit: Crunch!ed! All of Us! Perhaps the-Price of Civilisation eh? Deficit….Keep-ING *moving...*'

'Dow-Jones: Dogging…'

'Goldman-Sachs! Merril lynch…'

'…and the rest!'

'Poor and Standards'!'

'Same as I.T.'s ever been!'

'Bringing in the-Harvest!'

'Or not...*Global-Failure!'*

'Local: Of The-Banking-System...

'Global. 'We' are told…*this*-time...Private and Central-Banker's City-Trader Scam! Big Bang! To –In-Vest! Freely! The Government-Banks Federal-Exchequers' Peoples' in-teres(ts)…'

'…whose Peoples?'

'International Monetary Funds'...*' whistled from account-to-account: fraud and laundering: hidden-stains washed-out:*

'The-World-Bank: Domestic to Global-*Productivity...' barriers-battled freeing dovetailing relatively all peaceful worlds...*

'Producing-Everything! Processing Food and Furniture factoring Logistics Wholesale…Turf-War(s):' trans-porting-Portal…*retail*…time-as-energy: Futur(I)Zon: selfie-ID-online profile: banking and medical appointment(s): building learning-machine(s):

'Movable…mobile…'

'Nuclear-Cell: Family-Home.'

'National-Sovereignty…'

'Protective: Global-Corp-O-rate: *operating*...system…*working*...privately-owned and…'

'Dis-credited:…'

'Home-Bank!'

'Self-insuring…'

'People! All of:'

'Them!'

'US! Give *Them* Our-Money to Loan-back to *Us!'*

'All of Us!!! Loan(s)-War(s)…'

'Now *truly*-Globalised…de-*Regulation:* Free-Trade:'

'De-Centralised: local-controlling: City-Trading: Companies…'

'In-Corporation(s):…' mobile-*computer: Home-Office: Box Floor face-face dealing between: Brokers with pots of shares-and no-cash...*

<*Binary-Broker:* Pro-duction Chain-of-Command (PCC):…

>High-frequency…short-term *timed... by digital milli-second screened*:

'Joke!'

'Multi-National(s): Corporate-Interest: Investment: Old-Time Firms and Big-Bank(s) directly-entered safe: man-made: un-safe: *Natural*-Disaster:…'

'The-Life of: The-Market: pre-post: scarcity passed-on: Price-Rise(s): On: Credit*!*:…given…gone!'

< List: *bubbles-popped...*

Re-play…

'Saw Nothing like this! Triple, quadruple...*many* times *over*-rated...'

'And with Selling-Commissioned-Bonus on Top of That!'

'Paying Taxes? Who pays Taxes in their right-mind? Eh?'

'Who can get away with I.T....'

'Other-People's *Money*:...'

'On:...'

'Credit:...' *on-line daily- amount:: automated-algorythm...' di-scretion-agency: in-cretion protecting the causer-of-harm from the harm-caused: self*:

'Be a: Big-Boss! The Biggest-Boss that ever Bossed the World around!'

'On? *Cash*! Coin(s)? F-folding-Money? Credit-Machine? Overdraft? Debt?'

'National-Debt. *They didn't know what they were doing...'*

'Re-investing on: without insurance...'

'Re-insurance...'

'Like Kings...'

'And Queens...Sheikdom! Caliphate! Presidential! Any-0ne Can!'

Buying and selling-on digital-information from computer-screens spread across the desks passed across to others who knew nothing...

'Government? Except*...unless*...of-course? You're The-Revenue? Police or Thief eh?'

'Both? Maybe? Selling to the *developing*-Worlds' corruption and scandal(s)...'

'As: Ours' developing still...gimme what you've got?'

'Bribe?'

'Debt(s).'

'For Special-Protection Racket? Eh? For their extra-pay, eh? Paid: so *bad*ly be-fore?'

'Money? Police?'

'Ambulance?'

'Fire…Social-Worker for all I care, Government-Army. Generals and Politicians for: n-years elected to:…'

'Life-President…until…anyway or not all…'

Missile and Missile-Defence Systems sold-O-ffensively as-if: protecting…

'Defensive? Us and Them?'

'Never had the chance to say: No!'

'Not-working anyway? Foreign? Off-Shore: Convenience-Stored?'

'All ways. You? The In-Land *Revenue Police*? I don't *owe*...tax re-investment innovation route chosen…'

'Tax?'

'Not. Taken.'

'W*ith:* The-<u>People</u>'s *<u>Future(s)</u>…L*ife.'

'In-surance?'

'Buildings *Ass-YR-ance?'*

'Certainly: Banks' *holding*-Pensions' Social-Security….'

'Health&Social-Care. Welfare-(I)nsurance?'

'Mortgage-Benefit?'

'On the next generations: Now! Corruption and Fraud…

Schools and Hospitals never get built, bridges collapse, filled filed: infra-structure land-deal(s):…

'Non-existent. Market-Places mass-manufacturing using cheap-materials…'

'Who: Pay(s)?'

'Who doesn't *have*-to: *eh?*'

'Who-cannot.'

'Privatised…'

'Sold-off now…'

'Government Bail-Out?'

'Asking-askance…'

Capita: Royal-PLC: Bonded-Contract(s): sham-Democracy:

Security-Weaponry: Defence and Assault: On:

Social-Economic and *National* Security-*concerns…*

'Prison-Analysis…'

'As to: *know who to* say: no: to…'

'City-Analysis: Who: to say: yes: to…'

'Too?'

'*Secret-sanctified sacred:…'*

'Secured?'

'All Over The World…'

Scared-stochastic! Scholastic! Proven!:

'Never take a Risk…'

'Un-believable! Why-not? To make *more*-than-*enough?'*

'Why?'

ssssSimply:

'To: Live or Die.'

'Too-complex too-much…'

'Too-Big too quickly…'

'You-watch. We'll be back…' *quickly*, on the-button:

'The Midday-Conference? To: a *small*-few will it actually *be* midday.'

'To: a very small-few will they ever agree.'

'Agree to differ, perhaps?...'

'Least-worst, is best, yes.'

Set-an- ex-ample.

Everyday referenda-endlessly: for proportional-choice not non-democratic permanent-power minority cheating-death: must have their own-war(s) make-enemies more than friends' known-about as every King Queenly Presidential and Prime-Ministerial: to any One: N/n…N/nnn…

Material: Weapons of Mass-Destruction…

Big-Time Risk (B-T R): Financial any…destruct:…

'Ever-One: N/n self-Value Worth and Winning(s)nnn…'

'No such thing as too-Big: Or: too-*quickly*: bang!bang! Big-**Bang!** Bonanaza!!' *jumping fore-ward then backwards as if shot both now in the knowledge assumed of the other:*

'Stunts? Take a beating. That is how They do IT! No-Risk.'

'Only 0thers'…Un-*believable*!'

'Reign-In! Don't see IT.'

'Or THEY!'

'IN-and-Out. Last-Night! That is All IT IS!'

'Rogue-Citizen! Police? Thief? Global? Army?'

'Global-Citizen? Now?' from *that* last night to *this* morning:

'Need Bread? Need an Ambulance?'

'To Eat?'

'To: Spend…To: Take…'

'Buy and Sell.'

'Pay-up or Banged-up!'

'So?' Both now assumingly knowingly unknowingly yet simply *pictorially*-imagining that morning the scene as unchanged from the night before.

The-*same@* ID-ent(i)cal: for-All: now as far as either of them or anyone on: The Train. As: there, or anywhere-else known of as of dealings of *intricate:* Commerce and Business: *small* to medium and Large: as that evening *previously…*ceased then as now inside:

The-City: **Stock-Market***(s)* building: heavy-teakwood-mahogany doors tightly-closed hermetically-sealed a normally *fluorescent* glow inside turned-off except for a single computer-board screening presence there remaining: *b-linking*:

'Market Closed.'

'Charit(y)ies:…'

'Free.'

6. Nursery School and Work.

He'd taken: The DownStairs with: The Children two-at-a-time one in a pushchair the other just learning to walk, and turning outside pulling the buggy *up* steps to the road level they headed off together for The Corner Shop.

Turning at the top of the road, pushing the baby buggy uphill, the almost unmade pavement now in disrepair, showing the lack of *maintenance* savings through *the good times* as well as the now financial recession…

Telling *The Walker* (as He and She said to each other in jest *the children laughed at that...) commanding-tone* but *The Walker no longer holding on to the buggy* called-out to:

'Hold on to the buggy' *answering the constant questions*:

'What is this?' and:

'What is that?' *and having to say:*

'Be careful!' *every second, and*:

'Stop!...making me have to say:

'Be Careful!' every second!' and they giggling together, at what, He knew not what.

Not-even *imagining(s):* A Time: *when:* He and She would not be going to work, and The-Children: to School and Nursery and then keeping Them into: Our-Dotage: *probably!* Going to pick up *the fallen walking running-off:* child grabbing the perambulator again, and continuing walking on the uneven pavement road:

'Do Not Run! You'll *Trip! Over…!*'

The walking child hearing only the middle word:

'Run!'; and wondering what all the shouting was about, and running:

'Stop! at the edge!' hearing all the words this time: *thoughtfully*:

'O.K?'

'O.K.!'

Trying-out these new words heard from them and at: The School:

'Stop!'

The_Walker:…running now and stopping at the pedestrian-crossing to get collided in to and rolling on the ground giggling *The Road!* getting up and running off laughing, looking backwards,

'STOP!'

Having crossed the crossing turning confidently the opposite way,

'This way!' onto the next junction,

'Stop! at the kerb!'

He catching up, pushing the pushchair ahead The Walker hanging on, over the kerb and into the road.

Looking both ways all ways and then both ways again. Then back again, one last way this time: *too quickly...going to Run!* The way the traffic was headed, moving slowly, one car stopped, and let them across, to a wave returned. Watching-out, for all three and to the oncoming traffic split, by traffic lights commanding: *Stop, Start, or Pause...* Walk! To the other side safely chasing on ahead to The Shop. The 'Little-'un' in the buggy trying to get out to follow, screaming and pointing with one then both index-fingers toward the road,

'Taxi!'

swivelling around almost falling-out. Pointing, ahead:

'Bus!' the other returning, giggling:

'A. Bus!' correcting, and then as they passed The Shop pleading verbally and non-verbally tugging and whining for *sugar*(y)()-sweets:

'Helicopter! Kit-for-Kat!'

'Coca-Cola Ambulance! Tit-for Tat!!

'This for That!!!'

singing, and pointing and swivelling around again:

'The Shop!' the other:

'Sweets! categorically. *Usually not until they came home from school and nursery. Even then only some days, and if they had been good at school or nursery. But always worth a try....*pointing, jumping up-and-down, on the buggy, the other falling out, buckles unbuckled, by the older one:

'As long as you behave yourselves today, and they're not too bad for your teeth, and you clean your teeth!' *they knew that* giggling all the more, at some reference only they knew. To the words, the noises, and the tone of voice, the bedtime:

'Clean your teeth! *Proper*ly!!'

'Clean your teeth! *Proper*-ly!!'

The *Youngerer* One: repeated, and they went into more fits of *giggles…*

Into: The News-Agent-come-Grocers' and Confectionary Shop and sometime Licensed off-Licence Liqueur and Drugs Store where He and She, and They, stopped each morning, for a quick pain-relief head and stomach-ache: *fresh* bread or newspaper.

On the way to nursery and school, when it was his turn, always the possibility of sweets as well. As they crashed through the door the older one getting deliberately, or so it seemed, in the way of the baby-buggy. Asserting rights and responsibilities over the other smaller and weaker, and released both leaning up at The Shop counter.

Not unusually but always predictably in the morning rush *with so many other things to think about* the only thought, unable to think about anything else:

Food shopping tonight? Newspaper? Sweets?

The BabyBuggy: almost tipped over in the raucous, the older one falling over the younger, strapped in, strained at the straps, snapping painfully back.

Letting out an ear piercing yell.

The Older One: un-still giggling, until the younger lashed-*out as only younger siblings know how too* and the older one let out a *Yell!* then a *Scream!*; apparently exaggerated explication of pain from both now, and claims of *unfairness idiot! etc.*

'Come-on you're The Older One, you should know better! Do you have to have to fight and argue over everything! No sweets!' and then He knew, as soon as He said that that: He was *A Beaten Man.*

A yet louder exclamation set-up.

While: The Younger One: *looking on in vigour and glee, quieted and puzzled; twisted turned looking upwards to* The Father for some resolution to the questioning plea, and fell out of the buggy, unbuckled:

'Me a' well?'

Looking up from the floor, the older standing and going to stamp on the younger, smiling sweetly now, the other sprawled on the floor as if felled:

'The Smiling Assassin!' He called-out from the front of The Shop in common reference to the older child and to The Shopkeeper grinning in collaboration, and who was stacking shelves from remaining stock.

He, holding-up the regular: National *Financial*-Newspaper: The Shopkeeper called:

'You may as well keep that!' to the loose change being handed over the counter:

'...it will be like one of those free ones!'

Hearing and not listened-to until later, scanning the headlines:

STOCK-MARKETS IN CHAOS!

The money placed on the shop-counter chuckling, when the remark realised:

'No, I got it!' minding: The Children...who were not fighting but pretending to steal sweets *not knowing any better yet*, knowing better, laughing and looking palpably guilty. The Shopkeeper bagged and handed over most of what it was they-wanted:

'There you are, for later…your Dad's change!' the customary sweets as a gift now *in-change sometimes anyway* for a small note passed across the counter. From the Shopkeeper, to them, and then him:

'Daddy keep it...for later'

The Children looking *pleased*, and anxious also that they too might have to 'keep it for later' with only then the conditional:

'And only if you are Good today! All Day!!' *the emotional and ethical merged into puzzlement*. Sweets given to The Father patiently waiting to get off to nursery, school and work.

Again consternation, put-on, by the older child to The Younger. Pouting, dropped lower-lip. Acting-out, pretending, face pulling. Puzzled at, and copied by the younger. Both laughing at this, and between themselves, at something they did not really know: what it was *to Be Good...*

Today or: *all day*; or how or what it was to attain this.

6. He.

They had stayed together, a family and with two little ones, one of each, girl and boy by the time they're both about to be in school, they could not risk another to bring up, and the cost of it.

They only hoped they would hold on to their jobs, and worked hard. Difficult hours, and few days-off. Where the rota's didn't workout for childcare, family, or neighbours, parents now friends of the children's friends who lived conveniently nearby: The Social Network...from the cradle to Nursery School and Work.

Diapers to Di-p-loma to District Directorate...

They had met when things were starting to get a bit tight, get difficult again. Meaning the situation for most working families, for those looking for work, and those in work, things had not got any better, any easier really during the so-called good-times, and both parents were needed to work to keep the family going. Voluntary social networks became all the more significant, and reciprocal. Shared-care with child and adult adult-er-a-t-ioninteraction, thereby social and meaningful: shared lives between people, and gender. They had both kept their jobs in, more or less essential services, although not without their job-cuts and reduced hours, or expected overtime at the same or no pay, ever-the-less, never the more, in real-terms...

When: The Bakery 'Factory' went on three-days week, and pay to match. He had more time to be with the children, and helped the same with others still in fulltime work, or her awkward shiftwork.

He had done some untaxed building work on the odd-days to fill-in. She had done some shop and garment-making work before then when they were no-longer hiring, took re-training... Ambulance-Driver Her current-Work: She hurried toward, as did He his as a Factory-Baker.

Then they had moved to His folks in The City: suburbs really, inner-urban, something-like-that. His mother had worked at The Old Mill and got her a job there; and then with him at The Bakers' Factory at the top of the road, near the nursery and school, when they had moved in together; and had kids. Turn right, then left, and a few more turns, before The Factory Gates.

His Father's Family had been Millers too; before that Gypsies as EveryOne before once... Did well. Moving around...

Funnily enough He-thought *like Government-Corporate People nowadays do... Business-Trip Metings Decision(s)...*looking across the busy roads beyond, leading to The-City.

To The-Airport *to visit SalesPeople to The Retail Outlets: Shops in other words: Big Business. Marketing, and Sales. By plane to meet clients meetings here and there and everywhere. Cities all over, to do deals on a massive Global-Scale worth millions, now worth billions and trillions of whatever the currency dealing even in the currency itself. In the past when the work dried-up his' family 'moved along' or stayed with their stores, shares of the crops of the fields and water, natural and free from the well. Waiting for more or different labour or better paid to the costs of running the household...*

He thought *of them, and his own family. Out of work, they always found something. When the work was finished, they moved on. Along the waterways, they not dissimilar, but also different from her family. They had a farm in the countryside for a while, and the parents still lived there. Hers. He and She, now, through the Industrial Future. To The Soul of The City. Across The River, across the tram tracks, and railway, by the station.*

From The Heart of the City, the Financial Quarter. Settling in The City outskirts. His self-employed, their own bosses, worked on the building sites of towering sky-scrapers, lining The River. Then employed. Not their own boss. Both their families on some land, renting from their pay together. Then they, He and She eventually, buying: homeowners now. Investors in their own future, and their Children's' children...

7. Shop.

She'd pressed the OFF switch, and They all had left for school and work. *Now,* closing all the windows and door behind her, a short while later and going where those others' had set-out and others still were leaving front doors for the days school and work and buying and selling activity ahead.

Outside and downstairs, through the piles of discarded rubbish and the door wedged open. To the blocked refuse-chute, to the stairs and the *If-it's-working* lift down to the ground floor: t*he worst thing standing inside the open lift door not being sure if the elevator was going to work, or not. Or go crashing to the ground, like everything else today,* She-*thought.*

He was *on-a-late* and so *He was taking the children to school and nursery. He would not be collecting them later today.*

When Her shift finished. She could normally do overtime but today to clock-off to collect them. *If there were no emergencies, that was*. Then She would have to phone one of the other Mothers or Fathers to collect their Children as well, *if* they *could?*

She entered The-*same*-Shop He had recently departed with The Children. Only a few minutes, but crucial lateness seconds earlier:

'Got any Bread in?'

'Not your turn to The School today then?'

'Early-late…' She re-plied. The-Shopkeeper:

'You may as well take One there only One-Day-*stale* so-far…'

'One-Day?'

'Since Midday…' *midnight, half-that*:

'Yesterday.'

'The Midday: InterNationAl-CON!-Ference…'

'C*on*-ference? climbing-down off a stool-from-stacking-shelves:

'It's gone stale already hasn't it? Never-mind: The Bakery!'

'Haven't seen them yet today!'

Today: The Shop: Open: *as-usual ready to stock-up again with the usual days-supplies that had been 'phoned in the day before* this*: or rather*:

'It looks like it is *whenever The Bakery turns up*!'

Then, not for the first time:

'Your better-half works at The Bakery doesn't He?'

Then:

'Saw him with the kids earlier, no sweets until after school!'

Then:

'My significant-*Other.'*

'Mine went out early enough today to: The Cash and Carry: then: Bakery. Because they haven't turned up or answering calls, gone there to collect *ourselves…and* not back yet! I phoned-in the order. They put on a message eventually: *said:* 'No Deliveries yet Today. We will keep you up-dated…then online frozen. Nothings' moving yet...looks' *like:…*'

Then:

'Going to see if we can collect bread and cakes later baked! There's a Midday-meeting at: The Bakery Factory. At: The Food-Queue:'

'Food-Bank(s)…'

'Probably!' *pointing at the dry loaves on the shelf*:

'Going stale!' momentarily paused, then:

'No Cash, No Carry!'

Exclaimed:

'Fresh is Best!' concluded as The Shopkeeper continued to Her:

'But *this* we get from Your Bakery, you know, it doesn't last! Gets chucked' *chuckled.* I *Have:* to: *Health and Safety* it, or give it to *The Bin-Raiders* out the back! They have it! Still, can't blame them can you? Poor beggars…I leave it for those that take it…' *homeless, dis-advantaged immediately mostly you know, or out of work, on: Welfare-Ben(e)fits that go nowhere poor and hungry and Hom(e)less...*

'That's where we'll all finish-up...'

'If we're not careful!'

She called: The-Shopkeeper: re-plying:

'The Army of Homeless@...they take the out of time, toast out of-date bread on one of those outdoors braziers, you know? They sleep under: The Bridge-Arch(es) you know. It don't seem to worry them...'

'All yesterday's bread has gone: barring-One! *Panic*-buying!'

'Panic-buying? What already?'

'Only that one loaf left now. We won't get another delivery today I dare say. And I am told:

'We don't know when!''

'Well, if '…they don't know? Only: The News'papers delivered so far, and I haven't paid for them yet. Only pay for what I sell: nothing on re-turns…'

'How's that?' doubly surprised at the apparent revelation: *that not everything had to be paid for up-front: Credit. Re-cycled for the next day...*

The-Shopkeeper: came towards the counter of the shop, and continued:

'You can give me all the money you've got if you like. No change though…sweets instead, confectionary, like the last time! Inflation!'

'For; The Children…' *continuing...*

'The Banks are not-open. So, you won't be able to get any F'foldin'-Money or Cash Out of The Machines *anyway*. Never be able to sell *This*-Place now. You know? I've been trying to sell-off The-Shop and its Stock to Pay-off Loans and Bills on The-Shop: and on the stock; but no buyers. Not yet. Not now. I'd have to sell-off at too low a price…or perhaps too high...maybe...'

Then:

'I'll just Up-and-Go: sometime…' *leave it all behind.*

'Family? Any Buyers yet?' She asked, not listening, heard it before; *and not just This Shopkeeper. All the Local Shops were known either by the name on the front of the shop, or the Legal-Nationality: Sovereignty Ethnic-Ethic: Identity of the-Family: that owned, or rented that shop, and its' stocks and shares, and did their business there small retailers, family-run Businesses across The Globe: despite the SuperMalls and HyperHeroes Markets' still the way most Trade finishes up: from the roadside, to and from: The Town and The-City Market-Places lined the streets in and roads out and, of course, to the Stock-Markets and Money-Markets...*

'Waitin' for the Price to Drop even further ... '

She pondered.

She looked at the front page of the newspaper unfolded, and thrown onto the worn-*light* dark varnished and metal-trimmed wooded surface.

She glanced at a cartoon which depicted The Finance Ministers heads in hands sitting on stacks of money; no words needed, but a comment She read for free, without intending to buy, on the inside page:

The Inside Page:

> In the last weeks and months there have been queues in shops for scarce goods, rationed by ability to pay. There have been queues to spend, instead of investing, pay, pensions, and profits, before they became worthless. The prices of goods and services have increased week by week and day by day, as *more* as ever again…

She pondered again: *Don't we just know it! So what's so different!*

She wondered, and said:

'So what's so different!' to no-one in particular: *how the small shops and retailers and service providers like health and social care, whether small cottage hospital or fast-food chain.*

How the small shops managed at all. With all the Hyper-Markets; Super-Markets Out of Town Shopping Malls and Giant Chain-Stores…that everyone shopped at, because they could not better afford the prices and: Scamming Special-Offers…

Hyper Super-Markets' paid up-front but cheaply, and only what they thought they could sell at a good profit and what people could afford paid not at all on what they did not sell or could not purchase…

Fixed the costs and prices in theirs and no-one else's Toffs at the Top and Favour: sold-toxic chemical-manufactured plastic-medicine shit-fertiliser intensive meat-and-dairy dis-integrated organic-Earth: intellectual-property patented re-parented cross-seed global-generational multi-cultural food-crop(s) e-Quality…tech….

The Shopkeeper had continued without stopping hardly, and stocking the shelves and the final aisle way finished:

'...that's it! Everything is out. I'm now officially almost out of stock!' *apart from what I've got in the back for me and the family for a few days...*

The shopkeeper pondered the arrival of a starving family…his, starving family as any other:

'...and that's it!'

The *Train* of *thought* returning to re-stacking the meagre shelves with the remaining stock, and with some finality:

'Not getting in even enough customers to cover the household ourselves! Existing loans on capital, stock and shop; rent is un-paid for the *year...*'

Back at the counter, handing the money-back:

'Go-on, you may as well take it! Here, why don't your Other half bring us some nice freshly baked bread to stock up the shop with?! That's where He works, it is isn't it? They 've closed the works. Again, did you know?! I owe them anyway, The Bakery, The Cash and Carry, you name it! I'm well into negative equity now! The amount the shop owes...is owed. Never sell up now, have to give it away!'

Then:

'That is where He *works* 'though, isn't it? The Bakery?'

'Not any more it seems...' her sullen answer.

The Shop Keeper then with a renewed finality:

'How about a Free Newspaper, then? Everything else has been taken from us, they've bled us dry!' the Shopkeeper exclaimed.

She exclaimed, without irony; restrained and mixed with anxious mirth. She said to stem the merriment:

'HaHa...You know We don't even get bread re-tail from The Bakery: nevermind *free*-Newspapers!'

'Have to steal it then?'

'They are All *that* tight with *their*: Profit(s)…and Credit for Wages!! Credit or Profit for What?! That's what it is! Like you have to work to buy food before you can eat even if you're starving! Even although He *works* there!'

The Shop Keeper and She added together:

'How *stupid* is that?!' un-*caring*-for-your workers and staffed as cheaply as searched for any takeouts!

Hired&Fired. On the spot! Stealing-loaves…

The Bakery: wants to make as much profit out of *Us* as they *can*…

Same as the Hospital! And That is lives! Not-*lies…stealing-lives! Saving! Lives, All!* out of all of us! Never mind the *measly* pay! Anyway... pointing a thumb back through the door:

'If The Bakery works are closed, no-Bread...'

'And no Cake either; not today, at least!'

The money for a small loaf was put on the counter and the large sliced loaf in its *mould-inducing plastic wrapper* and the newspaper with its banner headline declaring:

STOCK MARKETS IN CHAOS

was carried-off.

'Will you be going into: The Rally?'

She texted when she had left The Shop, and called His mobile cellphone with photograph stored-number *gazed-at* longingly*:*

Voice-message command-ready: as speak-texted back-alerted:

Ting.

'No-point going in before I'll *not* be getting paid-off any-way! Maybe?' *seen, re-dund-ant thought…*

From The-TV: pipeline disputed: Halted. Soon. For-now…

'Controlled. Transport infra-structure built…'

Modernised for:…

'Re-Building…'

'Started: Between All of U(S). In-vested-in…'

'The-Vision:…'

'Full-Employment…'

'Living-Wage, Hours and Conditions.' *chosen& taken.*

'*Claim*-Control…'

'Social-Care&Common-Wealth? Education, Health and Homes?'

'Un-believable! Only: Hotels…and: Market-Place(s)…Blown-up!'

'*Brought*-down…'

Explosive: Armistice; Armaments mining brutal new raw-materials and manu-factoring plant(s) occupied: taken: bombed-out:

Oil-platform and market-re-finery: clean:

Clean: <u>*Water*</u>-Wells: *NOT OIL WELLS!!! fighting and peaceful remonstration between sibling's squabbling...screened:*

Green-wash...muddling-through management-speaker-energy hy-genic clean-water:

'For: People! Food and Health. Space: to-move gypsy-like Refugees...'

'T0: The-City(ies)! You only have to look *there*:...Who spends most? Who makes the most Servile-Serf or Murderous-Rapist prostituting Robber-Baron! *Re-Publican: Democratic: Presidential-Monarchial...*

Guillotined. Shot hung out to dry. Shackled hand and foot in Communal Slave Citizen-Cabin:

'Debtor: Proxy-Prison...'

'Death-Penalty! Civil-War!'

'Not goin' to Prison just because Taxi-Driver(s) and Bus-Driver(s) and ...'

'Ambulance-Chasing...'

'Genetic-*Lottery...'*

'Brewing-Bakery born...it's in the yeast. Mouldy sour-dough: Food-rations Weapon(s)-Factor(ies)y: Market(s) Place(s): given:...'

'Blown-up!'

'Market-Places...'

'Bigger-Picture?'

'There is *collusion*?'

'Collision...'

'Between a Bullet and a Hu-Man-Being?'

'To: Bomb: a Building with People inside on a Religious-Culture. Clash?'

Controlling the Numbers…lost their pensions insurances not-assured lost for good…

No Home, Food-Bank: starved living in the trailer or a tent not in the campsite or the trailer park, but surviving Survivalists…

In The Woods…in The Mountains…

'Re-Legion! And they're coming to get You!' *You…Us…We? Armed...and loaded-legged-it...shit for-brains though:*

'Too busy striving for surviving…'

'*Mush*rooms! Fed on Shit in: The-Dark…'

'People! For-Food! Cannibals! No-*brains* at all…'

'The God(s) of Money!'

'*Them We* Need:…'

'The-Goods...Stocks and Shares…pricing: Food-stuffs…'

'Food Banks…' de-*serving*-poor:

'Quantity: The Homes…'

'In The First Place…'

'Off-Grid. Food and Homes. Welfare, that is what The People want...our-own!!!'

'Well Fair…'

'WarFare?'

'Equally? Quality?'

'Badly-*enough now!* Social-Right(s): *useful*-employment…'

'Responsivities not-shared:…'

'Then you can have your-Responsibilities…'

'Duties of Care:'

'Health and Happiness!'

'Dream-On.'

'Rights and Responsibilities…right?'

'So where's Yours, now? The Media? The Votes? The Majority dictating Markets? Value for Money? Paid-for elections…'

'Whose? Ours or Theirs? My vote?'

'What de-nomination?'

'Re-ligion?'

'Government. Social-Insurance pensionable self-reliance limited Safety-Net…'

'Culturally Charitable-claused: caused: *Institution*(s): Exempt…schools ' re-moval of any prohibition arranging for functions to be carried out by a body whose activities are carried for profit.'

'Privatisation!'

'For Us!'

'The few only…'

'Not-for profit Votes!'

'Dis-enfranchised…'

'Charity!'

'Donor-Fund?'

'Bailout!'

'Pay Your Taxes!'

'Poll-Tax Government!!!'

Banker-political:

Reform! Opportunities'

Over! Back to the Shrine! Back to The-Streets!

Fighting for Human-Rights!

Fighting for Peaceful Responsibilities!

'Peoples' Rights?'

'Peoples' Re-sponse(i)bilities…'

'Banks.'

'Left-Banks…'

'Corporations' Media&non-Media (M&non-Media).'

'Governments!'

'Sometimes *rarely…*'

'And/Or Liars! All! Even:'

'Un-even. Un-equal not even near: Un-fair. Every Vote Counts!'

'Proportional: more…*Democratic…' absolutely sure the majority never but the least worst lose out all lose out but the few::*

'Identity. Every piece of Gold!'

'Iron Poll-Tax!'

'More-than and less-than!'

'But Own IT ALL ANYWAY!!'

'If at All.'

'All Vote(s): *count...*'

'N/nnn...'

'The: Never-Ending: Auction-Race...'

*'Racing-Auction:...*gambling with-life: all-*running...*'

'To the Top!'

'IT goes:...'

'Highest-bidder...what's wrong with that?'

'Lowest common-denominator...taxes...nothing: to-Bid with?

'Exchange and Interest -ates *dropped...*'

'Optimism *spreads like WildFires...spending...'*

'As-pessimism...' burning-off the opposition:

'Promising...'

'The Bearer...'

'Pall-Bearer...'

'Giving to Get...'

'Lending-Investment for Dividend...'

'Share-Holder voting by buying and selling virtually...'

'Trust...confidence...breaks-down...'

'Rigged? As mis-Trust? Biting on Byte-Coins?'

'Mostly over-reaction based on *bad*-information…' mis-*information…*

'Not *Freely*-given…'

'Lies, paid-for…'

'Birth-*Privilege…*' dis-crimination pre-judice: soft/hard levers…:

'*White*?' 're-cycling re-producing re-processing…

'You are what you are.'

'**Black?**' re-cycling re-producing re-processing…

'*Confidence…*' im-*posed*: on *Others*'not-*photographed:*

'Paid-for….'

'Trust is what keeps E-*verything* going…'

'But a little *mis*-trust may save your Soul…'

'Your-Conscience?'

'Memory.'

'A little *false*-information?'

'Then coming up with The Goods?'

'I believe all souls are basically good…'

'At not getting caught…'

'Is that all this is? Lies that don't pan-out long term?'

'Lives. Crashed! Minute-to-massive:'

'Money-*deals…*'

'Only *really? Castigation!'*

'But No-One Suffers?'

'Every-One does! We All want Food…'

'Home: *goods…services…*'

'Producers and distributors…see?' in *own*-world *normal*-room.

Play-Station: Rock-Pool: Sunset fish and creatures stand and sit perspective pick flowers reach out and pick feelings?

'Birth-*Privilege...*' re-cycling re-producing re-processing…

'*Confidence…*' im-*posed*: on *Others*' not-*photographed:*

'Paid-for?'

'Trust is what keeps **E**-*verything* going…'

'How. But a little *mis*-trust may save your Soul.'

'Your-Conscience?'

'Memory.'

'A little *false*-information?'

'Then coming up with The Goods?'

'I believe all souls are basically good…'

'At not getting caught…'

'Is that all this is? Lies that don't pan-out long term? Crashed! Minute-to-massive: Money-*deals*...0nly *really...'*

'No-One Suffers?'

'Capital Investment Trust Fund (CITF):'

'Enriching us all?'

'Re-ducing poverty…'

'Not.'

'Every-One does! We All *need* Food…everyday. Home…' *goods...services...producers and distributors in our own owned world normal-room to live*:

X-box. Play-Station: Super-NiN…esss Z+

Social-Media Network(s)': Rock-Pool: Sunset fish and creatures sand and silt hand-stand sitting perspective picking flowers reached out to the lower branches and pick pocketed *feelings*?

Imag.-limit(s)…drawn and codeed head-set screen-move sub-merged:

Enterprise-training text-speak spoken-instruction padded-cell:

Health&Safety@ *risk-room sensor moving around wi-fi hand-set controller auto-postal fraud from Prisoner to Prison ...*

Criminal-Offence: due-diligence target criminal-deniers personal prosthetic games prostitution to virtual-reality. To: *real*-reality. Tin-can powered by our own body smart faster quicker artificial tendon e-calipers powering motorised armed with: Weapons of Sport: proxy-War: Knives Guns and Vehicles. Of-Sex: *e*-motion:

Net curved-Ball Batted: Hit! Score: VR nauseous-CyBot. Cyb-athlon. Exo-skeleton military-connection difficult hacking with live-pilot drone nano-part-i-cu-late: push-pedalling pulling-to: get to target away-from:

'Banks and Building-Site! Factor(y)(ies):…' Shut-Down. Closed.

Hot Laser: Radio-Chemo. Burnout cyber-sickness. Mu-t-ation...un-controlled un-controlling particulate. The Other-Part controlling-well enough...successful to this moment...

Multi-task-ing: reading-signal-air-social-sleep memory-mood. A-ttention tens-ion...

I/im-plant: underneath the-skin electrical-input diode and anode electron-holes lit-up pixelated nodal to motion-limited control-Avatar: with thoughts'

Brain-Stormers: making-*waves...*

Virtual: VoodooMagic Predator under cover com-puter-memory-maker: **SMART**: *safe and secure...*

Internal e-mails

In-formation on everyone in the world...

'Transaction-Cost(s)...@

'Price? For what we *have* to have to Buy?'

'Paid-Employment with conditions attached:…'

'Staple(s): of course, energy, food and water and roof over our heads...'

'Welfare-Share(s)? Fair HealthCare…'

'Credit(ed.)?For what? To Who? Debit(s)…see?'

'Well?'

'Fair? Or Not?'

'Car-Pool? All Of Us?'

'Automated. Not-likely...not if We can help IT!'

'Collect and Re-turn. Driverless? How about it? Allies? You? Rational or Equitable or both?'

'One of five or or six really...in any sector…'

'Globally…'

'World-Wide…'

'Ally? Right here? Right now? The: *City*?'

'Specifically?'

'SMART? Me? You?'

' How do we get there?'

'Not how…Where? Apart from on *This The*-Train?'

'The-*City*? Share-Prices? Dropping like rocks…'

'Or Bombs…'

'Nuclear.'

'Confusion is all IT takes…'

'No-*confidence…*'

'Informed: *con-fusion…'*

'Creating-*inevitably…*'

'Fusing-the-0pposition?'

'Fission nuclear-fuels…'

'Fueling-fusing: con-fusing…'

<N/n/N/nnn…com-*plexing*:

'Doesn't have to be. Made to be our way Out of Global…' *warning warming…*

Swarming: as Geo-Political: economic-disaster: *thermal*-meltdown: *rising…*

'Carbon-capture…'

Oxygen mask *connected…*

'Hydrogen: electric-fuel and Nitrogen-Cycle(s): Oxy-clean water-based life de-salination pro-crastination di-v-iding and de-ciding and de(v)eloping-further… '

'Sea: Ocean-Land Level(s): year-on-year…'

'More: Desert *less*-trees…'

'Slimmer: *shady*-hot…'

'Day-by-Day…'

'Money and Trouble-and…'

'Strife! Married!!! Bread! Cake! Today!'

'Benefit-from: The Stand-Still: *ceasefire*-to: Buy-Out: *then* stabilise and…'

'Business as usual? What about : The Big Buy-Out? Cost-Price Analysis: Placement and Promotion! Penetration, De-velopment and *Di-Versification...*'

'Verification? Product?'

'Money…*then...*'

'The-City...Society...' where Brokers and Jobbers…

'Buyers' and Seller's…'

'Buy and Sell...'

'Break-out…and make IT!' *gophers' runner's-rumoured and listened-in true whistles-blown. Bells'-wrung.*

'*This Capital-***City:…***flight-to: …*'

<The-City: *Option(s):…*

Trumpets, horns blew from afar. Behind-self and other-construed cloud constructed amorphous as from behind closed-door screened newspaper curtained-off then heard from back behind: The-Banker was dis-appeared peering from behind and outwards as if to, and from:

The Train as a whole.

The Other-Passengers and drawn Mechanical-Carriage: *Fuelled and Staffed.* So with fares-paid and terms and conditions *tacitly* agreed by rules and regulations and Laws of The Land and asked:

‘*Great*-Game!’

'Is it All a Great-Game then? No-*Real*-risk...then?’

‘Serious consequences…’

‘Limited-*liability…*’

‘Tech? *Harm-ful*-Tech….?’

‘A rt-i-ficial….’

‘To: n/N/*nnn…*

‘Responsibility? To Your Shareholders or Only To Yourself?

‘You-too. Virtual-Reality Hy-Brid…’

Starchy-Nano: mole-cular: Wacky-Races! Image: confirming:

‘Your-Debts.’

‘To be, or not to be, anymore, is that the question? So, what is to make of it, now, then?’

The-Banker: avoided eye-contact now on ear-piece bartered furtively and openly and loudly and confidently *confidentially flashed* a look across and down into the opened laptop tablet as if commanding from the top of a *mysterious:* thrilling: Money-Mountain…Magic Money Trees. *Mysteries…*seemed like they were *given*: true.

Conspiracies. Brute-Logic. Full Reason. New World-Order. Hunted Slave-Metics and Dove-tailed To: The-Leader(s)’ *dependency* on-People:

As People on Them before break-fast…

In Life as in Death.

8. World Markets in Turmoil!

As in: a-voiding *Total*-War.

Day-in and day-out Battle(s) to keep Society together and not collapsed *that* much, but struggles everyday…

It. Was obvious. Then. Then, again. Mutilation of the-Multitude *afraid-of* unless…*making*-peace.

Set-sail, oil powered and marched on-land slaughtered drowned at sea and alive converted or not tried in absence then exiled presence at:

The Gallows…swapped hand-signals and *punched* the air...*slapped both*-palms together:

'High-fives!: We are in the ten's...six...seven-Billion if you will…' and holding a-hand over the heart openly-palmed, and as sat bowed slightly winked, a single staring-eye, as stooped to:

'Trillions…Con-Quer! And: Deal!' with *on-screen* confirmation apparently…*re-directing...confirming...* password…and printed-off paper-copy waved-frantically financial-agreement-stipulating:

'Beat The Competition! To dust! Only to be: *signed-off...*

The Brief-Case: re-*veal*ed laptop lapped as reading-off as The-Clerk now speaking:

'But The Market(s): are closed? Shut-down…'

'Only to the outside world...*details* only to be added then...'

*Complex completio*n…then: out-dated:…

'…simple really but make IT look *complex*...I.T.?

'Trillions of Money! *When.* The Markets Open Again:…'

‘When. The: *International*-Conference?’

‘Details! Live!! Love!!! *The Small-Things! A*nyone can!’

‘All: billion(s) of birthday(s) of: US?’

‘One for Every One of US on this Planet…’ un-mutually-*assured*…

‘Trust…’

‘Democratic:…’

‘Auto-Cratic. Constitutional-crisis. Executive-Orders…too-many!’

‘To be ratified.’

‘If you were getting a tax break for you and your friends’?’

‘Party!’

‘Too-few…’

‘Too-Many: Work(ing) for Pay: Profit(s) Price: Pay-Tax-*funding*: Government…’ Research-and-Development: Safety and Security: pro-tected from harm full-radiation:

‘Sulphur-chlorine…phosphorous-hydrogen cyanide…mustard-gas…’

‘Poisoning: Anthrax Sarin *spore…perhaps…*’

‘Industrial Venomous X-nerve agent: *flesh*-attack…’

‘Nuclear atomic-molecular particle-cloud breathless paralysis respiratory-collapse…’

‘Re-taliating re-tailing: *threat* over-gaining potential-(A)d-vantage (C)apability over: The-Enemy(ies)’…’

‘Allies:…Defence-in-*assault*: protection: from: -fear: inspection embarrassment cover-up:…’

‘Arms-Race anti-dote: respirator-hood: Antropine-jab:…’

‘De-commisioning inspection embargo…’

‘Condemning as after-sale: protectionist Tardi-Grade(s): Grafters: Grifters:…’

‘Chemical.’

‘Biological-Weaponry…’

‘Fertilizer-Pesticide! Mutually Assured Destruction: *cell*-burst! Mad-Hellism!’

‘Waters Processed-Heavenly! Recovery!’

‘Being and Nothingness…’

Re-covering The-Other *continuing existential…*

‘Closed-Down for a while. Not! *Di-saster…*buying-up…’

‘All the *little* people! Great! Again!’

‘Like you?’

‘Like-Me!’

‘You?’

‘Could be…’

‘Super! Hyper-even but: All of Us!

‘Super-Man! Wonder Wo-men!!!’

‘Of course! All-People. If We want To Be…You want: Shares?’

‘That is The Name of the Game?’

‘What? The-Game?’

‘Buying-Up and Selling-Off Shares? Certified Managed Debt-Account.’

In People and Work. Bought-off cheaply freely-landed in-dentured apprenticed traded tortured sold-off: land and goods favouring certain under-writing judgement(s):

'Life! Managed-Certifiable! As Ever!'

'Same...difference! Certitude…as ever:

>Gender Age Fitness and Well-Being:

The New-Slave-Drivers: listed: and over-seers...fore-man and (t)wo-men…savants and servants' risk-takers:

'The People!'

Re-fugees

Trafficked Ex-changed: for: The Good-Life: goods and services' stock-recommendations: in-surance auto-driver(s): living in certain geographical areas with specified proven employment occupational and National-Carrier: selling:

'One: Global-Store': *online huge-volume operating costs-minimised to between 10-20% more/less pay hours and conditions of that incurred by smaller competitors buffeting bunkered-down bullets and billowing raining clouds of*:

'Success!'

'To the-Buyer…'

'The-Seller…'

'Fun-Fair&Free!'

'Trade. Set-*Price:* Buyers? Seller?'

Market-Place(s)…forward-traded bribed for *forced selling long-hours low or no-wage: buying cheap child-labour migrated-to:…*

'Domestic-bliss: Globalisation…' fuel-fumes choking drowning hypothermia at sea pirated smuggled desperation taken-in processed minimally financial-aided for:

'A Life: The-Dealer and The-Buyer not-*equally…'*

'No-shit.'

De-®(i)(v)atives:

Time-Bomb again. Arms, legs, ears deafened and eyes blinded felt the pain:@ Lorry-bombs…mainland not anywhere: Capital-City:

'Again.' borrowing to buy? Again? Hiring? Spending…borrowing-Wars?

'Talking-Wars?'

'Liberal Free-Trade:'

'Taking-on:…'

'Wars?'

*'Battles…*dealt-with: Amnesty…'

'Everyday. Peace-Debt.'

'Cash-Call.'

None-in-Hand…'

'No-Hand(s)…'

'*Killed*-off...'

In-trigue(s)…poisenous like-a@Terrorist-Assass(i)nation: of worthy and un-worthy *cause*:

'Bought-off?'

'Bought-Out?'

'Me?'

'No, not you. For You we have a special-Arrangement…don't we? Tell me what you *know*…or-not…'

'What I say is my stuff.'

'What you hear is your stuff. OK?'

'Debt-Co-Lateral: *Raw materials-in* Goods: in-and-out...Get You In?'

'Get me In? What?'

'Money...*itself*.'

The-Business-Information: analysis…k*nowledge*...

'You…*have*? Knowledge?'

'Insider? *Prediction*. From*: retro-spection…Plus or minus...that is all IT is…*

'Deals...' re-gardless of what IT is…

'Shit. Shit in...Shit-out...'

'To-add you must subtract…'

'We! merely Fertiliser-to:'

*'To: Shit you must Eat…*or: die.'

Hit!*ting* a button-key: door-card: air-conditioning drapes: light.

Dinner: shower-bath: rational-cable: Power-trip. Fetching-collected wiped security-*footage…*

Artifice. Ex-pression. Likeness. The The Real-World…Nation-of-Law(s) of images…Gvt. Cyber-Admin. Block. Family-Account(s): Bio-*metric*…hand foot print: eyes button-camera:

>Deal(s):list:...

<Done.' *and with a nod, laterally entrusted, undisputed, and further endorsed over-lengthy client midday luncheon tied-in as-if gifted as;*

'Charity?' by-guilt-association...pending…expense-account commission un-accounted-for and through electronic-signatory: password name and number recognition and as a matter of public-record only-*details:*

'No longer negotiable...or ever-were. And only the final -*details* to be *added*...then: taken. N-away…'

The-Banker:

'Then?'

'Then?'

'Re-Naging Deal(s)?'

Then:

'All. Traders traffickers to-be *ironed*-out today:

'The Suit(s)…'

'The Shirt(s)…and ties…'

'By the all The-Clerks' and Leaders of all The-Worlds' Works!'*: mis-information-kwiki:..*

'Blame it on the Judge!'

'President?'

'Checks and Balances...'

'Democratic-Trans-parency: liquid-like...' solicited.

Solid as an assignment. Proposal. Proposition. Projected through The *Cloud...pending* thieving conspiracy that is where the missed-truth mis-trust lies…fudges. Hedged first casualties…in-escapable:

'Send them back…'

'Debts? Where? Home?'

'Not-here.'

Station-stop pulled-up. The last one before the-bell was rung for-departure for:

< The-City.

Then as a *warning* to anyone last-boarding the the next Station-Stop: Train-Doors' closed: The Train-Carriage: sealed and seated oppositely a-side again faithfully facefully *fatefully*:

'I don't know what to make of 'It'…yet…' *pause...pregnant...*

Then: from: The-Clerk:

'But I'll *bet* we will find out soon-enough anyway? Don't you?' the-*thought* snickered: *slightingly* to-Self:

'I think we already have. Ill-legal-immigrants? Re-fugees?'

'Health Plan?' re-cuperated:

'Economy, stooped.'

'Stopped.'

Each spoken now and heard, and now seen:

'No going-back now...'

Both, now considering the import of these words, the more thoroughly, thoughtfully, perhaps, than said and heard; those out-spoken, aloud, as to the-*enterprising* enquiry requiring further-reply. In-turns? Or not? Now the previously *saved* in-memory and as the *first respondent* again The-Clerk ignoring the possibility again of turn-taking, with another supplementary yet: elementary-*question*:

'Why?'

'Why? So? Who?'

'Is...What?'

'Me? Now? Business-as usual?'

'Business is *not*-as-*Us-u-all(y)...*'

*Puzzl€*ment seconded now by both-speakers triplicated as almost-identically *mindfully* apart re-flected against all The Others' on The Train. In The Train-compartment *visible* through adjoining compartments and conversation and music-tinkling and beats' *thudding* pro-social financial-networking and attempting quietude: eyes closed as if neither further-apart or closer to, as to:

The-Clerk and The-Banker from: Each-*others*': Truth and in Each-Others' *minds*: and *all this meant what? Exactly? And how soon? How soon, is now? How much is-enough?* And: *How much is at stake here? Exactly?* as instantly both now regretting the opening-given to the exclusion of anyone-else in:

The Train-Carriage. As both-enjoined as advertently now in a two-way dialogue of which at that immediate-point there was persisting, yet only:

'Limited-*information...*'

'In-sight.'

'All likewise:'

The Banker and The Clerk: *momentarily* inadvertently and actually *advert*-o-rially making eye-contact: *flash*-framed each-other and through the closed shared-window as in bright- rainbow and sky-coloured mirrored; as, through each of-themselves *en-raptured* recklessly perhaps to be wrecked or saved as over-crossing:

The Great River(s)' Estuary- Bridge(s): un-noticed perhaps by anyone-else in:

The-Train-Carriage. *Un-cared* for if-noticed-or-not by anyone *else* at-all. Now each *in each others Thrall*:

'Dis-Connected?...'

'You too?'

'Same…'

'Di-versification...'

'*Innovation*...and That hat, is all what is needed.

'Un-charted Territory...'

'Lived-in…'

Imperious: Racial-Colonial#: *violence*:

'New Preference-Functions:...'

'Privilege. Doesn't much matter *what* It is...as long as IT sells...'

'New-*Product* or staples...'

'New-Markets...'

'New-Algorithm?'

'Fat-Finger? You?'

'Me?'

'You?' *Mistake?'*

'Error-message?'

Anyway-horizontally and vertically to the same outside-world moved-past moving-past and through, oppositely and thus as inevitably differently viewed...

As if re-plicated the future re-freshingly really...

Relishing as then focused-away both to the outside-world as indifferently similarly perhaps yet inevitably indifferently: from The Estuary-Town now staring beyond and both towards the as yet unseen rapidly oncoming-City:

'Through-The-Roof!'

Then:

'It Fell!'

'Off The Building! From the-Bridge! Mental!'

'Into the crowded restaurant below of the clerks and bankers below:

'There are the already the well-*drowned...'*

Avatar and-Royal: each of Us: part-in-harm measured in-love all askew and a scrivener looking over: The-Abyss.

Branded aircraft and ships and bull-dozed roadways slipways runways production lines of new goods and scrap re-cycled from foreign parts tariff tax-free trade-fare fair or else prices rising as ever again...

'Price-inflation Tariff-abroad...'

'If You can *Getaway* with IT Again!'

'Pay-Gap Trap. The-same: Again!' *not croft-ed* crafted from forests and desert hill borders *frozen*-legend(s) on-screen: *names* and places...times, and as instantaneously:

'Meteoric!' *collisioning, folding up/ down-wards and inward out-ward side-way(s) full-fell Green&Brown mud-sliding ramming and mined:*

Basement-cellar: filled and built upwards to:

The-Skyscraper*(s): Earth-quaking...shaking bursting volcanic red- flaming...livid: geo-thermal flooded terra re-forming firming farming&man-u-factoring:*

'Once-lived! Dreadful-de-ciept on re-ciept of bad-business low stocks and shares:'

'Will be-Lived! Again! Balancing-The-Books is *all*...'

'Government wants:'

'Experimental! Business! Always! Innovation...that's what make IT Ex-*citing*...'

'To make as much money…'

'For as little as possible…'

'To add-Value?'

'Quality!'

'USure? Tax. Every Time…4War? Peace. The-Same. Each Season *bring(s)*...' *near-far world wanting to buy forced to sell…*

'Import-Export: Food Health and Social-Care: Education: The: Global-Village: Town and City and Coun-try-sided…'

Out the window continuing:

'Lovely. One and A.N. Other…as ever! Bought-Up!'

'Bought-Out!'

'Shafted. Sideways…' *like-Religion...*

Science... Government and Big-Business ...Faith...

Sliding-off the-Screen(s) lit-up with numbers and consonant abbreviations and vowel(s) plural one to another: punctuation and grammar: spelling:

'Com-pre-hensive…' a-*wondering*:

'Business? Trade-takeovers? Farming? Making?' *flaky* common-sense:

'Pharming?'

'Yyyyes…'

'Selling…'

'*Harming*?'

'No!' *uncertainly* to:

'Dia-0besity…'

'Food-*Phishing*?' *bulk target backed-blame: whole-area judicial in-discretion: discriminatory en-forcement:*

'Road-Kill.'

'Can't You See?! 'We' been in a Car-Crash!' then as wittingly un-wittingly:

'Car-Crash? Train-Smash?'

'Do-No-Harm?'

'Un-less *harm* done to?'

'Who?'

'Un-Lucky then. Do harm in return…'

‘Where does IT End? First-Principles: im-perfect information: an Act of mis-Trust: *fixed*-in=Advance…’

‘Fixed-Odds Gambling-Terminal…’

‘To: lose…’

‘So, who wins? Democracy? Autocrac(y)ies?’

‘We do.’

‘Fuck.’

Swearing instant-honesty:

‘Like: *Fuck* we Do…not all of us. No, not all of us...Trade: Free and all that…’

‘Fair-Share(s)?’

‘People-Prost(*i*)tute(s)!!! For how much?’

‘Fare-*fee*?’

‘I*n-vestment best-meant: any inter-action so it seems:’*

‘You and Me...perhaps? Sporting?’

‘Hunting and gathering point(s):’

‘Vote-Money. Big-Phood and Pharma-Farms piddling phiddling the proof-numbers…’

‘Phieving?’

‘Should think so.’

‘Why?’

‘Killing their same but betters randomly non-Gang member…’

‘Advertantly…’

'Caught…they always get caught!!!'

'Time…'

'Postcode-lottery: NNN/nnn/000: Intellectual-Property (P(I)P). Patently…'

'Did you hear the one about the *starving*-Clerk who stole a chicken to feed the family? A stranger called and asked to share: The-Clerk asked: 'Who are you?'?'

'The Stranger answered: 'I am Life! Trust in me!'

The Clerk says:

'Why should I? As you are un-free and un-fair in life and do not share that which I have to steal for me and my family to live? What, has Life, done for me and my family? What have *We* done to You for You to let Us starve?'

'The Stranger says: 'I am then Death.'

'The Clerk says: Sit down, then. As we shall all eventually die you,Death, are Free and Fair on all of Us! Sit down and eat chicken!'

'Free and Fair shares, then, for All!''

'Only when you're Dead.'

'Exactly…Business as Usual...'

'What is-Usual? *Then*? Eh?'

'There? Eh? *Who* is-Usual? *Normal*, eh?'

'Naturally. You!'

'Me.'

'Me.'

'Your-Company. Lawful-Animal Vegetable *Plant* Mineral-Metal…'

'…and dead-Meat!'

'Con-struction & Dot-Comm.(s) still of-course:…'

'Alive! *National: Private-Priestly: fetial: finial-de-corated: festal: foetal: detail: re-tail: fee-paying: Tax-paying…'*

'Abroad. That is why we import? Make more with Tariff: Tax Free-Trade see…'

'Free. Multi-Media:'

'Oligarchial: Try-Con…Global.'

'Phishing?'

'Fueling?'

'Armaments?'

Keeping: The Capital-Company-Line…

'Pro-moting: *false*…Fake-News:…'

'In the: *National-Interest…'*

*'Advertising-lies? Just causing-*War?*'*

'Against-pillage and in-vasion…'

'I was here before You sat down.'

'Im-perfect. Government-Officer? That's 'It' isn't it? Doing the-Governments' *dirty-* work: The-Peoples Work!'

'Voters All!'

'Vote them out!'

'How? In The Tax-Office? Government-corridors? Got The Ear? Pig's ear! Sow's purse?'

'Daily-sacrifice! All of Us!'

'The Peoples' Purse-Strings!'

'Purely, in a Democratic Barrel of Our-Own Making…' *each stock and commodity and bonded share price passed...each sell-by date out-dated...*

'Crashed! Blown-up! People killed!'

'Yes, I know..' *remembering: as lower and lower price-marker losses moved across electronic-boards against rows of banked fan-tail desktop screen-closing: listing: acronymical and apocryphal-foreign and un-pronounceable or mis-pronounced: home-grown and familial on-screen pictured read-off:*

'Government...'

'And *their* Peoples' Property! Lives!!!'

'All! In this together!'

'As *their* Peoples...All.'

Falling into the same *Raging*-Pit...

The same *pithy*-Core of Being...*that evening previously with prices continuously rising steadily being-bought and-sold relentlessly on-commission and sold-on again and again where did IT-end?*

The-Management: fee-taken already as socially contracted suddenly stalled stilled stopped:

'Taken from Us! Each-Time:'

'On-*inflated prospect...*'

'Exaggerated. CON-fidence:…'

'*De-flating*-prospect now...'

'That is all…'

'De-valuing us all with a c*on-fidence* un-done.'

Looking down and into a lapping lapped blank screen: with *realisation*-rising dropped in free-*fall: looking-up:*

'Un-precedented price-rises blamed...'

'Then?'

'Wages-drop…'

'Stag-flation…'

'Stag-Nation?'

'In?'

'Everywhere. Zero-rates of ex-change and *interest…*'

'Civil-(i)-sation: Business's Now! Basic-Income: To: Live!'

Collapsing in-itiating un-mitigated…

'*Di*-saster!'

To@ the-(i)n-i-tiated: just another: Day's Trading that strange and unknown incantation of: Corporate-Commodity-Capitation: announced: *and de-capitation pronounced thereof: dis-proportionate re-sponse re-cording:*

'Midday…. '

The Busy Body-Politik…

'Business…'

'Trade: Aid…' as *religiously as-politically…*

'Pull a Stunt!' *as ever hanging-on: The slow-Scientific: Economic split:*

'FAIR-Trade?'

'Price and Cost: that is all it is...what is 'I' is over between those is: Profit-Interest excessive of-course…

'Improve better and perfect working conditions…'

'Like watching mere-Daisies' *growing...'*

'All you need to worry about…'

'All *We* all need to worry about…Who? Is going Top!'

'To make the...Daisy-Chain? Profit? Balanced thus free and fair yet…'

'The Top take-more…'

'Loss. Exactly.' *simple as that announced with comparable lamentable-loss...laconic, iconic, as compared to a nano-second earlier, and no sooner or later than:*

'Timing...*mis*-timing…'

'Is no-timing...as <u>Today:</u> Too-*late?'*

'Now! Immediate-closure. There, and Then...' *e*-photo taken:

'No warning-signs?' *and at that-place...as in each and every other Big-City-Exchange. In their own-time and place there was for a-change in the stifled stilled emptiness: an assumed and peculiar-pecuniary, and utter quiescence of now political-religious: tragic almost comical, theatrical proportions. The Parenting patronising-*secular promise: pictured: an unpromising condescending candescent screen-saver stilted stilled as on paper-writ:

Market Closed.

crumpled as some witticism *baiting* as some as yet *unrealised*-victim:

'Ignored to:…'

'Now! By Greed! Blown-*up! in: Your-Face*! Out of all proportion! What-for?'

Knocked-down *traitorous-villainous:*

'Heroic! Un-Heroic! Martyrdom!'

Dead. On-track, now *toward where dealers in-Global-Commodities: Wheat and Gold, Diamonds and Cocoa, Coffee and Tea, Soya, Corn and Rice:*

'Food&Fuel.' and rare-metals and mineral gem-market(s)...

Frozen-screened re-heated:

'On *false*-Figures?'

'Official! False *fake*-figures! Fake? Or-*True*?'

'Accounted-for?'

'Divide and Rule? How do you know?'

'Exactly! Info-Nation!!!'

'Infotainment Scams! Not on your life! Fraudulent! Corruption!'

'Organised-Crime! This is what keeps this whole caboodle going! Trace-able? Buys and Sells? Bought and sold...that's all...'

'All?'

'Time?'

'*Due*-diligence…' *after:*

The-last-Event…knew nothing…

‘Analysis? Knew nothing? Directors?’

‘*CEO/CFO/COO:...’ pidgeon-steps:*

‘ShopFloor PayGap mark-up made-up: 50-300%: to:...’

‘*Not-saying:...’ mostly unknown un-taxed evaded avoided... ig-snored:]*

‘Tax Re-turns?’

‘How about a share in the-*repossession* then? Same-Again? How's about *fair* shares then this time?’

‘In the Losses?’

‘149% Homes De-fault reached! Don’t tell everyone! Risk to Losses…’

‘Chance?’

‘No-Chance.’

‘Equal?’

‘50/50?’

‘Zero-Sum difference!’

‘Out-Go equals-income…’

Game-Playing:

‘Top to bottom *fair*ness as: Pay-Gap: Globally: *generally* acceptable?’

‘Brain-surgeon to car- mechanic street-cleaner re-cyclers…’ f*arting*: following-through…

‘*Shitting*: Time and Money! Life! Work and *then* Play! For Pay!’ looking-up into the eyes of the original protagonist now turned antagonist:

'*Nothing* is for Nothing.'

The-Banker: *looking down into the screen of a half-opened brief-case then speaking into the blind yet not-deaf-space between them*:

'If You don't...someone else will.'

Marshalling-Yard: prowess, and the-dark-arts horse-back ridden, risen over grass-lands roots&green-shoots...

Actioning: Dark-*Mountain Project*: myth *mystifyingly undermining, transition-culture... Collaps-a-nomical...*

Drilling-down: optimism projected...against pessimism re-surgent: emotional-rhetorical: Climate-Changing-inevitability...

Migration-Movement muddled spiritual-debate: of confident-faith-boosting happy gamma-decoding brainwaves...into abstract-reasoning memory...re-locating...after any event has passed pasted into-history: productivity-rates births and deaths…

Acted-out as previously run-backwards before a backdrop of multiple-windows gold and silver-grey screen-graphics security and multi-tasking capabilities (not necessarily achieved) : a patchy grey-hazing jagged-green shining outward sprouted trailblazing digital-numerically downward to-ward: The Burning Centre of The Earth: taken-root.

Re-routed, deeply-inside and on carbon black luminous background: pixilating-light screen black-to-red blue-green: simmering onto a dark slate heat-light dotted... warming… *cooling-off:* fading-into: pastel-yellow grey-cloud softening over Mountain and Hillside and as: The-City skyline re-*imagined* as:

'The-Logo?'

'R/e.'

‘E.R.?’

‘E/R? Markets Closed? Equitable?’

‘Rational?’

‘Is all that’s *needed...*’

Ridden-towards: as at the start of *a brand new-day* The-Clerk asking now:

'So. How did 'We’ get into this *Mess*?’

'What Mess? This cycle of in-debtedness again?’

‘This dis-*array*!’ into the out of cloud screen device:

‘Fast-Action...Slow- motion...saw It-coming?’

‘Pile-up. Hit the buffers. Off-the-rails...’

‘Slow-motion wreck...’

‘Train-wreck?’

‘This: *little-Turbulence...*’

The-Banker perhaps unexpectedly uncompromising, in response to: The- Clerk:

‘Wrecking-Ball! Hurricane!’

Re-covering: The-Banker:

‘Global-*Turbulence* is All.’

Ghostly...ghastly...infinitely messy fractal vortices:

‘There is a Market-Situation@ *known as Demand and Supply…*’

‘Where: if a company doesn't have enough shares in stock to distribute and sell...’

‘Then this increases the price for these as a result...’

'…and this is known as a Bull-Market.'

'And this is what we have? A Bull Market? Cow? Or perhaps *had*: Ursa Bear-Market?'

'Or perhaps a: Dragon Market? *now...anyway...*

'Tiger-Market?' *Panoramic*:

'Tiger-*ish*…a growling Jaguar squawking screeching-Macaw-monkey market if you like! A Lioness? Li-gerrr! A Tion? A Lie-ter…Bonfire? Of The Vanities! 'It' doesn't matter what you call 'It'! The bigger picture...*thinking*-outside: The-Box:...'

'The-Cage?'

'Bigger: Picture-Box….'

'This is a Movie-Film?'

'Cinema?'

'Big-Biota: Algic-bloom: Enzyme-Crash!'

'Rioting-*Viral*...this is not a *script(ed.) ...'*

'Cover-up.'

'Secrecy: intellectual property confidential:'

'Big-Pharma:'

'A*nti*-Biotic….'

''Flu jabs give you:'

'In-flu-Enza….'

'Homeo-Pathic!'

'Astronomical.'

'Astrological…'

'Made-up. No all…'

'The-Money?'

'Debt? Hospitals re-cyling Life and Food-Factory:'

'Banks.'

'Admin.'

'Best? Better?'

'Advertising patenting-design: *I-magi-ne-ing: Tech. Machinations:'*

'Agricultural In-dustrial and Techno-Digital…'

'Social-Evolutionary…' *assumed*

'Pragmatic. Goods' *consumed*: *badly allergenic histamine-hormonal-warning(s)…*

'And: People. Each Personal-Battle(s):'

'Life!' *particular(s) in an all-out:*

'War(s)! All-Day! EveryDay!!' falling-backwards…

'To: Battle! The World Order!! World-0ver!!!'

9. Your Debts? Your-Bet? The Bait is Laid.

He called-in to: The Bakery and after sending the text about going-to: The Rally. As: The Walker walked not-ran toward The School-Door since: The-Teacher was now in-charge, and He: settled the younger child into nursery and out through The School Gate He met a Work-Mate also, going towards: '*The Works'*: The Bakery: The-*Factory* as it was known: The Bakery: The Factory-Gate.

From The Nursery School passed the old religious buildings at the top of the road.

Now a Friend and Neighbour from the same Residential Housing Street walking in the opposite-direction and now shared: The Journey Home:

'Not going in ...'

The Other had said:

'No Good. They've shut The Factory again!'

'Remember last time?'

'Few more out of work, three day week again? I Know only too well! What now? Zero-hours!'

'Work for *No-Thing?*'

'The last time, and the time before that!'

' 'It' has happened before!' was the blunt reply without irony. The Other replied:

'Its' *Close-down* Time for good *this* time we reckon…'

'There is A Meeting mid-day...'

The Other continued:

'The Factory-Gates! We'll find out then!..' and *laughing*:

'See you there!' shouted as they passed closed shops and each to their separate homes *laughing* at what they could not be sure *like The Children: waving and laughing too, at what they knew not what. Awaiting midday afternoon when they would meet up again. Or would: The Rally finally put pay to all their carefully laid plans for the day? The Children…half-day…*

He remembered…The Midday Inter-National Government Conference: they had walked back towards their homes.

Passed by other shops nodded and said hello:

'Hello' to The Shopkeepers and The Paying Customers standing around inside and outside on The Street as they passed:

'What's going to happen then?' Another called over:

'Nothing!' He called back. Then to The Friendly Neighbour walking alongside:

'*Nothing*...again!' Then up the stairs to the apartment along the balcony walkway. When He got indoors with the key, shouted:

'Hello! Home!' only out of habit and out of habit switched on the T.V. and He: started to clear-the-breakfast-things away.

She had already set off for work, with a sandwich and the last of the bread remaining calling after him, and He then thinking: *Did I say I'd bring some bread home? She'd said earlier:*

'We need bread!' laughing:

'And bandages! If you're hungry...even if it's stolen!'

'If you hungry from work...you hungry! If you *hungry*-before...*I'll get some in later anyway, in any case if there is any left over, anyway, I'll have to to take it and risk my job...'*

'Sour-dough here!' She had replied, and She then:

'Don't lose your job over a loaf of bread!' thinking: *it was lucky I got some in yesterday. He* thought: *or sheer skill remembering what She'd told me before I went to work the same yesterday...and I* didn't *forget...*

Then, to now: *and now it's all gone!*

But this time...tomorrow... and as He settled-down with a *last of the bread* wrapped bandaged toasted-dry sandwich in front of the television to watch events unfold:

He wondered: *or did I just imagine that? From some Other time, yesterday? or at all, anyway...*

*Anyway: What does it matter. We need bread...and I'll get some later...*then mindful *of: The Midday Meeting at work and collecting...looking-out for looking-after: The Children...*

Shopping later at the supermarket wondering: *what would happen if there was no bread. No work? No money to pay for the bread, the shopping? The mortgage?* worry reserved-not for what would occur anyway...which as yet He did not know for sure, for certain, what would happen today.

Only what *might* what-may occur. What could occur. What Can occur kicking the-can down the road.

C*ould*-not would occur which was all He could really think about existential angst...compre-hension-essential...what *should* occur?

What Shall Occur...Hopes and fear meshed with Love&Hate!

Home, and a sandwich at this very moment…with whatever is left in the bottom of the bread-bin and some *half-empty or half-full jar or a tub of something and back to work...*or not. *Before the meeting at midday...collecting The Children...half-day telling her...*reading quickly, scanning the front page of The Newspaper paid-for:

> **STOCK-MARKETS IN CHAOS!**
> Today, there is so much owed by so many, that cannot even start to be paid-out, or will ever be paid-back. This morning the stock-markets are closed. Once more world trade has ground a halt. All financial currency and credit/loans trading, the trading of stocks and shares that in recent times has left prices at all high time levels, overnight have collapsed. We are in the *Greatest* fiscal and financial crisis, ever; and yet, *again…*

At-Home: *no hurry yet* He realised: TV-Home: *Food-First then…again: Street and Super-Market: if or if not before, this time: that He didn't have any cash.*

Only a couple of plastic notes the cash-card machines would be empty. If The Banks were closed, and there had been panic withdrawing, as well as buying yesterday, there would be none left, and anyway risk going around and topping them up with new notes now wouldn't there? Money riots? Pillaging Smash 'n' Grab! Striking-first! On-Strike! Lightning! Wildcat! Same thing...something: stoppage looting...on TV-information like a game being played-out elsewhere:

Going-slowly…the: Armoured Security Vehicle: bullet-proof cars, dark and light brown, black and silver striped, dusty rumbling over the go slow cobbled pedestrianised street as seen*: shops either side walking down the centre...*the *imagined* seen-crowds *emerged into: The City Square: emptied except of Troop carriers and Tanks.*

Automatic Teller Machine...emptied well before…so simply locked and bare barred yet empty. The security-vehicles will be headed-back or staying in base...keeping all the money for themselves! Under-Orders no doubt. Police escort definitely; and The Supermarket would not be open anyway. Since most people paid by credit/debit card. There would be shortages already, on the shelves, after one day. They were all virtually 24/7 anyway…of the day everyday…week, month and year. It would all be Gone. Bought or or robbed or hoarded frozen in the freezer for later…

Possibly: The Bakery Factory: raided with violence.

For: Work. Bread and Hospitable(s):or unpaid taxes who'd know! No deliveries anymore...they'll be closed. Waiting with all their stock for the prices…

'To Rise-UP!Take-Control!!' He exclaimed to himself. In-image of rioting threatened looting, hundreds, thousands of shoppers stripping the shelves of everything *paying, or not.*

The-Supermarket? Could be open tomorrow; if everything was sorted-out by then He wondered *If? And how much would everything cost, once it was all sorted out? With what pay? None? What about the food and everything? Ourselves? Our families? Our Mothers and Brothers…and Sisters…*

Compadres...duty-bound, to each other and to Them to their *Stock-Holders…Workers-Groups! Ourselves! Yet, individuals with individuals wishes and needs and selfishness. Anyway paid and pensioned-off if we are lucky in and finished work...putting the prices-up they'll tell us! To their-customers who are US! Trying to keep prices down they say…Price wars? Shopping Wars! or colluding…colliding tender-Gender War(s):* almost: brutal-*Battle(s)-of-The-Sexes Game-Show: Logic analysing: Guessing…*

*

They themselves He and She and The Children and extended-Family: Friends and Neighbours: Other-people we meet on the way, and lose, EveryOne: event-u-ally: *would have enough to stock at Home and then be broke again and if we don't get paid into The Bank and then to The Shops, then what?!* and suddenly He thought less calmly.

They had to get some money from The Bank and The Mortgage had to be paid: *would The Mortgage be paid if The Bank was closed? There was some food in the kitchen, and water in the tap. He had a little money. She always had some...usually...*

So they should be alright for a few days? Perhaps? The-Banks had been shut before. Bank Holidays! That's all! It would get sorted out. After this enforced holiday...the shops always open the holidays to grab everyone's Cash while The Banks are closed anyway. The Bank(s) are never closed...auto-money that is what it is now…

Online…go to: The Supermarket. Closed. Tomorrow, when The-Banks would be open again and shelves and cash-machines re-filled. Like fuel-stops, and cards and online banking re-commence…again:

'*After all,* they are not going to want to lose business' He said out aloud and to himself:

'I get paid so that They get paid and They pay people like me to pay: The Prices to Pay them back on Credit: *and so it goes around...*'

'Everything-Cost(s)…' To: no-one else there except the TV screen in the background:

'Basics:Staple(s): Fuel and Foodstuffs...'

'Health and Social-Care:... *' when markets back in the black...from the red...credit...screen*-blues and yellows and greens *flashed* across the *screen… '* a-scream! On the T.V. more reports from:

The Stock-Market(s): around: The World. Those that had closed, or opened and then closed immediately:

'The City, the Financial Quarters...'

'Are awaiting *instruction* from The-Government(s) and Big Business's...'

'…and: *The-Market Street and International Experts to give their expert Opinion… ' opining:* minor-officials from: The Banks and The Governments' made statements to the effect that:

'The Banks were: Closed…To: Day…*as if anyone did not know that by* now…'

'Unless they were brain- dead; or living in the middle of the jungle or the desert-fossil(s): or on top of a mountain with no electricity, no radio-signal, no fuel for *smoke-*signals:…'

'Government –0fficials are meeting to discuss:…'

'The-Crisi(s): Around The World...' from the TV screen:

'To: Day:…'

'The Statement at Midday…'

'…would Calm *Fears* of Looting...' etc. *never mind looting that had already happened and was about to kick off again somewhere, maybe even here.*

Maybe our street, our Home-Food: in the Kitchen-water:... in the tap shut-off through non-payment…

The News: continued to come in from around the world and was broadcast *simultaneously*...raw and un-edited reports on audio and video from Cities and The Country-sides cataloguing *unfolding* events. The sound and pictures of people meeting, being interviewed. Ready to comment on the announcements and their responses:

'Temporary shelter tents etc. food and water...'

'Women and children are at The Railway Station fleeing...'

'Stock-piling…'

'Trade-Ears!'

'All! Food-Riots!'

'Water!'

'In the dust and debris...' and the like:

'In the fields homesteads and out houses...buildings on fire...' suddenly from The-City streets:

'Convoys blocking the way...in some places Economic-Political Religious Race-Rioting:' as sides taken…the assumed poor stealing from the richer…lootings as stabbings by- *force buildings burned: Hospital Doctors and Nearest Electrical Rational-Engineers; Architects and Builders their Work undone Ambulance gone to help the last emergency emergency-services attacked for trying to save: Police or Army casualties and The-Demonstrators!*

Blown-Up! Killed! Shot at with Buck-Shot Tirade. It didn't matter who they were. Mis-understood, dangerous-language, perhaps, uniforms. Phrases, trying to make the situation more understandable, not less:

Any excuse He thought and then heard:

'Shelling gunfire...fields land-mined...cluster-bombed...'

'Attacking or Defending?' *Fighting-back. I always understand how my enemy thinks. And when you truly(?) try to-understand also you love them impossible not to love as they love themselves…*

Afraid you won't understand. Afraid you'll lose. *Attacking obviously* He thought:

'It is Difficult to Tell...' from the T.V.

N*ot from here it isn't* She thought *fighting back against Governments, and The World Bank and Global Trade-Markets...as they see it.*

Necessary as they made themselves seem but it wasn't necessary at all except for themselves and the competition from the people:

'Accountable! No Surrender! No Trust monopoly! Price! Rate-fixing…Global National Sovereign Governments and Big Business Corporations and lending-Bank's leaders meeting face-face. Others via satellite links...' *telephones and facsimile machines whirring and humming helicopters buzzed in and out of The InterNational Global World Conference-Site:*

'Freedom and Justice!' all specific and vague:

Policed and Army feet and heads and heads Air-Force 'planes and Drone-Heli-Cop-ter:

Quad and Space-Craft Stations in Village Town and The City-States Nations' Army Air-Force and Navy: on*:*

'The Pirated High-Seas…' this next solution was expected by each side or another…not whether, only when:

'Oil and Environment, again.'

High-Rise *memory*-Bank(s): en-coded per son alities daughter(s)' lived; fil-ed re-corded: *strung-out*…laundry drying whitening in the sun darkening in:

#The-Shadow(s) in: The: Broad *Daylight*... concrete-bollarded: blockaded and surrounded by Army-Vehicles.

In Convoy with Police-protecting the buildings and streets beyond, on the emptied: Hyper-Highway Super-ways:

E-Craft: Solar-Lunar Wind&Wave Power: Helicopter and small Sesna's and other: light-aircraft too-off. To: : Space-Station: *deliveries:*

Management-Logistic(s): and Detritus: water and *waste*-removal: returned to: Earth: landed and took-off:

'At *The-International Global-Economic Conference:...*' the most well known and many totally un-known for-gotten faces for lawn and forlorn exchanged formalities; beckoning each other forward, back, or sideward's *in gestures of Power-Broking and Politicking: not even they know what is going-on...what is going-down...they* were made to laugh, coyly in public; at free hate-speech comments made amongst each other, shook hands, and slapped-backs:

'Press-Conference and Delegates'...*meetings Bull-dozed*-in...'

'Demonstrators' bearing-bourne-back borne-out...'

'Behind-Barricades...'

'Check-Points and Door-Security:...'

'The Governments and Banks however cannot agree Privately or Publicly between themselves or each other...'

'What *then*?'

'Some developments...announcements *will* be made before Midday...we are told...'

'To: stem uncertainty...violence and...anger frustration against felt-oppression...'

'W*ill they Work? Will they be believed?'*

Lines were drawn and withdrawn. Re-drawn and drawn, anew; and still again it seems:

'There are still, too many vested-in-tere(sts).'

'That divide, that could not in one or the next session get resolved, *yet...*'

From The TV Studio:

'The City Road and Railway Junctions and intersections...' *forked knifed and spooned to The City...seamlessly linked centre taped-off in yellow and black, blue and white, red and black, as through into a crime scene:*

'People are coming into: The City: Towns and Village-centres' gathered and emptied travelling in on motorbike and car. Coach, and Lorry…' a crime scene, they were made out to be:

'The Demonstrators and The Security Forces...' driven-into. *So-called…to avoid panic… security causing panic… un-Truth(s) wrapped-up as: The-Truth: until: eventuall-denied proportion or number of whatever……*

Outside, and inside CCTV cameras *reached the boardrooms leaking e-mails toxic enough: high-level: Toxic-Air! Puts and Calls being put-in drop placed:* donation: charity: lottery-research and development: large medium small: scale: The-Business of-Government:

'On Present: Presidential-Index:...' *texting…sexting*...un-moving credit-default...commission interest-rates and credit-rebate altering payment and re-payment...

The News: Broadcast: *broadcast and We seem to hold Our Collective Breath…*

'To await further announcement:...'

Blank-screen as if transmission lost for a moment then inter-*rupted*:

'People arrived to work to join the Meetings and Demonstrations that are already gathering in great numbers at workplaces, towns squares and piazza and village-streets and roads and streets in City Centres...

As the whole world it seems protests in Town and City-Square...Shopping-Mall…' and as cinematic as a musical theatre-hall on-line and in front of TV: The President's Face appeared: *more and more elaborate excuses and blame.*

Conscionable Self and The Other. Not caring for Them! or Anyone...anyway.

More Anger Fear and Blame. Self-satisfied, and lying, self-assured lustful delirium reaction at being caught-out:

*'The-Crisis...*This-*Time.'*

It was difficult to tell if at the beginning or end or an almost endless sounding speech *perhaps on loop...*

The-President looked drawn. But was adamant no-changes or some changes would be made, after the previous offer of limited change had been ignored and *the speech went on and on, round and round* and faded-out. TV-Journalist:

'The Presidential Security Forces...'

'*Why?*'

'In-*secure*: The *Secular and Religious:* Rebel-Rogue: Fighting-Force(s)…' *as well as ostensibly with sophisticated vulnerable: Scientific-technology...radio and TV press-releases...social-media...weaponry… in the crowd:*

'What? For? Or Against?'

'Allied-with Government and Big-Business. Separating: Religion and Science...' *heard*:

'Help-Us! God!'

'Science Help Us!'

'Un-shared:…'

'Nuclear! Fuel! *Common*-Sense!'

'No more coal gas or oil?' left in the ground.

'That is all that will Help-Us Get through this!' shouted into the camera, out of the screen-*screaming*…

'Reports and interviews, speeches, and the chants of gathering crowds. The delusional claims of The proclaimed: Leaders Government and Religious: Officials, Politicians and: The Market *Ex*-pert(s): alike. As-if *confidence* in the markets was itself marketable: which it was, until, now; supplanted by declarations from: People: on: The-Ground.'

'From: Work: Place *meetings and city centre assemblies and World-Wide Television (*WWT*): net-work(s)...*

Wires on telegraph-poles and satellite(s) in Space...

*I*n some places there was the sound of police sirens, and at others the rumble of: Water-Cannon:

'*Local Strong-Arm Militia...'*

*'Police...*and...'

'Army, owned and funded by...'

'Us!'

Tanks and of Police Truncheons beating on Defensive-Protective Shields (DPS's) *as some shots rang-out from the partisan rooftops...*

On TV computer-screen(s) *blurred* and *faded*...rapidly re-booted: Smart-phone *add-on* screen wi-fi: the T.V. Wife(s)-picture *froze*...the personal phone-book: Dead-Hu(s)band: *quickly*-suddenly and UN-expected(ly): *emptied*:

Error message 303: *Invalid connection...connection...dis-connecting...closed...*

CTRL/ALT/DEL(e)ting...

No Escape-Possible...

Information: may be lost.

10. Train Crash.

As overcrossing an Estuary bridge unnoticed perhaps by anyone-else in the carriage. *Uncared* if-noticed-or-not by anyone *else* at-all. Except now each by the in-*Thrall*. Both likewise momentarily inadvertently, and actually advertorial making eye-contact: *flash-*

framed each-other, and through the shared-window as in bright-rainbow and blue sky-coloured mirror imaged as through each of-themselves.

Each Other enraptured recklessly, perhaps, or to be wrecked. As if replicated, refreshing…*relishing* as then focused-away both to the outside-world as indifferently, similarly, un-differently, perhaps; yet *in-evitably always* differently.

From the Estuary-Town Bridge stopped for shunting. Freight-Train many miles long. The one back towards, other-one now staring and beyond both towards the as yet unseen, rapidly oncoming-*City*. Anyway-horizontally, and vertically to the same outside-world moved-past, *moving*-past, and through oppositely, and thus as inevitably differently *viewed* as to what was initially referred to, and to make something of; that too, was soon made *obvious*:

'Un-charted territory…'

'(I(N)(n)ovation that is what is needed.'

'Staples?'

'Doesn't much matter *what* It is. As long as It sells.'

'New functions…'

'New markets…'

'There are the previously *drowned*-out?'

'Fell! Through-the-roof?'

'Hung from the-Bridge?'

'Mental!'

'Metal. And Oil and Gas and Minerals…'

'Plastics. If You can *get away* with It!'

'Oil! The same!'

'Global. Royal Presidential CEO General Chief of Staff: Oligarch(y)…Again.'

'Rational and Equitable.'

Crafted legend on-screen: *names* and places times and as instantaneously:

'Differentially Meteoric!' collisioning,colliding folding downwards, and inward full-fell yellow-brown red-and-blue gender greenwash mud-sliding and earth-quaking…shaking bursting volcanic *red- flaming…livid*:

'*Holy*-Stoning!'

Livid:

'Statues!!! Once-lived!'

'Lived-again!'

'Solutioning!'

'Experimental!'

'Always!'

'Innovation. That's what make it *exciting*.'

'Even Financially rewarding…'

'Or not?'

'EveryOne get's by…'

'Other wise we would not be here.'

'Each season brings experimental…'

'Weather?'

'New things…Experimental as in 'Scientific'.'

'Not: An Act of Trust?'

'Trusted-Trade.'

Functional-*formatic*:

'Political-Bureaucratic.'

'Stable. Fixed. Balanced. Protection.'

'So, who wins?'

'We do. Win-Win! Free-Trade!'

'The Richest World-Business Politician leaders are not free…'

'Newspapers are banned except for the official Communist/Capitalist information sheets…'

'Not at all of us be-lieve! haha. Lose-Lose. Everyday.'

'Everyday returns! No-Limit(s): every second counts…'

'No-Borders?'

'Currency? Any…'

'Money? Buy and sell that as well?'

'Fair-shares. Trad. Trade…'

'Somewhere-else: Not…'

'Worse. Out there…'

'Greedy, then? Usury! Not: Zero-Rate(s): Social-Interest…'

'Skimming, scamming off the top…'

'In-secure?'

'So, who is not…'

'Exactly, who is-*normal*?'

'Business as Usual.'

‘What is-*normal*, eh? Normal? Home? Se-Curit(y)? Lifestyle? You? Company: *Plant*? Eh?’

‘Journ(0)list? Keeping the Company-Line? Government Bonds…Whose?’

‘The Peoples’’

‘Government? Police?’

‘Defence Armies assaulting…’

‘By monetary-fiat…’

‘Power…Energy and production sales and re-couping…’

‘Re-cruitment? I was here first, then, you sat down…’

‘Government-Officer? That’s ‘It’ isn’t it? Doing the-Governments’ *dirty* work?’

‘No. Digging Holes? You?’

‘To fall-in?’

‘And I filling ‘em in again…’

‘All-Holy.’

‘Fanatic-Reverend?’

‘Revenue-Regulation?’

‘Tariff across Borders…’

‘Fought. With: The-Peoples Work! Soldiers…’

‘In the Tax-Office? Government-corridors and room(s) got the ear?’

‘Pigs' Ear?’

‘Sows’ sows ears? The Tax-Purse?’

‘The *purse-strings* you mean? Voted ourselves into *a barrel of our-own making…’* each e-stock and commodity Government-Bonded.

Share- Price passed each sell-by date out-dated: as lower and lower price-marker losses moved across The-Bridge: electronic bill-boards against rows of banked fan-tail desktop screen(s)-closing: *listing*: achronycal and apocryphal-foreign and un-pronounceable, or home-grown and *familiar*, closed.

The-Clerk asking now:

'So. How did 'We' get into this *mess*?'

'What mess? This cycle of indebtedness again?'

'This dis-*array*!' into the screen:

'Fast-Action…Slow- motion…saw It-coming? Pile-up. Hit the buffers. Off-the-rails…'

'Slow-motion car-wreck?'

'Train-wreck?'

'This *little*-Turbulence…' the-Banker perhaps unexpectedly uncompromising in response, to the-Clerks' questioning, reckoning:

'Wrecking-Ball!!' *banging both closed fists together.*

Recovering, The-Banker:

'There is a market-situation known as Demand and Supply.'

'Where if a company doesn't have enough shares in stock to distribute and sell.'

'Then this increases the price for these as a result:'

'This is known as a Bull-Market…'

'And this is what we have?'

'Or perhaps had…'

'Bear Market.'

'Or perhaps a Dragon-Market now?'

'Eagle.'

'Anyway…'

'A Tiger-market?'

'A growling Jaguar squawking screeching-Macaw-Monkey Market if you like! A Liger!'

'A Tion!'

'A Lie.'-*grrrr*!

'Acceptance, only Natural.'

'Bonfire? Of the Vanities!'

''It' doesn't matter what you call 'It''

'The Bigger Picture (TBP)…'

'Smaller.'

'Cake.'

'T*hinking outside the-box…*

'The-Cage.'

From apparently outside the carriage, momentarily looked blankly, thought and spoke, the-Banker through the glass:

'If you like. The *reverse*-situation…'

Looking away, and then back:

'What? Supply...then Demand?'

'Give and Take.'

'Take, then give.'

Not getting the reverse-irony from the pen-ultimately: simultaneously auto: *closing…*

'Un-concerned: Trade(s): anti-Trust: someone you know: Head of the Family at HQ. Trust-Buster(s): a long way behind the-curve: Consumer-Welfare:…'

Over: A-Bridge: *un-named…continuing* out the other end of a concrete cement volcanic: mountain-tunnel: subway sub-station airshaft: con-ditioning:

'A *Bear*-Market: this is when there is an increase in sellers…'

'I know *that*…and a fall in buyers:…'

'For: Shares: (i)nvestment(s):'

'Stocks? Stopped. Goods:'

'Services and: The money…*mostly...*'

'Cash?'

'Whose?'

'Toxic? Yours?'

'Mine?'

Bluntly:

'Every-Bodies'…' *savings pensions and insurance: investment: salaries and wage-rate(s): monthly... weekly and short-day: rates:...*

'This is now what we now have. Risk. Shared: The International-Banks and Economic-Zones: Government and Corporation(s): IT is a Global Market!'

'Shared?'

'Now the bottom has fallen out of it? No. Share the Pain? No.'

From the-Banker, a printed-card handed over with writing seen:

The Rational Equitable: *Economic. Effective. Efficient.*

(The-City Skyline Logo)

Nothing else: *clean*-edges…

'Valuable-Equitable? Equitable-Value?'

'You think *this* is *Easy* too?' as if practiced before.

The-Clerk taking and reading the-*card* noted:

'Rational-Valuable Market(s): Equitable?'

'Logistics. Import/Export: **Boom!'**

'Bang-Again!'

'Bang!!'

'And ***Bust*!'**

'Again!'

'Stopped. Prices…'

'Tax-Sub-sid(y)(s) or Sanc-Tion(s):

'Scarcity.'

'Starvation.'

'Sub-Prime: Mort-Gages: Negative-equity: stay for five-year(s): Homeless.'

'Space-Rocket Debt(s)!'

'Pay Pal? Then?'

'No-Debt(s) as such, you see?'

'You?'

‘Owing? No?’

‘Home-Debts? Mortgage? Home Re-covery? Car?’

‘Road and Rail?’

‘Tax?’

‘Of course, they would not be Taxes otherwise.’

‘Pay As You Earn (PAYE)?’

‘Or not?’

‘Then paid in advance 1-3 month deal(s): subs…’

‘Short-growing season…’

<1-3 years…

>5-10/12…longer…

<13…*trillion.*

‘Lifetime Rules! Base Metals and Pharma-Food Mineral(s): Priced. Valued: 3-5year(s): Harvest-Moon: Money is worthless. Currency only now.’

‘Taxation the same. Goes to the Rich…’

‘Tax-breaks de-Valu€ing: currency against *each*-other?

>Rich/poor list(s): pay-gap cost of living…

<Agricultural…Mechanical-Digital Log(i)stical:…

> Subsid(y)ie(s):

‘Worth-less to-they who-give.’

<Re-E-Valu(a)ting:…

>NNN/nnn/…

‘Bought-Up See?’ ><*Cheaply0(IES)*’ *falling*-in…

gradually:…

'De-bit: Cre-dit: *driven…*given re-mit: hit-hard, tortured, for *failing…*’

‘On-(I)nterest made:’

‘Un-made.’

‘Reasonable?’

‘Re-Paid.’

‘Credit-Debit: Paid again, see?’

‘And The Cash-Funds?’

‘Of-course, to draw-back on.'

Free-running now on all cylinders The-Banker let loose, re-covering, on the tracks, next-steps: ‘Buy-back. The Stock-Market Prices although always at some point in the past minimal seconded in seconds…’

‘Pica-Quantum seconds!’

‘Bought-back? Like the-last night?'

'Cheap. Cheep cheep chicken? Now. Confidence remains-*high…*’

‘Others' collapsed completely.'

‘As the others…’

‘Risen by more…’

‘Buy them up?’

'You got IT!'

'No, you got it…’

‘Money?’

‘Nothing…' *as the previous evening passed into-night and into this day* for The-Banker:

'From: First-impact. Trading instantly as a Body:’

collapsed.

‘In the moment *between* open and closed.’

‘Fortunes re-tained…’

‘And fortunes lost.

‘Not this One, saved by the bell…’ in that brief second-take before the closure *the final roll of coins landing face-or tail-up* across the-Globe without the *liquid* monetary-assets to pay or re-pay; or/to:

‘Cash-in debts? Liquidate. New: Target:’

‘Space?’

‘You Try It?’

‘Go Up in a Rocket?’

‘Yes. In case it blows up, you paid for it!’

‘For <u>*Asset(*</u>s) to be burned-off?’

‘All(y)ies-Asset?’

‘Whole-Corporation(s):

‘ Brought-down.’

‘Presidents.’

‘Governments’ Constitution!’

‘Even(s)!’

'Money Only!'

'Greedier!'

'To be sold-on…'

'With non-*existent* Credit.'

'Just: on-paper:'

'Only. Un-Just(l)(y).'

On-screen:

'People-Paradox: *near*-tautolog(y)ies: competition: author(y)ities:'

'Technical-offences small-minded simply:'

'Corporate? Rational-Equitable(s)?'

'Reasonable?'

'Efficient?'

'Economic. Financed?'

'Effective?'

'Economics?'

finished?

On-screen:

'The Credit *is the Country! Where We Are!!* All-Assets! Instant-Winnings! Win-Win!'

'All Put's made must Stay-on!'

'Stalled!'

'Precisely!'

'Business as Usual!'

'Trillionaires-Only!'

'Nothing! is *moving…*'

Looking-out of the window. Across oil-field pipeline gravel graveyard pitted mined hillsides. Concrete cement-based conveyer-belt-brick-buildings, smoke-stack flues…*venting*:

'With wider and wider differential-*ratings…*'

Deliberately looking again, forward through the window, directing the gaze:

'Stalled anyway between one day and the-next…'

'Not everywhere at once. Between one-place…

'As: *A.N. Other*.'

Looking out the window:

'Until this Day.'

'When the-*Bear* laid-down?'

'Or clawed Its way back…'

'The Markets?'

'Goosing!'

'Taken to the air…or whatever….'

'Crash landed!' and any other animal-analogy thought-of *statuesque yet misrepresented the otherwise rapidly turning-numbers turned-off, frozen and unrevealing shot-down drowned-out surfaced: exploded in slow-motion…in-pieces*:

'Shot-down!' market-marker board, and screen-seen pictured, mobile-camera photographed: on the train-travelling from where The Worlds' Stock-Markets' early-day trading, had or would have already begun. With the hammering of ancient cast-metal, a brazen-gong, heard.

A knotted-tied rope-pulled, a whistle or an air-horn, or an electronic *buzzer* air-vibration-*release*d…

Warning-signal…

'Red light…' ***black*** as the night, yellow-red, to blue-green, as to the light of *day*.

As when the field or factory-hooter: blasted pale pastel-*yellow* rising over the horizon. As at the-beginning, and then again, the closing-of-Business-Trading. The-previous-day, where-ever it was; trading-constantly throughout the world, around the globe, and then as with each evening. following-on morning, to the final-days' trade, and the next un-started:

'*Final*-Trade?'

'What?'

'Was it correct?'

'Or not?'

The-Clerk checking-accounts' screen: *clicking*:

<Accounts *closing…instantly* closed-down…

>Credit? *Advanced?*

<Profit in… T1:T2…

The Entire History of The World: Sherman-Tank and blasted mud and rock. Granite and Sand: Salt, Iron, Steel and Home:

'Still got a Home?'

'Vehicle?

'Individual, eh?'

'Home. Aren't We All?'

'Private?' no-chance:'

'Public: Limited-*Liability…*'

'Computer-Company: or chocolate teapots?'

The-Banker:

'Aces-in-their-Places! Done-deal. Commission? Profit-margins n/N…' *rapidly typing numbers and entering the fray…*

'Building-Risk:

'Bonus! Stays! Stay-Put. Until they are Put. Again?'

'All that is in the-*Future…*'

'Exactly.'

'Now.'

'So, it doesn't *matter*, now? Ker-ching! Blinging!' behind the scenes. Future stabilizing then immediately:'

'Back onto the Dealing-room floor leveraging core-competencies…'

'Play for-today?'

'Pay for today. Daily 'Me'…' *cultural-identit(y)ies:social-animal(s): species-specific furred and fuzzy around the edges…*

'Social-Media.'

'Back-to-Bankruptcy.'

'Ticket-*takeover:* Boom! *waved* through…'

‘Con-Tort and Ex-hort…’

Legal-Frame (e) L-F (ING):

‘Tax-Border(s):’ un-*certain*: commission: fees and *fortune*: all: shopping-list(s): mis-leading data not-open leading data *rushing…*

‘No-Going Back (NGB). Federal Trade Commission (FDC):’

‘Department(s): of Justice (DoJs)’

The-Train: *re*-freshment(s)-trolley. Bought and Sold. Hot and cold, coffee and tea, and snacks delivered paid-for placed onto: The Table: between:

'Well. Here’s the Deal…’un-questioning *intention* anymore:

'Further-loans at fixed-assured rates…’

‘Assured?’

‘To re-finance the debt?'

'What debt?’

‘Re-Venue(s): payment(s) made in data: puta(t)ive-takeover(s): Land Bank and Industry: flex(i)ble: FTC and DOJ.’

<Initial Public Offer:

>Initial Cost Offer.

<Imperial-Chemical-Corps: *seed-funding fertilizing me!*

>R/E/e: NNN/nnn/…###/ 000.

‘Your debt: cover possible-losses?’

‘Surely? Compensation-cover…'

‘Crowd-funding coinbits 4Libre:’

'Pyramid. Tax(A)ation…'

'Tax(N)(a)tion…'

'Guaranteed?'

'Never. Never use that word!'

'What never com-pen(sen)sation?'

'Personal-Private Investements' (i)nterest-rate(s): felled payments increased with *surety* of:

'Inter-Bank (IB) Inter-Governmental (IG):

'Self not-Shareholder paying fraud: Rate-fixing…'

'Price-Fixing?'

'Cartel? The International Conference?'

'Between: Crypto-currenc(Y)()(i)es…'

'Un-believable!'

'(E)l! World-Bank(s). Of course! Currency! National-Feds! *Electric*! Fixed-Price(s) Interest and Ex-change Rates (FPIERs)…'

'Will take care of that!'

'*They*?Will?'

'A-Will. The de-*claration* expected today…'

'Midday…'

'Or thereabouts…'

'Wher-ever we are.'

Re-called. Stepped-back, looked.

Stepped-up…and *in* again:

'No-*longer* Banking? Anywhere?'

'Anywhere. Ethereum to BitCoin…'

'Pay! PAL!'

'Yes. I know that! The Conference: To stabilize: Major Global-Currenc(y)ies: against each-other:N/nnn…'

'Exchange-Rates?'

'Debt. I know *that* too. Fake Start Ups (FSUPS!!!)'

'At some lower fiscal rate agreed?'

'Or not?'

'Higher?'

'And lower…'

'You got it!'

'No, You got It.'

'Pass-on. At the same time:'

'If *You got it…'*

'They got you.'

'What-if: The Inter-National Conference…'

'Can not-agree?'

The-Banker looking-up sharply and out of the window as if there were nothing there. Where farms and factory-buildings, homes and retail-parks *flash*ed-by.

Held. The-Clerk, as if sub-claused again, now. Left out-in-the-cold. The- Sun: *warming* hillside outside, shouldered out of the window reflection…moving-on. Attempting, open-jawed to fill the *void*…but no words came out.

Dry-mouthed, and with an intangible uncertainty, unfamiliar-*anxiety*, both, yet no so obviously one to the other, and again, anyway retorting to The-Bankers' incomplete statement, and asking again:

'Political-Priorit(y)ies: Propert(y)ies. Building(s): Tech.: Money and Mond Benefit: Online:

'Corporate(s)-Dominate:'

'Monopolise-Competition:'

'Scientific-innovation.'

'Terrific! Taxes.'

'People! Customers and Shops. And if they cannot agree?'

paused.

'They cannot, dis-agree. Interest-rates! Each personally…' then *not even thought about*:

'Justly-Rises! Which they must Do!'

'They will! *Their* will, of course, they must!'

'Otherwise?'

'Enormous-*Clout*! We will prevail!' photo-shopped elastic-banded *sprung-back* missiles blasted into hordes of hired-mourners massed-crowds gazing at a passing poster advert, both:

'Proportionate-ratio's N/nnn…'

'Stock-market…'

'Super-market…'

'Hyper-Market:'

‘Global…Market. MasterCard Express…’

‘Then CyberCoin…coining-it in!’

Mechanical data-banks whirring and buzzing information between every conceivable individual thus family and community society dead and alive and thus, Culture. Gender and ethnicities essentially mixing in Cities and Country all over the World, all over.

Globally the *top* five or six, no longer, not the lowest of the low and no-one between, either, where ever, the same, without sharing the Ven diagrams endlessly, familiarly and seemingly as is to each of *our* infinityies…

‘Token-sales made between currency token taboo and totem carrying Armyies…’

‘At points and places…’

‘Gone. Bull:’

‘Bear-Eagle…’

‘Drowned…’

‘Dragon?’

‘Making-out the-*odds*?’

‘Does the Deals. In money…some may-not return…’ *everyday shopping? Going to the cinema, theatre…*

‘Bear-Cage.’

'Bull-fight.'

‘Mexico-Eagle. Komodo-Dragon:’ di-urnal solitary carnivorous hunters of pig and deer, hunted. Water-Buffalo, and *fishes* out of the house-waters, to eat…

'In the soup.’

'Some adapt…'

'Some do not.'

'There is the *fight*: The-Benefits System in Sovereign-Wealth: Fixed: in *their* advantage.'

'Corporate-Government:'

'Gamed.'

Bounced back and forth:

'…and then it is over. Then, there is the *mental* fight.'

'Real or imagined?'

'Over, and over, in-*detail*! A lie? *Changing* the-story…'

'Does not *Bear*-witness?'

'Ohhh Bullish!'

'Dragonic. Only the-*Truth*! Truth will prevail…'

'Eagle World-Justice: will-*prevail…*' *no-matter how un-likely driven, as being still, waiting for things to happen:* ee-action. Response. Consequences. Re-(d)action. Unprepared. Prepared. Predictable: Un-predictable: scenario:

As if behind a paper curtain hidden, heard, *anger*:

'Storage since the inevitable: Pay-up-and Get-out!' the-Clerk now sub-claused: The-Banker:

'Currency currently and con-currently worthless in name but shares worth the value of the product:'

'Goods?'

'Services. Not-making Primaries: but Secondary: Initial Re-Sources:

'Food and Water.'

'Shelter.'

'Home?'

'Work?'

'Welter-Services…'

Helter-skelter-ING Moibus-strip…

'Goods? Fire and Ambulance. Army/Police: Hospital and Social-Worker(s):'

'Welfare?'

'Food-Bank. Re-volving Door(s)…of poverty:'

'Family?'

'No such thing. Species only…'

'Social-Security?'

'Hot-Spot(*ssshhh…*).'

'Safe?'

'Health?'

'Stock?'

'Money?'

'None.'

'Relative to others? Not of-themselves *toxic*…'

'But *toxic* of whatever *noxious*-currency they are being bought and sold-for!'

'Exactly.'

'Or-*not*, as the case may be.'

'Nuclear!'

'Exactly!'

'Negotiable, shall we say? I am a Great Negotiator!'

'A Great some thing?'

And the-goods? The-property of whoever has bought or been sold-out. As: moneyed-share(s) in the first place…'

Except now…

'Money. Locked-up. Worth nothing.'

'Hardly…except the actual goods?'

'Good?'

'Got to get them moving…'

'And the only way to do that?'

'Price-War. Shopping-War(s): Trade-War.'

'Pay-War? Tax-War Benefit(s)?'

'Averting-*Disaster! (AD!):* that is what: The Conference: is All-about: creating the conditions for:'

'There was no-disaster…'

'Disaster! US *first…*'

'That is created by You! All! Your Country Needs You!'

'To Pay Your Taxes: Everlasting.'

'E*veryday…*in both our favours, then?'

'Sure…

'OK, so 50-50 then?'

‘Of the profits and the losses. OK! Profit from Losses! You got It! No…’ *patent-*Profit: stolen as available WorldWideWeb: from *shared*-academy-styled: *research*:

<**R/E** Government. Big: Business: S*hares*-falling…no longer rising so fast…as unknown before…a-*moment*…then:

‘Big-Bubble. Payback…’

Time!@The Big-Banks: National and Private: Family-International: Global Co’s CEO: Limited-Liability Partnership(s): Presidents and Prime-Minister(s):…

‘The-Government(s)?

‘The People in-Corporated.’ *in the background…foreground: pulling the strings…* (Is) suing-suggestions: modeling modest debt-reminders of cash-flow and cut-off threats if-necessary: *sanctions….*

‘For-Fuel-flow cut-off…’

‘(N)ecessary?’

‘Bargain: Trade-*Agreements*:’

‘Trade-ins? For what?’

‘Farming-Subsidy…’

‘Pharming!’

‘Plastic!’

‘Money!’

‘Oil. *Fracking*…con-*sidering*…’

‘Gold?’

‘Taxed?’

measured measuring…

'Charged. Call It what you will…'

'Ex-tracting…'

'Money.'

On screen:

Deep-Mind.

Deep-Water: *troubling…*

<Nautilus Minerals: gold, zinc and copper, lustrous alloyed silicon metal(s):…

>Healthy-Diet and Social Re-lations…

'Making: thing(s).'

'Metals? Minerals?'

Insider: Industrial: Digital-Machinery: made: Goods and Services: made-in: and sold where?

Internal-Market(s): Territorial-Water(s): slurrying slush silted: contractual-difficulties: /MB Holding Omani and MetalL(i)o(n)Vest:

'Russia:…'

'Share(s)? Stock(s)?'

'When? Highest-bidder:…'

'Harvest?'

'Manufacturing Good(s) and Service(s):…'

'It' gets more-*serious:…*'

'Stock-*broth* and Bread!'

'Medical-supplies…'

'Could say that…'

'Trade-*stop*page?'

'Stopped!'

'As Embargo Sanctions stopped:'

'Re-started: food-shortages and no-water, how about that?'

'Siege-Currency: as-Sanctions.'

'Market?' Money-Bites@...

'Market? For what?'

'Currency?'

'Food!' *wet-and-dry*:

'Health Securit(y)ies…'

'Market Authorities…

'Data!'

'We Grow Our Own!'

Out-growing…

'Stable-door(s):'

'*Healthy*-(E)conomy?'

'Thanks.'

'Whose?'

'Your(s):…'

'*Social-Stability…all p*urely-Financial-Agreement…'

The sly City sky-line glimpsed in and as

Other glanced-at surreptitiously…

Or openly *simply un-challenged*:

'That is down to others.'

'Politicians…'

'All? People? Buy for Votes!'

'Or Sell? Buyers or Sellers' Market?'

'Both. Country.'

'Army?'

'Weapons?'

'Depends, if you are a Buyer, or a Seller! Boom! **BOOM!!**…'

'…and **Bust**. And **BOOM!!** Again!'

'Until it's time to go **Bust!** again…'

''It' is all about when you get-in and when your get-out…' in the background now: *E*-Car engines racing against:

'Each-Other…'

'*Natural*-selection?'

'Our-Sel(F)v(i)es: Digital-Asset(s): each alternative private currencyies…'

'National *de*-selection!'

'Natural Re-selection!'

'National-Selection?'

'Elections?'

'Societyies. Express. Free and Fair.'

'For later-Life learning:'

'Health: and retirement from work for *Leisure (Time-Warner): Enter: Tainment(s):*

'Re-search:'

'De-volving…'

'De-velopment…'

'Re-velopment…'

'Push the Envelope?'

'Whatever that means…'

'No share-busting cropping…

'Blame?'

'Social-Care?'

'De-centralizedd…Re-! For-*eternity*?'

'Historyies. Herstoryies…'

'Societyies. Familyies. '

'Could be Society: Communal (I)nividuals'

Crypto-wallet:

<Credit/Debit NNN/nn/…

'Family-Farm? or *Something*?'

'Something!' as a small-Business *flourishing…*

Mocking? Seriously…

The-Banker accordingly, affordably, breaking-out of the cyclical-contortion, as if for nothing-else in-particular, except attempting-testily an explanation of:

'The customary re-normalising-writ to be re-presented.'

'Of what may be implied…'

'Not: in Real-terms:'

'Un-*Realistic*?'

'True?'

'Then…'

'You could say that. Monetary-Terms&Conditions: Trade(s)-Union(s): *and that which will decide this*-Day!'

'This Day? Cartel-Guilds again medieval…'

'A 'Periodic-Existential-Crisis of Capitalism….'

'Communism. Failure. Of: Collateral. Land. National Investment-Banking Services.'

'(NIBS) Goods *and* Services!!!'

'Accounting-for: raw-*material(s)…*'

'Metals and *minerals from the Earth*! GasOilPlastic (GOP)!'

'Nuclear Daily!'

'People! Now Money itself! Pica-second by second…'

''It' seems…'

''It' is only having *that* Competitive-edge.'

Elect/ric:

'Naturally.'

Naturally:

'Nationally?'

'I see it in you. You're a Natural!'

A bit too sarcastically, or was it ironical, or even:

'To be honest…Anglo: Kings' Country.'

'Queens'? National-State? El-Presidiente!'

'And otherwise?' Irish: Scotti-Skandi: Western-Russe…'

'Each Generation: does its' best.'

'Med-Evil?'

'Med-Good? Good. City?'

'Country. To be *honest…*'

'You mean you haven't been up 'til now?'

'Too honest, perhaps!'

'Who?'

'A.I. re-placing doctors and drivers, bakers and buyers…

'All of us?'

'Or none. Everything I say is false…'

'You think?'

'Never mind.'

'Only if True?'

'Eh?'

'False. Only if True.'

'Only if Naturalised! Nationalised?'

'State 'lyin' and cheatin' Human Nature: *Animal-Spirited…*' self-recognised. Self-fulfilling in the glow of a *naturalistic*-fallaciously held-privately…and publicly-renewed self-*admiration*:

'Free-Will?'

On: in-decision affectively effective freely-willing or un-willing at any stage:

'We prepare for 'It.'

'We Will.'

'Our-Will…'

Meeting head-on:

'Scheduled-in!'

'On what?'

'Commodities. This Stock-Market…'

'De-bacle!'

'Do you?'

'Or could you have been?'

'Prepared for this?'

'No. Only in the correct place, at the correct time, with the correct amount of *risk* to:

'As in: preparations for a failed:'

'Harvest? Software-Crash?'

'That's it? Isn't it?! Cover-up Conspiracy!'

'You want Me to fix the-software…Farm-Price2Pharma? Food—Price(s): Med.s: reviewed re-placed changed every eighteen months and going-down:

'Daily! like the Hardware! Second-by second…faster and *faster*…' no-one notices until the final seconds:

'What is that game you have there? War-Game?'

'WarFare4? No, WarFair4…only another Trading-Game: Bullets and Bandages…'

'Sold&Bought. Price(s): Quality-Control (QC): Un-equal *cost*...'

'Health? Home?'

'Money? Class?'

General Army-Class: Artist Labours' Humanitarian-Aid: good/bad: moral-high ground or low: G/B: h/l:…

<Ethical-*position: set by The-Government? Religion? Science?*

>*Common-Sense...*

<Green/*anti-discrimination agenda...*then...

'Human-Rights!

Red-lighted...

'And **Responsibilities-Boss**?'

'What?'

'Human-Rights…'

'Animal-Rights! Re-sponsibilit(y)ies…' hostaged by debt:

'Boss? We get out of here *alive?'*

Government(s) United-Nation(s): President(s):

'Secular: Nation-Sates: Weapon(s): Man-U-Factor: All going down unless we catch up with I.T! Homes, Jobs and Mortgages!'

'Atheist-Nation!'

'Agnostic is enough.'

'And Savings…' *going-down…*

'What savings?'

'Investment(s). Oh…'

'Family-Business? Livelihood?'

'Loans?'

'…and-Home? The Credit-Debit Personal: Loyalty-Card(s):…'

'Mortgaged?'

'Re-Mortgaged…

'Global-warning warming…'

'And the: Pay-Day Loan(s) (PDL): *debts* that go with…'

'So, what are the rest of us supposed to prepare-for? To be starved into submission like subservient Pariahs? To be Homeless? At War with the World?'

'Hu-Man Nature. No! Re-cycling 100%: So, each Re-Mort-gagged. Credit/Debit card, or cards never own anything else:…'

'Shop-cards. Loyalty-Card?'

'How many? Ex(e)cutive? Or: non-executive? Ex-Executive? What about the Banks? Investment-Houses *owned*? I mean owed?'

'But:…'

'Not the Shares: Pensions and In-surance(s): Re-in-surances: To: the highest-bidder. Get 'IT', now?'

'Do We not-*owe them*?'

'Do they not *own* us? We do not owe them. We Own *Them*! Of course! People(s)': Pensions' and Insurances: They are Our Debts! Ex-tortion. Ex-haust-ion:…not: in-sured. Under over-insured…' Circular-Power: Serving on the Board: President CEO of several different Family Fun-Run: Business-Boards. Shop-Family…

'Other-Executive?'

'Assistant Non-executive, you get me? Executive-Government(s)@?' *faction interest-group no political-part(y)ies…*

Caucus Cabal Bloc

Coalition-interest

'They do as they please…'

'They own Us.'

'They owe Us!'

'So. Down-to: Financial-Trust: again.'

'Financial-Gain…'

'Number(s) on a screen: They only want you to *owe*-them not: to: Own-Them.'

'Which We Do! Your-*might* with shares and insurances and pensions…'

'Salaries and Wages. If-paid at all:'

'Mighty most of: The-Economy! Least worst of the People…'

<R/e: N/nnn…

'Yes.'

Dropped-in out-now:…

'Owe Them?'

'Own them. The-Big and little banks…'

'Re-gulators' Corporation(s) Of Us? Customers?'

'Market-Floatation(s)?'

'Sinking…'

'Tsunami! Floods. Of course!'

'The-Bank's: don't want you to own them. They want you to owe them Big-Time with *interest*-rates and Corporate: Social-Authoritarian: Regime:'

'To pay for?'

'Police and Army Security:'

'Number(s) on a screen.'

'The Market(s)' mistake(s)…'

‘The Government(s) of The People(s) *the(y)* want you to continue *swimming* but not too quickly, not too much growth, to start with: then infinite.’

‘In a finite-World? Is it?’

‘Finite?’

‘This World, this Universe, Us? Continue paying-off whatever IT is. Subscription hidden-payments:… ’

‘Family?’

‘For eternity…’*thought…*

‘Bail-out, that is all they want…’

‘From?’

‘You…’

‘Me?’

‘Your Taxes, eh? Your debts?’

‘Government?’

‘Flat-screen TV?’

‘What about *that latest* gadget?’

‘Bought, or borrowed?’

‘Vehicle? Any other Property? Loans? Shares, and Stocks? Insurance? Stock-up, each week? Rental? Each month?’

‘Home? Bank salar(y)ies…’

‘Mortgage. Store-*share*?’ starving-out Ghetto Slum-State: re-fused:

‘Health and Social-Care. Goods and Services…

‘That as well?’

'Paid in arrears…'

'Work, done. Super Hyper Global Market(s).'

'Stock-Market? What do *You* want to be *known for?'*

'Credit-Card ad-vance on your-Debts?'

'You Want My Debts? Or: Tax avoidance for advanced R&D?'

'Monetising-Mars!'

'The-Moon!'

'First. Or; the next *Smart* 'Phone.'

'Add-in? Innovation more expensive, of course, to the last.'

'You owe *already*…So, why not continue subscriptions instead of paying-debts and taxes: *pay- yourself* in-company:'

'Share-Societ(y)ies?'

'Binaryies?'

'Debt(s)?'

'More than that. Family?'

'EveryOne Does.'

'Plus? What?' *to any cross-trading traffic immediately curtailed blue-green cross-trades as another parallel and crossing-tracks passed and rattled and rolled-over like passenger and freight-lines.*

Passing like ships in the-perhaps moonlit-dark starlit night-passing that previous-night:

'NNN/n. Margins-*called*:'

'Breaking-point…'

'Braking-point?'

'Tipping-point…'

For: *Profits* and silenced, skulked skull, sunken eyes and lights turned-out.

Screen left-on, referenced:

'For: Debt!'

'For: Life! Market Closed.'

'Only for the Day.'

'Until: Midday. Closed for Business.'

The-Clerk to the-Banker:

'Final-Trade?'

'Close of Play?'

'**Rational/Equitable**?'

'Time to Pay:'

The-Clerk:

'Time to *Play…*'

The-Clerk moving around tapping toes and hand mumbling, to-self or to the screen-talking unawares, into the earpiece-microphone replaced-lead: *talking to someone? Talking to Who? Listening to what? Is that, singing-along? To what song?* Singing? Singeing? Singapore. Who?

Burning:

'Watching, the-Game?'

'What-*Game?'*

Watched-in window-manifestation: manufactured: on-line *news*-updated…

The-Banker puzzled at the-Clerk head-down, no-further eye-balling body-contact, and

The-Banker *shuddered* at the *thought* of The-Clerk maybe getting a-head of the-*Game*:

'LoL'

'Ha-ha.'

'So, there, you haven't IT!'

'No, you have got it!'

'No! You have got 'It!'

'What?'

'The ball?'

'Bail? The-outfield?'

'The Umpires' Whistle? Managing the Game.'

'Calling: 'Time?''

Time-0ut!'

'Foul!'

'Move!'

'NN to nn Metre-line!'

'Out-the-Park!'

Dropping-down, the eyes, leaned slightly forward, looking into keenly:

<Enquire-upon…@…from the *Market-place…*

>Pricing…guidance…mortgage/rent…pay…skills

<C.V.…fixed…fixing…overheads…

>Capital-amount:

Your-Balance-sheet: …

>>Credit…plus/*minus*…Debit…*indebted*…to: Bank of You: *opening*…

<Balance-Book. Capital-*Asset(s)*: list…*to sell-off…then*…to cover-confusion…

>Co-Lateral: owed amounts: to: *lists*…out-goings…*that must be-have paid*…

<Owned?

>Owed. Horizontal.

<By Who? When? Why?

>Up-and-Down. Need-*cash*? because the-debt you *started*-with is the-one you're stuck-with: Life?

<May as well be…*already worth more, or less than one-second ago…not only increasing the-debt…but decreasing the chances…of-recovery…as the-likelihood probability, of that-debt ever being paid-off…*

<Logistic(s):Forcing your Currency to be de-valued:

>Which means?

<You get less-for-more: for-example: when you spend your currency abroad on-Your-*Imports* to *Your-*Country…then Your-*Exports* are priced-high to Others' Exports to You…as to *yourself* named: *list:* imports that you need, are expensive, to you…

>Only what I need….

<Never mind the-*Luxuries*…

>You *can-afford them*…

<You need: *items: list…*

- *Bare-necessities of Life:*
- Life.

<Your-Imports: Nn…pay-off…

>That You need to pay-off: Your Loans: list…and *your…*

Bank-OverDraft: Debt: Salt-Mines: *BootCamp Cheer-Leading Masochist and Sadist: N/nnn...and buying the things you need from abroad...*

<Are expensive! NNN…

>Buy currencies? *portable...*

<What money? <

>Anything…cars…TV…<

<Except your home…<

>Loaning money to buy with? <

<Those Corps shared in the Billions…

>Buy your bank and building society…

<Trillion(s): Now! Pensions e(n)surance<<Loans to pay-off loans…<

>Crashed. <

<Casino<

>Never. <

<Break the Bank then…<

>Break the Trust…then…<

<Mugged *then…*<

>That's about it…

<Buying-out *other(s)*< Sovereign-Currencies?

> Selling? Yes

<N0? :<Buying-up stalled.

>@Markets Closed. Cash-account…in the bank…

<<Uncashed…then un-*cacheable*…

>The numbers stay the same…<

<The value(s) changed…<

>I don't know!

< Why would I do that unless I was going on-holiday!

> Git IT! On Holiday!

<Health: employment based@:? Exports/Imports: n/N not-N/n… <Bonds?

>Travelers-cheques?

<D*e-values*…other<s against yours …

>NNN/nnn/###…printing more currency? <

<Homeless? Government-Bonds? <

>*Quantitively*-easing…like printing money…

< <Inflationary?

>*Devaluing*?!<

<Buy privately owned government bonds/debts unlimited but for agreement for government to write-off…Debts: Nn…*default* with Dignity? <

<De-feat, with valour! <

>De-values yours against them…in monetary-terms…<

<So, the monetary value of the currency against? Others< currency…<

>Or Currency-zone? <

<Yes. Or Country-Zones…

>Caesars-Sovereign: National-Banks:…

<What isn't owed Caesar…

>Is owned by Caesar.

<All: Federal-re-*serves…*

>Reducing: N…n… <

<Exports: for currency and the stuff currency buys…this is more-important than the actual goods< value of the goods…<

>Or the currency? *list…*<

<I want to trade for currency alone? <

>What do you want to trade-for-currency?

<Currency…

GoTo: …

<The-Bank<s: list: For Goods? Stocks?

>Servicing: National-Currency: *list...*

<Money? <

>To pay-off the debt, loan-credit…<

<On-paper? <*printing...*

>Feet of Clay…

<No hold's barred…

>Lost to the World.

<Erin Callous…

>Jimmy. John and Bob 'Barclays' Diamond.

<Joe Dimon character: 'Temper in a Teapot!'

>Fortess: Balance-*sheet*:

<Valuka's Law.

>Arrows'!

<Angelo 'Countrywide' Mozillo. Meryl, Ken and Hank.

> Treasury-Secretariat:

< Troubled Assist Relief Programme:'

< Mortgage:

> Fraud! Inter-Bank(s)…

< New: Sovereign-Presidential:

>Start all over again!

<Like: Change-Trade: Saudi-Oil: OPEC Prices: N/n…

>Bailout: For: Warfare4: Weapons of War.

<WarFair4: Weapons of Peace.

Quick aggressive move engineered through the Kaos!

Random-log normal-distribution:

<Global Banking: Federal: Re-serves: bailing out the Bank(s):

>Other: Fed. Res.@Presidents like own pockets…

<Plastic! Ours!

>Fred the Shred!

<Guerilla!

Office: >Gorilla-Warfare!

<WarFair4

>Peace.

On-screen: **The Country-Wide: National: Rational-Equitable**…

The Real-World: <Shares...*getting-there*...of the National wealth...*against*...

>*Supersubs*: Euro/Dollar/Yuan-*Mindi*...

<Sterling-*silver*:

#Gold-Rand/new-Ruble/new-Dinar/convertible:

<Peso's/ Rea and Rupee...: *forbearance* of your...Z:

'*Zombie*? Me?'

'*Servicing*-debt:' *choking-off further lending be-heading clean-cut ripping out the guts in front of boggling-eyes: as they used to do:*

'Rubles and Rubel(s)!'

'No-Humility!'

'*Bartering* Straight Swaps (BSS)?

'Settle a deal?'

'OK.: *Rates*-available: *list*...as above, or below, other short to long-term deposits may be made...'

<Savings: Credit...in the-Bank to be: made...

>Lending-for *investment* at a *reasonable*-return or simply-fore-going...foregoing...feigning...*fore-closing*...

The Cash-Till: action:

'Going-down...'

'Sinking-Ship:...'

'Titanic!'

'To get Home:' Solar-battery: charging playing-cellphones:

The-Banker held onto the newspaper, brief-cased opened screen. Sat back, where had been leaning-forward in some kind of *reverie*. Looked-over and stared the-Clerk directly in the eyes and between and around the other less-experienced in the ways of the world. Shiny-suited silver-grey not-dull-*charcoal*.

The Banker: a sharp-suited dull charcoal-grey power-dresser almost unnoticed rotund in-parts, like a tailors' dummy sharp-suited, three-dimensional 4G strung-out as a puppet *as to the Invisible-Puppeteer*.

Staged-and sound-designed as-seen self-motivated moving synchronous photographic phonographic form…textured breathed-in…and breathed-out…flavoured movably moved: *recruited*:

>**<u>The Rational-Equitable: …</u>**

<Hostaged…*to fortune*…exchanged: …

>*Terror*-transformer: *with Fear and anger: revolt revulsion propelling political economic and media-pundit…*

<Expert-citizen…per-citizen…the-Clerk clicked looking-down not into anguish or fear but deprecation with depreciation:

>Basics-required…*restricted…*: *simplified independent advice-orphans charging model…specific one-off advice: inherit pension-portfolio managed-fees…*

<Fixed-retainer or percentage-fee? Y/N?

>Y…for *larger*-amounts…

<Less transaction-fee-deal…*through home and small-business and personal-credit…*on-screen bundled-up again: obliterating…un-traceable credit and… mortgage's

and un-paid-loans…swapping. Loans/debts…. send-to*: confidential…. done. delete…deleting…*

<Vehicle? List:…*chosen: V*8::Done.*

>Home? Furniture (including radio TV and all digital and analogue devises media and games:)? Food? Water? Air? *even?* Evenly spread? Across Your Life.

<Lives? How many do You *wish* to Buy? *list: …*

>Everyone's? Lives?

<Only Yours…

>Selfish-Objectivism? Does not-*compute: The Panic of 2008:* does…

<Objective-selfishness…

>Subjective un-selfishness…

<Selfish-Subjectivism…

>un-selfish Objectivism…*computing all possibilities: now…*

<The-Market's: lists…of *lists…*

> *Deleting…*

The-Banker taken a-back.

Beneath-what were actually Gold-Gilt Bold CAPITAL-type caption-topping, and a clearly no longer tumultuous Stock-Market re-called.

The-Banker gradually and all too quickly, and suddenly and readily now recalling: implicitly getting-now, the pitiful irony of the newspaper headline:

WORLD MARKETS IN TURMOIL!

and the photograph below.

Taken, without permission, who would be-*have asked*? For: *permission*?

To the-Banker, now again, forcibly revealed, for the first-time, by the-Clerk, perhaps, *notoriously*, not only into short-term memory but now also into open-consciousness sight as of vision:

<*Access Denied…*

'As of this morning...'

'Has already happened.'

'What's done is done.'

'IT is what it is.'

'The Worlds' Markets' un-*doing…*'

'Is what IT is.'

Awakening as in a pent-up fury raging, invoked from the vestiges of the evening-prior:

'A phoenix, to rise out of the *ashes…*' speech-bubbled, spoken out loud?

Trimmed-wing's is, what the-Clerk thought:

'Business-as-usual?'

Both looking out of the still moving-window:

'Business-as-usual. There is to be a Declaration this morning.'

'By midday…'

'InterNational Meantime…'

'This-will stabilise the-markets…'

'At some-lower-rate….'

'Others' automatically-Higher?'

'And, and that is the-thing! What 'We' will do is simply re-align currencies….' the-Clerk interrupted as if boring into the brain of the other.

As if to satisfy some lust, or inbuilt hidden hatred unavoidable, as both, even as an *idle*-interlocutor:

''We'? Same-thing 50/50?'

'Or at another relatively higher-point?'

'Lesser? Or more?'

'You got it!'

'No, you got it!'

'And start all-over again…'

'At: *some* lower-point?'

'You give me the-nod on prices of one thing and another and I will do the rest, get me? Now then, those debts, who they with?'

'*Errr*, you?"

'O.K. Right here, right now' *as issuing some oratory declarative. Without clue of real-implication*:

'Known?'

'Collateral-damage?'

'Un-*intentional* consequences…'

'Like unusually honest politicians yet unaware of their truth…'

'Only that made up by themselves:

'If there were such a thing…as *honesty*.' *ready* to be barracked.

Self-deprecating and yet, as anyone appreciating of themselves, deceiving of-themselves. Implied depreciation of the-other. With the opportunity presented, as an explanation of the rise to glorification; yet also, thereby pre-emptive fall from grace: albeit: temporarily:

'As in current circumstances as *currency-account…' as simplicity 'It'self and with which 'It', would all be resolved today*:

'Lawyer-Banker: Politician?'

'Corporate: F(a)m(i)l(y) Business-Banker?'

'Free-Trader Independent (F-T I) of course!'

'The warnings given? Taken?'

'Too-late. For that.'

'Warnings unheeded?'

'Unstoppable!'

'After the event…'

'…and hold *that* Front-Page!' that nevertheless now could only now be seen from the-Clerks' supposed, and *likely derisive, and probably gloating, satirical perspective*. On the side screen-panels rapidly absorbed concerning the latest sports and business-media Celebrity-Star: photo of stage and screen, religiously-inoculated to:

'Keep up with the-Markets!'

'Keep up with the…'

'Other.' *through theft, and violence, on TV. Obesity, meals fluffed, plucked, personal-value, emotionally-in distress, in a consumer-hazed blazing marketing-characteristics: gentle gentile Capitalism, rough Liberal-Socialism, gentle-Socialism rough-Communism: as loan- sharks encircling the flotation-tank, gas-chamber, propitious-publicity, canary in a cage.*

Of the photogenic In-crowd the IT-crowd, and for the crowd of passengers generally-un-attainable.

Un-obtainable@ and therefore to be utterly-loathed, or loved, in equal unequal measure. Perhaps, as well as envied for their art or wealth, or both, and thus taken a part-of: most *alarming of all the guileless, seemingly-misguided, business trusted-bought:*

 # The-Newspaper-Owner: Media-Magnate.

Now the even more incongruously, and mischief-making paradox-inducing intent, of a supposed-Ally. not-Enemy.

Anyway, not-yet, anyway: The Tycoon-proprietor. The media-Mogul Magnate-Oligarch empirical pseudo-economist fine old art wheeler-dealer and owner. With-whom…only maximizing Profit matters…

Golf and Gold may have been shared-interests and at least and a singularly badly-shared literary-joke: this is not charity! Laughing together. Not laughing together.

'With influence…' *still marking cards, making-detergent soap, or string-balls. Media-Empire: whatever it was it mattered not.*

Although 'It' did. Betrayer, betraying even spiteful little-threat, whenever not-making-out.

At the end of the day: when push-comes-to-shove, no-one is or ever was your-Ally. Not even, your friend, not even your-family. Bailed-out. Bailing-out from the false-accounting phone-tapping mess.

From Power, corruption and lies…simple rate-setting, premium payment protection racket rocket.

Perhaps before anyone had tumbled…tumbled-in could have at least perhaps seen it coming. Could-have, perhaps should-have, acted with even-handed propriety, notoriety, *perhaps?*

‘Got away with Murder!’

‘Suicidal!!’

‘Murderous.’

Acting, acting-for as if with assumed-impunity, and as-usual uneven impropriety, summonsed-up and convinced and therefore convicted, in- their absence-of-wit…

The- Editorial Traitors! The Public: Closing-in. Closing-in…

'Closed-them down! I would!’ *and closed-down the print-run down, and deliberately stopped the newspaper and the train-company from delivering…*

‘For-Free!'

Then:

'No more Hand-Outs?!’ *let slip:*

'No more Bail-out’s!’

‘Welfare-Benefits Who? Back-handers. Re-cycling…’

‘Re-*purposing…*’

‘By and for whom?’

‘Super-Power: Hotelier? Medical-expenses? School? College? University? Health, and Social-communications…’

‘Media Suppliers…and re-Tailors…the-Works…’

‘The-Works?’

‘The: Rational-Equitable…’

> **Rational Equitable…**

<Store’s… and Stock’s…Good’s…and Service’s…Food…Health and Social-Care…

>Logistics…

<Wheat and Weapons’ *in silos and on runways out the window…*

>Civil-Protection.

<Military…*radio-equipment…opening…*

>AirCraft Carriers? Battleships? ‘Planes? Tanks? Soldiers?

< *Non*-lethal…*supporting…*

>No-Fly-zone: destroying the whole armaments' *industries…*’

<Simplify: as Boom and Bust leading to catastrophe beyond any Command or Control: except UK PLC and Nation Inc.:

➢ Steam-Punk Investment Level(s):

<Complex: *connections…*

Connecting…*connected…*

<A formidable Union of Defence-Contractors…

>Aircraft? Tourism? Premiere-Class. Business-Class. Freight? Military? Family? Too? To: Credit-Holiday! *Until things get back to normal, better, improve, not get any-worse…*

Both. One: not-connected…re-…connecting…disconnected…*re-directing…*

<>Desktop: *we are sorry that you are not-able to…your connection has not worked properly…*go- online to find a solution to this problem? y/n: OK? Y/N. *yes/no*?

<Defense of Democracy: No?

>Yes! *we are sorry that you are not-able to…your connection has not worked properly…*go- online to fix this problem…fixing? *click.*

>Double-click…fixed: *fixing…*

< *Soft-Corporatism: never Powerful Enough!!*

➤ Calibrating Competition Committee: Agenda: Monopsony: One-God! Only?

<Factional…*fictional*…almost…

>*Executive-Mono(p)0Ly-Sony: Non-Executive director…*

<O*n: the Board of Director(s):…*

>*Protracted*-Capital…

<Communal-Building(s): Land and Food. Machinery. Trades and Craft Unions built by soft souls and hard hats….

Building of pumice and rock, granite and steel and glass.

<Value/Risk: N/n… deposit/investment covered.

>Utilizing-maximum…

<Capita-*profit: after Tax: communal massive-violence, to the-engineering and on top of that: economic infra-structure risk-cheated public-private infrastructure sharing between Country to Country place and people to people populations and actual-goods and buildings' routes and ways…*

>Visionary: To establish perpetual-growth in-proportion to inheritance and wealth earned… *and taken: Industrial, Wage and Economic-Growth group-linked:*

<Tragically…

>Un-reasonable: taxation and poor working conditions…

Laboratory-tested Research and Design. Costs. Expenses. Price. Production…

Promotion:

>Shopping: for: Amazing-Bargains: Amazon: E-Bay: Ali-Baba: Armaments?>

<10% TenCent?

>TenPerCent (TPC)

<10%?

<WHat4?

>Why not?

< For: what?

>First-Step: Buy-cheap: as if poor: for: nothing: ex-changed for:

< Food.

> Fast-Food.

< Fat-Food: City-Epidemic:

<Glass-and-Steel.

>AT&T and IBM.

<Firearms&Frappuchino:

>Change-for the better?>

< State: Serco-Prisons meter-bids fail…

<We are: *Sorry* for selling-weapons of War?

>For getting-*caught*?>

<Forgetting?

>Not Me!

< Check-it!>

>I will…>:

<They will be used *against…*

>Killing: *innocent(s):* Parents and Children: and *real*-Martyrs:

<For themselves only led by others' Controlling and Commanding:

>Be-Sieged. Steel-girders, and glass and concrete:

<Dot Comms.' Chemistry and…

>(E)lectronic(s): The Future: *bringing out the past from sand and rock; water and wind and gas an oil: solar, wind and water (SWW): Earth&Sky heat and fuel to get off the ground:*

<Peace!

>Fractious…*fixing the rates…*

<By the Big-Six or whatever…

Everywhere:

<Within and *without*:

Civil-Government: Nation-State: (i)dentical across Geograph(Y)(ies):

> State of the Nation!

Everything-Else?

< Everything?!

>Every*thing across 91% time(s): surge-Price! Switch!!*

<Everyone…

>Everyone?!

<Of course, so?

>Everyone else pays…

<*A little each…*

>*Makes a lot!*

<*At 0.001 of a slight alteration…*

>Low-wage(s) long-hours…

<Gig for-War!

- On The Streets
- For-Wealth!
- Health!
- Not! Pragmatic-(*I*)deologue!

*Ethno-linguistically, gender and ability driven, strategic-*falsely *promoted tactics, using-history*:

<*Clash-of-Civilization(s)!*

- Economies.
- Good. vs. Evil<Love vs Hate>
- Evil. vs. Good>Hate vs Love…<

>Money! Not-wanting to *Lose*: any of it!

<On-*Fiscal in*-Security? Pay less? Or?>

>More? Military-Security?

<*Beat* them down!

>No-business operates on Real-economy terms, you must know that? Rather on simply…>

<*Pure*-monetary terms! Doesn>t matter what on…>

>The-Banks?'

<*Real*-Estate: Markets? NN/nano:>

>What >We> Will?! do…is simply re-align currencies?>

<Will >

< *We*>?>

In-contestably…

>Stabilise the-Global-markets at some lower-point and carry-on:

<Pro-Market Initiative(s): Everything will start *moving*…

- 'You may have to fight a battle more than once, before you win it.'
- ©onflict(s) of (I)nterest: Copywrite SI: significant-indifidual…'
- Player(s): One Two Three…

< Trade-Constraint(s): simple screening process: limited and pre-dictable: as evidence:

>Again. No longer Universal finger games, but on paper…

<Do you Buy or Sell? Simple…

>Stay or Put. Buy? I suppose?

<With what?

>Money!

<If you've got it!

>Eh? If you've got it?

<Flaunt-it!

>OstRich:' *head in the sand:*

<That is not-what I would do. I would watch the next one coming-along, the next one to grab at the opportunity: # scenario-2:

- To knock-them-outa court! I have got it! Natural!>

<That is all it is? *Natural*?>>

>The Rational…Equitable: That is what we do.><*Natural*?>

>Alright? Maybe you did not think CEO-Banker and President: *acting in their own self-interest* could be so…so…

<So, mean?>

>So-selfish?

>>Think they Rule!

< Greedy! The-Law!

> Think they are the-Gods that made all the living-creatures…><So un-caring!> As if on automatic:

>Scientific-Economics Game-Theory *pish*! only following rational-equitable order>s?> as dropping-*bomb*>s… on an unseen *civilian*-population.

Looking into the screen: hostage as *distanced* from…the *thought*…the-pictures: destroyed ancient-ruins, bomb-crater homes:

<So… Stupid!>

>Damn-lies…>

<Repeated *endlessly…*>

>Open-ended…

<Rigged-Vote(s): closed.

>Ended. Statistics…and…>

<Dead-Weather *reports…as unpredictable as each-other.*>

>Without analysis.> knots of data and patents controlled by one firm, one person, daughter, family heir-loom.

> African Diamonds and Gold stand for Money:

<See that *it* is…

Silicon: Creating Digital Markets (CDMs): empowering individuals: available on commercial terms to everyone:

<*That* is what You *work* with.>

>Not just, the-Money…you know?

<Un-Just?

But:

>Whatever: Stock-Good(s): and services' information: *you*-have:…

>Or: *think* I have? Get: my drift?>And there is a lot of it!

< A Loot! Of it!

- And it has to be the correct-information.>

<Got-it! At last! The Good-Truth!>

>Truth?'>

<Ethical?>

>Moral?>

<Legitimate?…>

>Even?>

>< Tactical-Strateg(y)ies, written-down?

<Of-course! Even-handedness?>>

Screen-up:

>Rational? Regulatory: list…*endless*:

<At least…Reasonable…

>Equitable: Not!><On the Open-*i*nformation Market(s) (O*i*M(s))?>

<Believe-it…>

>Or not.>

<Not.>

>*Soft-news…*

<Hard-News…> to charm, and almost-*paralyzed* with fear…and mis-placed awe, or not:

>Does anyone else know this?>

<Global: Climate-Change: Democratic?

> No.

< Who has the-vote? Republic: Peoples Populist(s): ‘

<ViseGrad ?

<Monarchist?>>Re-xit: Presidentialist: may as well be would-be:

<For: One-Term

>2!

<3!>Input.

<Output.

>>For: Good!><Only reasonably ethically morally legitimately-*hypocritical…*

<Then?

Head-phoned sarcastically…scornfully-mordant:

>Liar saying your prayer(s) again, surely?>

<Only: Natural of course.>

>Well?<Off-course!>>Of- course. In the rough!>In the trough.>Out of bounds!>

<Prying…>

>Nnnnnnnnnnnnnn…

The-Clerk looked-up: on-screen:

'Serious numbers! I don't usually ask twice, but do You want me to take-a cut-in the recovery, eh? Cannot lose? Be in on the next **Boom!'**

'Basic commodities?'

'Bust. Rare *Metal*s?'

'Food and Furniture?' there is more: rubber plastic Silicon: Oil and Gas under them there rocks passed generations…

'Generating-Energy: Fuel: based:'

'Clean Uranium. Plutonium…'

'*Polonium*?'

'Novo-cheque. Industrial: *or* Military-use?'

'Business?'

'To be *had*? Mining-minerals from The Earth.'

'From Space? Eh? Satellites and Solar-panels perhaps?'

'Who knows? Exciting-*possibilities…*'

'…and we do not think we have to be persuaded. Know what I mean? Just a simple 'Yes' is all 'We' need.'

'Who doesn't?'

'For a *comfortable*-Peace?'

'Piece? Of What@*Never*…'

'Never say: Never!'

'*What*? To: Trade-War?'

'Why-not?'

'Trade…Shopping-War(s):'

'Then? All the Time! That is War? Isn't it?'

'Buying and selling…Time?'

'Share?'

'OurSelves. Buying and selling constantly movement…'

'Until, now?'

'Life is just a Game to be Won!'

'With the most…'

'Not: with the least.'

'At the end of the Game:'

'E-Sport: the end unknown in advance:'

'When the end is known in advance:'

Dramatic:

'Always ends in death, eventually.'

'Some people want to die so they can be free.'

'Why would you not w*ant* Peace?'

'Like we had before *this*?'

'This-time?'

'The Last-Time:'

'Happenned. Cannot have *the*-same-again, ever. Every time…is *different.*'

'Of-course.'

'Equity only v*irtually-preserved…*'

'By *sullen*-Madness!'

'Mutually Assisted.'

'Destruction…'

'*Assured?*'

'Never.'

'Happens. Insured? You think you are? No? Your…breaking-point…'*snapped! broken, into-pieces:*

'The-Whole-Thing! Capital-Equity: collapsed…'

'Crashed prices no good for buyer or seller.'

'Whether-designed to or not-to…'

'With: Iconic-Catastrophic damage…'

'For *some-Sector(s):…*'

'All!'

'Ignored.'

'Ig-snored…'

'Not-All. See?'

'Cannot-be?'

'Again? Yet?'

Looking-out. Suburban-edges, trimmed-hedges, overgrown woods, and peeling whitewash walls. Compound 3 or 4 storied building, and alongside creosoted-fences, before the graffiti-walled enclosed-ditch, between poplar and ash-growing, pastures, and harvested-fields.

By the Railway-Track…looking-out:

'Killing Field(s)…'

'For: Harvest and Meat.'

'In: Country-Town…' *urbane.*

'Urban.'

'Towns&Cit(y)(i)(e)s…'

ChatCat. Nascent competition: out-doing and adding to: bought-out, merged…

Corporate-Merger: WhatsApp. Alphabet and InstaGram: Medical-Advice and Check-Up:

Educational: Literacy and Numeracy reaction redaction speed rate(s):

Space National Country-Wide and Global. Government and Corporate Scientific:

ISS (InterNational Space Station(s)): Empire-of-the-Earth:

Driven Test-Lift-Off: ex-ploded in *flame*(s): Forest-Fire Sale(s): Tsunami-Flood Damage: *swamping*-ancestor(y): HQ-Office: in every-City, or the Glove, every Country, of The Globe.

Passed through and beyond…and over:

'The-City@:Business as Usual!'

'So…'

'Stupid! Damn-lies…'

'Repeated endlessly…'

'Until now…it was all going so well…'

'Ostrich!'

'Head in the sand…'

'So, you knew?'

'What?! In the water…of course…'

'Boarding: *Statistic(*s): NNN/nnn…'

'Weather-reports as reliable as the day before…'

'As unpredictable as each-other.'

'Without proper-*analysis*. See that is it…'

'*That* is what You have to work with…'

'If You are not that Red Barbarian at the Gate!'

'The Big Green Giant? Hulk?'

'The-Party President-Monarchical Ruler…'

''Man in The High Castle'…'

Tuned-out turned: *away and down into the-screen*:

'Playing the-Game@'

'Big-Media:'

'**B***luey*-Meanie:'

'Alright. Don't be-*stupid*…'

'Government…'

'Crackdown on tax-evasion and avoidance.'

'Corruption.'

'Like Friendly-Fire?'

'Fraud, if you like…'

'Robbery?'

'As a Soldier?'

'Looting?'

'Police and Thieves!'

'Killing. De-claiming!'

'Sue *them* for Accidental-Damage!'

'Kickin' the Can.'

'Down the Road:'

'BRIG-Bank…

'Sailing-BLOC's…'

'Shipped as Flagged. Troll Fleet-Expedient:'

'Pragmatic. For: Fair?'

'For: Brick-*Bat*?'

Uber Re-Gulated Utilities (URU) a-*twittering*:' in-formation:

'Innovative.' *spirit: lobbying-cronyism: news-media corps.*

Seen:

'Looting the Public Coffers…'

'*Hoax*-loan: and *overdraft*:…' agreed.

'The-*Gambler* bets on what they *think may happen*.'

'The Banker on what has only just happened a pica-second ago…'

'That *others* do not know.'

'Are not *meant* to know?'

'Con-cierge Conscience?'

'Customer?'

'Share-holder?'

'Business-*hush-hush*...clandestine...*covert*...confidential.'

'The-People! Are not meant to know!'

'Playing-the-Tables...and all the Chairs and Tables of all those Generation(s)!'

'Society? 'There is no such thing as Society. There are only individuals and families...''

'National-Socialism is good...'

'The problem with Socialism: is: 'You eventually run out of other peoples' money...''

'Until you run out of other peoples' money! Peoples'Money!'

With an air of *un*-fulfilled un-*done*: Drone-Destiny:Training (DDT):

'Get *in-early*...'

>R/E:...loading:...soon...sooner...

<Inter: National: Corporate-Governance: *Own-banking currency(ies): listing:...*

>The International-Conference: *insider-information:* ...

'What if *they don't decide?* Done-dealing?'

'Never! Could not-stop ourselves, could we? 'It'...was just...too-Good! To be-True!'

'The-Truth?'

'Fair-Fee Charge (FFC).'

'Customer-Ownership: owing: N.n:...'

'Data and Pay: De-liver(y): Logistic(s): Nation-State: Pro_duct:

'Game-Over.'

'Enviably too-Big to Fail!'

'The rest of Us?'

'Too small to survive?'

'Society?'

'Politics of Envy.'

'You too?' *envied all the same...*

'Only, arguably…'

'Too Bad…'

'To: Fail.'

'Only *winning*-bids now…' *assuming:* Absolution: saving:…

Lion-roars! when it gets hungry! roaming...re-connecting...

'These *Loans*…then?'

'Credit-Debit: You sign for them:'

'Debit-Credit: Online?'

'You have agreed the agreements: *Form-Ally*?'

'Morally? Legally?'

'One. Or the Other.'

'Both.':

Ambiguous: E-motional:-E-thic(s): *calculator*: N/n.

digital signature:

7. Titanic!

Connecting... eventually all other parts of the Ancient-land and Land…beyond un-*seen* as yet from:

>Business-Centre: City: Nation-State: internal/external: Trade: Capitalism/Communism: saved from themselves shelving sheltering competition and co-operation:

<*Vanity*-Project: *soars!* Name: **The Rational Equitable**:

>Your-Business-Centre: Vanity-project!

<How so?

>The-Real-City: *named* after you. The currency named after your Town or your City…

<Equitable-Town: manufacturing and agriculture: mechanics engineering and *digital*-industry…

>*Currency: opening…*: Rational-City: O.K?: *Rational-Equitable*: R/e:'s…out by the airport…appeared prompted by-*clicking*:

<Building-*materials:* Food Furniture…

<Media…and Luxuries: *items…including*: Your Business-centre: The-Bank of You…how many floors? (give a number up to 100) and a number-given):

>NNN…

The-Clerk entered another number, by speaking, saying the number word, flashed on-screen and clicked:

<Nnnn…

>Loan? Nnnn…agreed…*dropped-in in a shower of coinage and paper-notes and: Bank-Vault!*

vaulting: The-Banker *photo-caricature cut-and-pasted from: …*

>Application's…*behind re-enforced protective-glass walls fluttering down the screens now…*

At the-Top Floor.

On the top of the building: from the top inside: The-Banker *as aviator: Vanity-Avatar.*

*

Sat behind a-*mahogany*-varnished desktable showered, with gold and silver spouting from and falling all over the World-Map

#Re-*flection*:

carpeted shades of black and white-light-brown and yellow and green deep blue seas and ocean cloud above, and beneath a blazing red-Sun.

Looking-out, and in, onto and through-out *modernist* strangely-angled sheet-light colour-stained glass and plastic-nano fixed-panel see-through from ceiling to floor.

Looking-out over, a bustling ancient market-place *fruit and vegetables and livestock trading-post's outpost's and stall's set-out with or without that which could not physically be brought-to market. Due to bulk-mass, type and value…*

In-Transit or still in-the-ground. On-the-ground somewhere elsewhere and never to reach here at all but boarded-out in letters and numbers in full transparency…hidden or chalked-up and under-the cast *wrought*-iron frame and steel-blue counter.

Oil-based: African: South-American: Rubber-Plastic: liquid-shampoo and solid: moulded unmolded sulphurous plutonium-bomb.

Golden-patterned sheet-topped tables…gambling-houses…betting-shops and *public*-houses brought-in full-size screened-Sports and places of Barter and Banter:

Sport and the Art of *ill*-repute and Goods of *re-pute.*

Lain-in laid-in and on and over the lay-of-the-land: laid-down, planned-over panning-out…from: Canal-River and Railway-Town.

Urban-Centre Marketplace Courthouse and Births Weddings and Funerals over-and-again. Built stocked, and abandoned, blown to pieces, the investment, the taxes. The…vegetable and fruits of the Earth and Livestock Market-Place…now, dis-puted: Vanity-Avatar-stepped-out through the window.

Stooped stepped-into an exterior elevator descending glazed window-wall fitted gated secure-cage to the underground basement car-park…

Nnn…floors down.

Out-driving…extraordinarily exorbitantly expensive-vehicle from *list*: The-Full Range: list…V*8 selected and clicked-on the *self-owned* now *advertorial*-character inside seated, persuaded, cheated into-gears…

Transmission: *automatic*: Hybrid: Self-driving on the Game-Pad: Console: buttons and switches *screeching-away between walls, and ramps, skidding-around to a…*

Halt.

Then around-and-out between buildings street-by-street through layer upon layer blocks of buildings…*ancient*…and New! buying and adding-to *all along* the way…railway bridged underpass, river-banks and Estuary-Tunnel: *through* to the other-side, turning, *turned,* and cliff-edged overlooking:

'Water!' screeched, *braked* and spun-around again, hitting a key on the steering-wheel: *fake*-landscape:

<Leverage!

>N/nnn…everytime!

>CCTV: Speed-Camera's…watch-out!

< VRN-VAR: Bet-time!

>V! Pay upfront…

<Refused?

>Refusal may cause…

<Anger!'

In-red. In-blue:

>No Offence:

<No-offence. Get out of prison Free!

>That is what 'It' is? Go on the offensive!

<Credit-Time! Best-time! GO!

>What for?! *hitting:…*

<Tax: *breaks…*

>Mining: virtual-machines under and overground transport controlled from the cabin:

<For: Building: The-City:

>City! Never-*neglect* the-Defences:

<Doing the Laundry?!

>Washed-up?

<Spin dryer-Machine?

> Algorythms…

<Advertising…sold…a-*pup*! (never shown the advertising effect, nil.All of Us: *conned* into having to buy or sell enjoyable, some, when they make a laugh out loud: F/B Twitter Run!: LoL.

>Where did you get that from?

<Gangsta-0-family…

>Cleaning-up?'

<The-Cleaner? Me?'

>You got it…

<Clearing-out…

>Not. Only…

<If You want to bring in rich-investors…

>Investment-in?

<Yourself!

>Tax Cuts!

<Public Service Cuts!

> Washed-up? On THE BEACh?

<blEAK?

>Tax-rises…*scares them-off?*

<Compensation of laborious Transaction-Costs and Logistics…

as if without-prompting, without voting:

>Simply, as the visible natural agricultural- industrial complex, and countryside-landscape, naturally evolving-to…and from the…

<Coast. Down-river to The-City edges…*of Fielded Forest and Hill and Mountain…*

>This Time! *and at the Great-river lake, and scenic Oceanic map:* From the cliff-topped taking-off over the water and turning far out inland again. Alongside fields and irrigation-ditch to land-*afloat…*

On Equatorial swampland peninsular draining riversea estuary-basin:

On-board spinnaker wind-sail: Out-again on the water onto peninsular-sea…*mapping… loading…waiting…*

Motoring speedboat with increasing speed…*plummeted* plunged and sunk submerged:

Sub-marined to avoid various-objects (i)mperiled-on and in-the-water implied:

Shark infested-waters and blubberous Whale. Dead. Species, too late.

Mackerel and Cod. Sardine and shell-fished: *until there was no-fish left:*

<Non-vivi sectioning: Scientific: Re-search: *done.*

Caviar and truffle with wild boar.

Erased raised-*surfacing* and water-ski-ing wet-suited clad with the profit-motive: *tourism.*

Is that the…:

<**R\E** logo…*taking-off gliding with windsurfing balloon opening-up, and rising into the upper-atmosphere looking down over a country-town tour aloft overlooking casually and without due regard then straightening-up…ready…*re-turning towards The-City-airport:

Executive-transformation under-*performing*…

>Helicopter-view…

H-Block Landing-*perfectly* exactly on the H of the-now ready built:

<**Rational-Equitable**: **Business-Centre**: *roof-tops stretched out to the urban and suburban distance. In-between the factories and office-blocks beyond as far as the eye could see.*

<*Real*-estate: *beneficial*-owner: N/nnnnnnnnn… *in the clear-air…*commentary-spoken continued through head-phones…text/spoken:-'…' tapped:

>Choose? -text spoken…*clicks made over a ragged landing over field's…and Farm…in: Buildings: list…*factory or *You*- own…Home: Businesses: Centre: The-City: Bank: *the circuitous roads now heavy with cars lorries buses and coaches mechanized streets. Populated with identikit people of almost every personality-type and head and shape of every ethnic-race and apparent-creed and ideogram mixed as long as there has been and is and there will be…*

<Food and Furniture and Household-Goods and Materials for Making…*on the back of cart's and truck's, lorries and coaches and cars.*

On the concrete-built motorways container-juggernauts into-and-out of Village, Town, and to and from each, and The-City.

On the sea and land and awaiting at-dockside and harbour fishing-vessels, ships and supervised- controlled Hyper-tanker, and from the high-seas and Ocean waiting-off shore. Sea-port passed the coastal and inland estuary river-Town: *list: already* built-up: outskirts, and back to, in *lights*: Fat-Cats' Company: *excepted...*

The Rational-Equitable Tower built-up through river-way-lined embankment canal and railway-track up and along evermore and faster building-checking *maintaining*- control by-*braking…*

Gradually, spinning on a too-rapid action: onto the next…

Above: from: Satellite-Dish: solar-paneled beaming in below:

>Trade Banking Cit(y)ies (TBCs): Country and Countries: list:*in the-Cloud...the lofty City-streets and buildings now transformed from bricks and mortar...to pie-chart...*

<Projected-costs (blue) and Projected-earnings (yellow): Business-plan (Green): Balance-sheet (red/black): *on screen like towers-building...tumbling, and dropping, and re-built once more, only to fall:*

>You are within The **Black**-*Zone* stray into The **Green**-*Zone* and you are out-in-the-*opening…*

*Heard...fuzzy found-footage...in blocks and relief red and black with green thread's and lines like the real hills beyond and blue, beyond the columns and row's...*with a bright yellow sun in a bright blue sky, bright-clouds…

Not-*grey(s)*:

<All *this* City and Town and Countryside-Village…*and hamlet... tokens taken the place of the buildings and roadways black and tan, green and yellow fields and trees digitally-transferring between and across spread-sheet and balance-sheet number and text-wrapped boxed and charted...*

Graphic's-mapping...where landscape and livestock...inside and outside and inside...on the single wall flat-screen backed room:

The Rational-Equitable Building:

>O.K. You are Trading: Private Limited Company:

Trading under the name: ...

<***<u>The Rational Equitable</u>***: OK?

>OK...Rational *classic*-actor: acting to: *maximize personal and others' economic-return-on-Investment:*

<*You*r-Budget for The-Day Trading:N...

On-screen: with Real-world updates:

<Real-time and Game-play-currency setting-up...

>Tough-*budgeting*: ...

<Not-budging...as long as there is enough demand to meet supply, or is it the other-way-around?

>Money or Goods?

<For goods? For money? *predatory loan shark payday Mafiosi...*

>*Cosa Nostra*

<*Yakuzi*

>*Bratva:Triad: Prohibition of alcohol and drugs: Euro Russe and African American: China-Gang: Violence: usury loan bubble economic power to legitimize political-power... interest ceiling against unfair lending special fee from Local Council State-owned People: owed The Banks' private lending market with exorbitant charges*

shareholder relationship open market pricing mechanism debt: pricing employmen second-slavery and religious-royalty bondage.

Joint-venture pirating and sharing in the commerce of profit and risk of loss, equity stake, for services provided, administration fee's, time and effort, of each party, equally to the effort and time or however calculating non-recourse interest free micro-lending: artistic craft skills covering every Industry Re-Tail and Mechanical-Mind: sober:

>*Family. Kickstarter Credit-Union*: collectivization for more freedom more land to grow and live…

<As the Earth shaped us!

>As we shaped ourselves! Cities!

< Furniture holding things up…

>Color of money: People!

< Or taste!

>Specifics: Gender Race of Humanity: Class-Id'd:

<Financial Infra-structure: Industry and Trade:

<Trades Union4Life!

>The Harmony of *Consumption*

>Torture-Game!

<Play!

Chrem(is)thetic means of exchange not unworked for profit or frugality sobriety deferred consumption of savings: stocks, and shares…

<When to stop-and-start (*I*)n-Game again and out of The Game, again.

>At what node?

<What meeting-point?

Shopping-Mall:

Page Up, Page down, side and right and left cursor-call, balling joystick socket and leveraging:

<The *Real*-Economy: *of the historic mills and factories and shops and fields:*

>Generating deal<*flowing…*

<Cost<Price *benefit…*

>Social-Public: Government Tax-Revenue…*for hospitals and schools, roads, and all that…*

<*Social-stuff. Public-Private. Make the World a better place:…*

>*Make?*

<*What?* War. Government-Product<loyalty…*key…*

>Different<0ffers…

<Built<in *obsolescence…*

>Buy all over again…

<Latest-model…

>Fashion! Next Years Model:

>When IT goes wrong!

<No! Re-fund…

>Corporations…

<Oligopolies…

>A few selling the same product!

<Virtually! None!

>Buying-Up All Competition!! Monopoly! Competition exists to create Monopoly!

<Fines: de-regulation <:>Over<competition: list:…

>Mortgaged to the hilt.

<Enough to take technological advantage…

>Advance? For how long? How long does IT last?

<Forever…

>War and Tourism:

<Peace Poverty

>Energy!

<Informations!!!

>Fake! Fraud!!

<Forger!

Securitised: Shopping-Mall Guards gated escorted vigilance:

Vigilante! Enrolled: Secure-Zone(s): throughout the World: host/guest guest/host host or guest: compl(y)(i)City: service re-lationship(sss: in Global Sy-stems

A few weeks…and a day.

One<Season<Ticket-Technology: *made to be kept for so long, before the next model*:

>Innovation? One and two years?

<Eighteen months?

>To start with…and *de-creasing*…

<Folding? Monthly?

>Weekly:

<Daily:

> *like* today?

< Advertising the latest model all of us, latest:

>Dot<Comms? Mobile<phones, laptop tablet personal ergonomical agronomical] *computing…*

<Power? Need: Power?

>Constant *innovation…*

<Triplicate and tripl(i)cant, again.

> Needed: or not: Healthy *peaceful, relatively for most…*

>Naturally!

<Society?

>Most the time, maybe…

<Standard(s) and Poor!

> The Rise and Fall of the Markets…

< Why Capitalism and Communism fail(ed)@

>Everything has to be used<up…to be sold<up again at a frantic pace…

<To eliminate the competition.

>Algorythm(s): seek-Monopoly:…

<*Aggressive*-marketing:

>Setting the price(s)….

<High as you like!

>Low, now….

<Low as you like!

As you find them:

<Snap them up!

>Precisely. Still familiarity bores, and brings on the new; and not a bad thing… Except for the detachment from real life. The attachment Politics and Religion, Economics and Technology.

Protecting-Civilians' Securit(y)ies: providing food and furniture of life. To make *this* our country safe

Again.

You'd would think it would be:

<To make OUR country safe first.

>It is! KillBox: Lemmings obstacles floating climbing blocking bombing basement minefield digging real-time strategy-gaming

<Grand Theft Auto GTA! Access-coding: following leading to safety…

>But it is not!

That's the *point*...

<It is to make Our Country Great! Again! Our Nation! Empire!!!

Crossing the ravine-borders, mountains and river(s):

<State!

>Name?

< Nanny-State!

>What? Money-State!

<Father of The Nation!

>Mother!

Safe at Home…and abroad?

<What?

> War-abroad4Peace-at-Home.

<*Peace* abroad?

>At: Home

<War and:

>E-sports': Home.

Front: Hierocracy, hypocrisy, theocracy: *breeds contempt, contempt, hatred.*

With pictures and reports, in and from city and town squares there:

>The World All One!

<The World at One.

shouted into the air as news broadcast: *started*: continued:

<Investment: Sale of profitable insurance-contract *deferring use of funds as percentage of principal paid-back…*

>Pay-Out: State-Bank: Fixed-Deposit-Receipt (FDR): price rate(s): *capped*: con-current with Economic-Growth (EG) to safeguard momentum real and nominal no's and purchasing power with inflation frequency dynamic range full duplex relaying forced development re-quirement(s):

'Yes is more.'

'Less is not.

‘Stopping the World: is impossible…’ however much there are wish(es) to stop the Train a swinging seesaw in 3d with ever more elaborate-Mechanism: tracing and tiling…

To: balance: nature-nurture: cheat with shorter and lesser transparency: Co(m)puting: name tracing config….

<Overnight holding rates…

>Broad quantity theory: spread…

<Interest and inflation balance N/N…

>De<valuation…<N/n

<In: valuation of the currency n/nnn…

>De-Inflationary…*admin difficulties…between high's and low's…between…wages and prices, usually…*

>Re-flation: Monetary-goals:

<Inflationary! Own-Goal!

>Today?

From kick-off to final-whistle we do not know the outcome of the game. This is not a pre-written piece future-secured. Paid too much, not on results, paid too little on results: Scientific:

<We want more rather than less…

>Full-employment *always something to be done…*

<A Home of your own? Coperative Corporate *temptation shared!*

> *This is IT!* <Unemployment-insurance…social-benefits…

>Structural:demand-and-supply: to max-out market-share *monopoly oligopoly Avoiding frictional-mismatch between choices…between employment and unemployment what choice is there…*

>*Cost-Wages and Raw-materials exploited at cost to: Prices at the Shop(s): Labour Payday-Loan?*

<People! For: Stock-Good(s)<>Cost-Price Stability (CPS) *dealing with conflicting interests across…*

>Sale-Price: *rises* on stocks held-and re-leased: false-scarcity: figures re-leased investment info-mation(s0):

< Bet(s): taken-out, on possible re-accredited (i)nterest rates: Evens/Odds…

➢ Some Future: N to one: in Real-time flashed-up: NNNnnn…

Digital-Time: YYYY/MM/DD/Mx60…sx60…12:00 midday… *minus*…

>NNnnnn…counting-down…or -up, whoever, what way you came at it midday from the past, from the- future:

<So, set-out your bargaining counters:

>Signal! You! Set-out yours!

<Your Bargaining-Chip(s): Nnnn…

Great Journey of Discovery… *completed...continue?* Y/N. 3? Y/N?

>3Y…..

<From the so-called Dark-Ages to the so-called *Enlightenment*...

>To the Space-age! Now! Denomination of Credits neutral one-to-one…amount? Nnnnnnnnn…Your password: AAAAZ: number Nnnn…again?: YyyyyXXX…

<Nnnn…Xxxxxxxy…loading…*first-re-colonising where only non-humans lived joining others and almost destroying although that patently not possible as roundly shown in figures, and statistics, throughout The Ages settling…living…*

On-screen. Buttons and levers pressed hand-held and pulled and push-pull for *imposing by simple-pressure:*

<Forced: enforce(ed.):Economic Religious and Political power:

>*False?:P*-Atomic organic plant life…animal…and-*virus…*

<Religion and Politics:

- Not: the-one without the-other:

<One cancels out the Other?

>Rich-Game-*change*r:

<Brain-*attack!*

>Without Religions and Politics, we would be Nothing!

<Exactly. Without *Money* We would be-*Nothing*!

<Without-Taxes…*something*?

>With Taxes, tithes and offerings…

<To appease The Gods?

>The Tax Man…

<Infinite-Jester….*either way. Red-line. Game-changer:*

<Tax-Pressure: on all-points…

>For: The People! Who Pay Taxes whether they like it or not, into pensions and insurance:

<For Military-Action?

>Who Pays?

<*They* do…

>*Humanitarian*-Aid?

<Mutual> *Sure…*

>Fraud!

<Robbery!!

>'Not!' *heard*:

'Save!'

'Action!'

'Regime-Change…' *that is what it is all about:*

'Totalitarian Militaristic Regime (TMR): change for some other: Dictatorship of the-Proletariat (DoP): as for ourselves: all…all the time:'

'The Ruling-Class€(s):'

'Famil(y)(i)ar. Elite. Natural.'

'You know who *you* are?'

'Arbitrary-Power:'

'The Excluded-Middle…'

'Non-identical Family. Families: Elites arbitrary reporting-arrest dis en-franchised:…'

'Inside, fear and loathing, as well as Love for the Cause…'

'Which is?'

'Me; and then everyone else…' *keeping clear, anonymous or else:*

Head above the parapet:

‘Super-Powers…’

‘The Rest?’

‘The rest don’t matter…’

‘Oh, they do…for the purpose of global wars without boundaries, across boundaries…’

‘And within?

‘Grass-skirt.’

‘Grass-court…*of course….*’

‘Civil, as well as Global Wars.’

‘Corporate-Competitive:’

‘Tax-regimes…’

‘Global: Tax-*burden*:’

‘Accounts?’ pattern-patent.

Patented dis-cretely con-cretely for internal and international:

Global-*Fraud: de-frauding: The-People*:

‘Tax *re-lief*!’

‘Big-B*urden* on others.’

The People:

Violent-Sectarian Party-split to be utilized…

‘Government Official(s): Bailed-Out The-Bank(s):'

‘On-advice? Again. Not the next ‘though 'IT' Dot.Comms. *was last and first of the Millennial-Bubble(s) including: Government and* Bank(s):'

‘*Was* the-B…

'Not-now…'

'Then?'

'Corporate: Competitive-*conformity of rates bonding…*

'Neutrally stated…'

'Sovereign-State: National-Pride: in Ourselves as Ourselves not not-*Them…*'

'Who are unnatural mans/ inhumanity to man? Why?'

'Naturally?'

'Family? Me? No.'

'Yes, well…'

Family-Bank(s): of Mum and Dad and sibling(s):

'The-Banks then defraud in the-Government: negotiation(s):'

'R&D. People.'

'So, IT *is* the Government: Financial: Military: At all different Time(s) and Place(s): Yes/No?'

''Us?'

'You?'

'US? The-Banks *de-fraud* the people…Saver(s) and Lender(s):'

'Pension and Life-Insurance…'

'Fake-Fund(s):'

'Tax.'

'Fund. Trillions…'

'Quadrillions! The Government-Bank!'

'Their own People!'

'Don't we *know* it!'

'We don't own it!'

'Government?'

'Bank. Pension and Insurance Fund(s): New?'

'Frauding or de-Frauding?'

'Family-Frauding again…'

'Are they?'

'De-fending funding: Borders, edges bleeding edges…'

'Cheap Buy-Backs. You watch: Dark-Mountain: *secrets…*'

Touching the side of the nose and nodding, eye-to-eye both, instantaneously inside, continuing: outside heard-spoke:

'Liquidity. Sold-off…bought-Back *cheaper…*'

'Double-Asset stripped!'

'Ripping-up The Rulebook.'

'Whose?'

Striped: barcoded: stipend:

'Crimes! Crimes-against-Humanity!' *chemical bio nerve gas-factory sites facilities on-screen:*

'Money-War: (s) Crimes: Be-Sieged!'

'Sieged!'

'Where? Geneva?

'ZuRich! Here! The City. That's where the money is:'

'Jakarta, HK, Australia. Shanghai-Bejing…'

‘Tokyo and New York and Buenos Aires…’

‘Seoul. Papist. Islamic. Christian and Judaic:’

‘Capitalist-Dictatorship(s): Syria-Secular: Russia and China.’

‘Dubai and Nairobi and Johannesburg?’

‘We are only assessing the situation…’

‘Only hoping to discover The-Truth.’

‘Only Truth? Not the lies too?’

‘The truth of the lies?’

‘Lies?’

‘The Truth about The Lies, then?’

‘As Good as it *gets*. As *bad*-Regulation…’

‘In-Law: on:-*Commodity*-Futures: then: N/n…'

‘Speculation:’

‘Re-regulation.’

‘Re: de-regulation:’

‘By-Law. Rules and Regulation(s):’

‘Global-Cheating?’

‘Yes.’

‘Yours' or Mine?’

‘Mine not-Your’s.’

‘Then? Neither?’

‘Someone else’s *problem…*’

‘Contradictory-paradoxical?’

Managed-Economy: *Free*-Market(s):

'Free: *Cash-based:* economy: Managerialist: Cruel-Dictatorship:'

'Symbolic (I)nformational Meaning (SIM) or not…'

'At the time meant-to be: covetous.' Greedy grasping hungry:

'Avaricious?'

'Rapacious.'

'Materialistic. Die! is cast!'

'Family. Security.'

Acquisitive:

'Family?'

'Friends?'

'Tribe? Commu(n)ut(y)ies'

'Not unlike People, self-made, made in self.'

'The Excluded-Middle.'

'Identical.'

'Not.'

'And/Or.'

Looking-sidewards out of the window and across again to:

The-Banker speaking, interrupting:

'Why do people *rob*-banks?'

'Because that was where the money is?'

'Not-anymore.'

Recovering from this *slight*:

'Now all Cash-Machine(s), eh?'

'Shop-till…you drop!'

'Now?'

'Cashcard…steal.' *oxy-arc explosive bank vault wall, heaving heavy metal door with locks and wheels…*

Express-Visa: Card-Reader:…

China: Diners' Club:

'*Where the money is…*' nodding, glancing-down at first one then the other computer-screen:

'And the-Time?

'Is now.'

'Prison-Time: (PT)?'

''prisin' time.'

'Social-Security?'

'Benefits?'

'Everyone?'

'State-Security.'

'*Nasty*-Squad?'

'Then *forgotten*-about.'

'Made sure.'

'As difficult as possible.'

'Complaint?'

Exchanged for *passivity* be-littlement a burning fuse of *re-sentment…*

Sub-limating awe, gritty grey-bitterness, *angry*:

‘Then?’

‘De-regulation…’

‘Again?’

‘This morning the International Conference of Business and Government leaders…’

‘Re-regulation *surely*?’

‘Shirley?’

‘This morning in Geneva, there is to be an announcement of The International Conference on Monetary Compliance (ICMC). P*ossibly* midday…’

‘Who *knows*?’

‘International-Time (IT): NNNnnn…’

‘Yes.’ *looking-down…and into: @Corporate-Government sponsored enterprise the-National-Bank: list:* list: >*Currency*-Exchange-Rate (CER): list(s):…

Both:

<Currency-*exchange* rates: *list…*

>N/n%…

<Banks? R/e Investment Houses:

>% Private-Assets (PAs):…

<Public: Want. Water *waste*…re-using…rotten shit-fertilizers pharma re-cycling…re-porting:

>Journal of Economic Affaires:…

<Toxic de-salinating de-toxifying…

>Cleaning-up…

<Re-using…

>Rainwater?

<Pay-for:…

>Loan?

<Energy?

> Sunlight?

<Wind-*power*…

>Re-wind: for *electricity*…

<Between Food and Medicine…

>Sewerage: *nutrients*.

<Safe Water and *decent*-Sanitation…

>Built water-stands and Pumps, pumping:

<*Clean*-water:

>At a cost:…

<Coal-Gas and Oil *to the surface* short-term free-lance zero-hours employed:

>Re-Plastic: Social-cost: serial-number: NNNnnn…

<Working-*Costs*: re-purposing byte-based *gig*-economy…

>Buying-up…*re-fining*…

<**Black**-stuff…

>*white*-stuff?

>Red and Green-backed as well, see: list…

<Like flies on-Shit.

>As Well as that?]

<For *Quick*-returns: N/n…

>*Personal*/Company-accounts: *list…*

<Government-contracts…always pay-up, in the end.

>Even if they don't? Or have to fight for decent pay-off…

<Or *pay*-at-all?

>Voluntary-sector…

<Mandatory through Judicial-Courts…

>Sovereign Due-*processing*…

<For: Tax-re-imbursements?

>No Tax at-all? Paid-up…

<Threats enough:…

>Unless…

<Unless, what?

>You are a Country? Nation-state?

<I am not…

>So, you are a: Hu-Man-Being (HMB), after-all?

<You could call Me that…

>*Compensation*?

< For what? Hurt-feelings?

>Compensating for paid-up Insurance-bill: claim(s):

<Credit timesheet invoice: to close-of-business: date: closed Factor(y) Shop and Home.

<Business-*transactions*:

>Global-Commodities: *lists…less is more, more is less: timing-important:*

<No Pay-out: on: N/n or n/N:Economic: Significance: list...

>Larder-Food. Betting-Shops? Funeral-parlours n*ever Parlous: P*eople's lives…as…*number*-of…N. to n. or n. to N: >N=N. n=n: may as well do.

< What-for? Starting-price: N/n:

>Commodities: List: Television and: Radio: list:…

<Machine-fuel *lubricant...*

#Computers

Desktop…flashing-red… *green-light*:

Forward Operating Base: Public-affairs Office: Vehicles: *updating*… every second…

What-Day? Week Month Year:

<Second-*ing*

> *Poll: gun-toting...*

<Poll-Pot...

Polling-Dictatorship: *perpetually insecure and hopeless helpless and threatening the rest of the Peopled*

World!:

>Torturing rape and murder:

'*Spies took* a bigger Hit! *look*: Bigger-than…'

'The Big-Ones too. First-World…'

'Second and Third and Fourth-Estate:'

'Worlds' Lies?'

'I did not tell any *lies*…not like the-*others*…'

'About each other?

'That's Business.'

'Black?'

'As usual?'

'White-*lies*?'

'Red-Lines.'

'Legal-Referee?'

'No Prescribed Drama. Doctor, Do no-Harm? Co-operative-harassment *fails* your-team first and your-*opponents* all of them: Opponents-fail: lode-lose…'

'We: Win-Win.'

'Fair cheating Sports and Game(s)?'

'Impossible! To the whistle, to the bell…'

'Your own-team fails. too. Lose-Lose? You?'

'Not. Quite, as good as: Win-Win.'

Others, not dictatorships exactly, but *shambolic*-democracies: Communist Capitalist ruling-minorities. Social triading and searching the family-homes arrested and exiled-to offices of: Human and Women's Rights Organizations (HWRO). As: *Responsibilities'*-Organisation (RO's): Political-Prisoners and Activists: PPA: peaceful but dis-ruptive as dis-tractive, attractive, destructive; or otherwise, threatening-destruction, continuing to Kill. In the name of *single-conjoined* family party politic(s). AllofU(s) (AoUs).

Issuing and eventually, killed. Be-fore carrying-out such threats, having-to: or not, exaggerated for *political*-purposes:

>Speech?

sooner, or Later.

<Ex-Colonially de-invaded: Democratic Socialist-Dictatorship:

From the first time elected then: Military-Puce:

>Conscripted against their will.

<For?

>Metals: list: minerals: list… *except* in the case of democracy, not-*Sham!*

<Monarchial-Presidential Re-Colonising: sheiking-down:

>Aristocratic the-leaderships have only seconds, minutes, hours in which to decide: dis-ingenuously, indigenously inevitably, candidly whether it will protect and/or capture Oil-Wells and Gas-Plant and Pipeline. Food, fruit and vegetables. Salt, nuts, raisins and wine. Gold&Silicon&Silver. Logistics-Prices: Trade-Routes and for everywhere-else:

>South-America and North America. Africa: Middle-east…

<Euro-Russe Chinese and Skandi: Indian Viking and Anglo-Saxon, Greco-Roman. Franco-Prussian and Italian Spanish Portuguese: Africa: again and again…

<Australia.

>BRI-CKS BANK(S)! Federal-Reserve of: The Peoples' Republic of China, and Australasian Pacific *including*…

>North-Atlantic Trade Organisation:

<South Atlantic African-American: British:

>Ex-Colonial everywhere at some time and place until now…

<Oceanic *plastic* mined metals and minerals, and grown and reared foodstuffs, alternative energy-sources, and *technology*-powering mobile-phones, camera, music-store

collections, reading-matter, and messaging, social-contacts and place-name, *favourite*-sites and networks…*calculators*, all…

>At the Fat-*Cats' Table*: innocent, trusting, honest, sincere, forgiving, *naive*:

<Manufacturing: *steel*-girder and carbon re-enforced, unforced, in-force laws of nature, and society, similarly. Learning. Maintained, no-mistake: *owed-a-debt*-of-gratitude: in the first-instance next: *financially*…

<Borrowed: NNNnnn…

><Borrow-to-Lend?

<Since the Pyramids, the Arches and Strut-Beams and wooden Stake-Posts in the ground…

>On the ground, people here and there, and everywhere, almost…

<Mining and extracting…

>Virulent-virus, epidemic-proportions, obsessively envious-of-the-living…keeping-up depressive anxiety addicted…

To: the screen:

>Paranoid-*schizoid*…

<Dual personalities all..

>Triple-Kaos! Except some more than others…

<By-degree at any point in Space and Time. In one or more of each case, and case-*history*…

>*Money-mania*, and suicide over unpaid-*debt*s…

<*Unnecessary!*

>Unilateral…

<Me! Me! Me!

>Materialist, systemic-failure of financial-*systems*…

<Mis-selling mis-managed: *no*-competition: free-market rebelling reveling any which-way…

>Promoting: In-Equality: Revolution?

‘Against The Government!’ shouted loudly from a crowd of yelling and bawling demonstrators:

‘Insurgency! Across-The-Board!’

‘Again?’

‘Crackdown on Companies and Corporational-Government(s):’

‘Tax E(v)asion?"

‘A-voiding:’

Ignored:

‘In-vasion…’

‘Project-value: foster-posterity *and* protect-our-people.’

‘Home.’

‘Global-Response-Centre:’ like a soldier a player de-claiming: stealing from the cookie-jar:

‘Red Barbarian at the Gate!’

‘Orange-Sunny Delight!’

‘Blue-Boots.’

‘Cut!’

'Green Giant!'

'Corn.'

'And prices so high 'We' simply cannot afford anything except the basics or not at all…'

'Broken-biscuit. House and Home? Rented? Mortgaged? Credited in-advance:'

'For: Bread and Soup Poor? Not quite yet!'

'This situation is termed as a Bear-market.'

'I know that too!

'There are others.'

'Like?' *hooks to hang ourselves-on:*

'Narrowing-margin(s):…'

'For: Social-Good?'

'Widening: Openings Too!'

'Correct. You Got-'It'.'

'No, You got-'It'.' not *faltering* now, either.

The-Banker *chortling* unsure yet con-ceitedly *self*: or other: de-ceptively or not: inter-cepting:

''Buy' or 'Sell'.'

'What?'

'Do 'We' buy or sell?'

'That is your call isn't 'It'?

'Not this one. Your call. What do You reckon on?'

'Simple. Buy? I suppose?'

‘With what?'

'Money. If You've got it. Eh?’

‘Incorrect. Information. That is what You, can get, for Me. For Us. Together. Then worry about the money.’

‘If you've got 'It'.’

‘Information? No-worries. Flaunt-'It'. That is what I do! I have got 'It'!’

‘Natural. That is all 'It' is.’

‘Rational...That is what we do. Alright? Maybe you did not think CEO Investment-Banker(s): arms acting in their own: Rational: Self-(*I*)nterest:’

‘Could be so…’

‘So?’

‘So, mean? So-*selfish*!’

‘So Natural, see? behaving in their own best interests…’

‘Alone?’

‘Why?’

‘Not even the interests of the Share-Holders Customers and Worker(s):’

‘Staff? Not even, not by far.’

‘V*oted*-in, weren’t they?’

‘No?’

‘By purchase of their own knowledge…’

‘Information, see?’

‘On: The-Board: Government-Committee? Lobbyist? What Corporation?’

‘Family: Company-Business. From The Country. Not: in the *know*. Not able to be, because: ‘It’ is all made so…’

‘*Damn*-complex! Unfathomable to the customer. That is the idea. They all do it. Politicians, Church People, Military, simplify! ‘It’ is simple!’

‘What? Subs! To: the *Ordinary* Share-Holder(s):…’

‘Business Pensions and (I)nsurances and Home(s):’

‘Not! Bonus for Fuck-up! Pensions and (*I*)nsurances…so, un-caring about themselves, their Famil(y)ies:’

‘Others’!’

‘So, Natural. We know that now.’ as if *only following orders*...as if dropping bombs on an unseen *civilian* population: hostaged.

#So, distanced from the *action*...performing a rescue, taking lives, to save lives...

‘Hopefully.’

'So...’

‘Stupid.’

‘*Damn*-lies...’

‘Repeated endlessly…'

‘Be-lieved of All!’

‘President(s)’’

‘Economist.’

‘’It’ was all going so well...’

‘Ostrich! Head in the sand...’

‘In the water...’

'Boarding...'

'Statistics…and...'

'Weather-Reports…'

'As un-predictable as each-other:

'Predictable? Without Analysis?'

'So, cannot be?'

'Unpredictable?' on-screen:

'See that is 'It'.'

'That is what You work with.'

An uncomfortable pause, *pregnant.*

For the-Clerk affronted, check-mated, and taken.

As for the-Banker, afforded:

'Not just, the Money, but only of whatever Stocks:'

'Services-(*i*)nformation: you have or think you have...'

'Get my drift?@and there is a lot of it…'

''It' has to be the *correct*-(i)nformation.'

'And I have it?'

'Futures?'

'Got: 'It'' distant: *instant:* but only now *felt*: mis-trust:

'Fixed: Extreme(s): Evens?''

'Odds?'

'Not-evens...then?' dealing-in *fantasy* and *fear* the-passive: reflective- *thought*: and then again the-Bankers' *anger* looked back upon:

‘By closing-the-markets’ building-mortgage and credit-crisis. Crashed. O.K.?’

‘Credit-Crash: Re-insurance and -Pensions as Life-Saving(s): Home-Mortgage(s):’

‘Home and Office Building:’

‘Over-Production: low-price.’

‘No-production?’

‘Famine? Growth dwindling...’

‘Single Industr(y)ies’

‘Blowing-*Bubble(s):* that is all.’

‘Why the Government-Interference? Why the Market-Closure?’

‘Regulation(s):’

‘Law?’

‘Orders. Dragging-down whole-Corporation(s):’

‘A-(ir)lines. Fallen out-of-the-Sky.'

‘Sub-Prime. For Sub-primes’ were ‘It’s’ Biggest-Beast!’

Whole-Industries Businesses Transported to and from:

<Driven: Logistics-Corp.s.

>Transport Home-and Abroad.>

<Logistic(s): Lorry. Ship-Owners>...>

>Stock-Holder(s): Share-Holders>

<Bargain-Partner(s):>

Before the next listed:

>OwnerShip!>Portside:

<Sold-out>.

>Sold-off!>

<Sunk!>

>Crashed!>

<Collided!>

>Mired in the quicksand...>

<Of information!>

>Onto the Black Rocks! Of Doom!>

<At the bottom of the deep blue...sea.>

>See: Bonanza! And Blow-out>s? Over-ripe…for the taking…Scamming. Shamming. Spamming computer-fraud.>

>Without permanent circuitry, no trace.>

<Intentional...>

>Of-course.>

Dry hacking-cough.

From the-Banker: *viral*:

‘Spear-fishing...’

‘In a barrel...’

‘Lake.’

<Red...Ripe!>

>Green-*Light*.>

<Blue-Stocking: Hard>

> Soft: Orange-Sun>

< Leaving the Liberal Free-Market (LtLFM) bad apples *to-rot*!> *crushed* collapsed...*fermented* on-paper: drying-out: i-goggling new(s):

<Capital: Stock-Market: *collapse...*>

>Again.>

Denial of service...

*

‘They were...’

‘You were…’

‘Drunk on ‘success’!’

‘Whatever *that* is!’

‘Not happiness?'

'Or sorrow?’

‘Success breeds success'

'Other-*Success* breeds money!’

‘Other-Sorrow breeds Money!’

‘Money breeds more-money.’

'Money breeds Greed'

'Greed breeds success…’ or abject *failure*:

‘Not. More success than happiness?’

‘Happiness more than success?'

'More equal?'

'Ecology? Whenever is enough not enough, eh?’

'What if 'We' lose?'

'The *process may not be perfect…*'

'But 'It' is still 'adequate' under the *exceptional* circumstances of the day?'

''We' already, eh?'

'We are all inter-dependent...'

'You speak for yourself!'

'I do!'

''It is like a pyramid, at the top...by: Conquest: Conquistador: Constant-Conquest!'

'Matador! Kills the helpless Bull!'

'Tortured and killed, for dinner!'

'Create wealth...Easy! Capital! What chance does the Bull have?'

'Or the Bear, baited?

'Every chance.'

'No chance.' '

'The Super-Powers (TSPs) remain quiet or loud: *roaring…*

'Lion(s): Subdued.'

'Not-*howling*, and baying, for blood?'

'Finite-Population of Worker-Bee(s):'

'Only One Queen!'

'And pies! More-pies!'

'Buyers and Sellers.'

'Presidents and Royalty: born-blood:'

''Fealty' to one or the other. Head of this or that...'

‘Only if They can get away with it again!’

‘Everyone thinks’ they can.’

‘The screens and the board will *light*-up again…’

as: they did. Un-*frozen*: the electronics at boiling-point:

'Almost:’ at the Relative Speed of Light! (RSL!)’

‘And the Economic-(i)(n)(t)eraction between People...’

‘Now! that is at the-Speed-of-Light!’

‘Quantum (Q)!’

‘Sold. And: Quality.’ at a rate exceeding human vision...

‘Or a human beating *heartbeat* skipped...’

'Zepto. Pepto! Laser!’

‘Then it will go Ballistic!’

‘As soon as the-Bell goes!’

‘Trading...*dusts*’ itself down..’

‘Again! and starts all over...’

‘Again!’

‘*Feeling*: The Hunger.’

salivating…

Succouring the already done-deal:

‘Done deal.'

Feeding now …to see who is holding on… who is selling…and who is buying-back…and who is biting now?

Fired-up, now, and onto the feet, across the floor for everyone else to *see*.

On the screens and boards all-around surround-sound…*vision-statement*:

'The Whole Global World! (TWGW!)'

The-Banker now awaiting no response from the-Clerk that was *serious* at-least:

'Product to Market?'

'Consumerism:'

'Consumer-led.'

'Consumer bled.'

'Everything that happens <u>must</u> happen...Naturally! Think about it…the naturalistic fallacy…is 'it's' self, a fallacy! All is *unnatural*?'

'As well as natural. This is both happening naturally and *unnaturally…'*

'Con!'

'Cocted! By each of our senses...'

'Could be something-else?'

'Not-happening?'

'Apparently? Now…then: happened:

'Cost-Price vs Sale-Price.'

'Sale-Price vs Cost-Price?'

'Yet? You see? Human-made!'

'uNNATURAL!'

'Teflon. Everything, including our thoughts and ideas and what we see…'

'Rational-Actor?

'Irrational!'

'So? *Purely* un-real.'

'Until seen.'

'Then 'It' is too late. Perfectly. Impossible! Nothing is so-Pure!'

'Nothing? <Mis-buying. Or return to Common-Sense: State-Nationalist-*values:*at Cafe and bar at Railway-station and Airport, in Motor-Cars and Helicopter; Fast-Foot and one of the Fleet, unchecked, and on foot; and on the ground, people counselling each-other or ignoring, remaining ignorant removed from ignorance, by more ignorance; intended, apart from law, or restriction, or now, for a brief-moment in time: one-day.

Without any fiscal-law to take for granted or seriously against *each of Us: representing a felt tenet and point-of-personal-morals and ethics argued from-opinion or of a point of view of a particular-incident event or granular pixelating happening(s):*

Consuming-all consummate: Public-No! (I)(n)terest-in-repayment of compensation: for every stage of that:

<Mis-selling: on-*Commission*…tied-in for Life.

Once bought and sold and signed-up:

>*Direct*-Debit or Credit-Payment Sub-scription?' *managed...*

'Managed-Funds?'

'Actions?'

'Bad-Behavior?' forced-feeding extreme-diet:

'Minority!'

'Militia. Significant-Minorit(y)ies:'

'Elite-Majority. In: significant-individual.'

'Voting: Decision-making machines…'

'After the Event realized!'

'Ethnic-Zones at the Border(s).'

'Safety?'

'Always a good bet?!'

'What? Risk? By who?'

'Natural Disasters?'

'Like Today?'

'Or a: Deliberate Act of Sabotage?'

'After the Event: Terror-Threat:'

'Scare-Tactics!''

'Handmade. Hu-Man Made.'

'Like: Global-Warming: diseased dry Desert-Wasteland and granite glaciers melt flooding the Oceans and Continents:'

'The Global Economy. Commend: Climate-Change: Command&Control: Hu-Man-made:Climate-Change in the ex-tremes:'

'Species of The Devil!' *debauched…*

'How is to destroy to create?'

'When: to create is to destroy.'

'Or be un-created?'

'From Nothing? Impossible! Irrational…'

'In-the-event rationalized.'

''They were wrong before...as to say:''

'They were wrong before.'

'What? That ''It' can only be natural'?'

'They were All-wrong. Admitted it.'

'Who? Under: Economic:-Tort(u)re! Stock: supply-withheld prices held superficially high. Stock re-leased onto the Market. Oil for example: Prices rise from Cost Price to: General-Store(s):'

'Price rises again: price falls from cost price directly to General-Store: once ubiquitous Department Stores and online:

'Those that said 'It' was only excepting those under Others' control:'

'Natural-Catastrophe!'

'Not: funny.'

'That's what I mean...anyhow, possible:…'

'Any mean(s)? Un-seen? The-Rich: give *nothing* to the poor.'

'That is: not-true: Charity-works too, you know? Charity? 'We' Love-Charity!'

'Great-Publicity: for when 'It' all goes wrong…again. What about: paying: Government-Taxes?'

'Here? Peoples' Taxis. We do that. Benefit(s) Everyone, says they do.'

'As little as possible? Evasion, or Avoidance? What about all that Tax-Charity? What? 10%?'

'1% Charity!'

'Starts at home...' as a kind of: *Heroic*-Martyrdom.

Without: *knowing* really why, what for, or whether the outcomes would be favourable or not: N/n:

'Others'...'

'Homes for Workers, eh?'

‘Fit for Heroes? Of course! Working Heroes! Fit for purpose?’

‘’If’ they cannot manage their own accounts, as well as others...'

'Office-*orifice:…*’

‘Cabin-Cheated! *Out-of...*’ *of course...even our-own customers’ managers’ share-holders’ stock-holders’...*

‘Especially: N*othing*.’

‘Well, to nothing left, almost…’

‘Everyone *cheats*...or steals…paper-Clip(s): a little, perhaps, from their Employer, do we not want a little layback for what may or may not-be:’

‘Too-much.’

‘Everything!’

‘Everyone!!’

‘Greedy!!!!’

<In: Customer-Value (C.V.): (Y)/(N)?

>(Y):

‘Actually-nothing. Actuarially: Credit-Debit cancels-out:’

‘Everything. When it comes time to repent.'

'Or: re-sent.'

'EveryOne: Personal...’

‘Security…’

‘Life-Assurance...’

‘Re-assurance...’

‘Pension?’

‘For when I am old?’

‘S(i)K.’

‘Savings-invested Kredit.’

‘Re-invested...’

‘Savings?’

‘Debts. Ha ha!’

‘Profit! Debt-Holiday?’

‘Of course, retire-young, protecting, the investment…’

‘Market-Share: Import-Export:’

‘Export-Import: licences and licensed-to…’

‘do-*Business*!’ the hands-palmed.

The-Clerk rubbing a thumb and the finger-tips of both hands, as if counting bank-note(s):

‘De-regulating man(i)pulating: analysis.’

‘For Trade-Offs (TOs).’

‘Trading-in?’

Looking-down:

<Allies. Looking down into the machine, and up again, quickly:

'Now. You’ve got 'It’.'

Looking-down...again@Corporate Government sponsored enterprise:

>Currency-exchange rates:...

<N/n%...

>Banks? Investment Houses? Private-assets? Public?

De-salinating, de-toxifying, cleaning-up...re-cycling…air-conditioning:

Pay for rainwater?

- Food and Medicine. Safe Water, and Sanitation.

Built: Waterstands and Pumps pumping:…

Clean Water, Gas and Oil, to the surface….*buying-up*…refining...

‘Red Blue and Green: backed' as well, see!’

‘Like flies on shit.’

‘As Well as…’

‘For: Short-Term (to@pica-seconds:’

‘Quick-returns...

‘ Long-Term 3-5 years? Slow: Re-turns…

‘Government contracts…’

Bonded, always pay-up in the end. Tax-re-*embursement*? Compensation: Insurance: Corporate: Social-claim(s): to: the close of business…Today signed, back-dated.

Business-Transactions:...

‘The Hardware-Tech.: re-placed every sixteen-months, days or even years, the same product, slightly improved slightly less-good: 90% Price-rise with steady cost(s), until now: 32-bit…64/64 quanta-switches, trillions of:

‘A few weeks to months only days for the *software*...

‘Delivery-Good(s): the-Commodities are important...

‘As Larder-food. Peoples’ lives:

'As Televisions and Radios...*list*: machine-fuel lubricant:

'Personal-Computer (PC): Desktop: Vehicles and…

Updating... every week somewhere!

'Everyday: Choice, and Competition, see: promises at the brink of reality:

' The Bank of Reality: re-package re-issued must have, must have, like children: Shorted-on...

'Shared: Odds-on favourite quick re-sale.…

'They change-in-value day. The-Gods'-made…eh?'

'Can you find a new mark-up?'

'The New-Find(s)…'

'New-Crops. Seeds or Fuel-Source:'

'New Bio-Bacterial-Fuel:'

'Organic: you heard of *that?'*

'Meat&Vegetable(s):'

'New drill-testing?'

'…and mining…' … *information* …

'Shafting?'

'Re-newable: *shifting* for quick returns…'

'To: keep the whole thing running…' *tenured-lands…and building's…grabbed, built, knocked-down, whatever. Sometimes takes-time…n*eeds some patience:

'So, some Short-term, some Long-term?'

'See? Spread-bets…'

'Bets?'

‘Investments I mean. on good information, before anyone else gets it!’

‘And requiring government, regime-approval?’

‘Which? Police or Government Military-(I)ntervention…’

‘Digital-Security: Spy-ware…insider?’

‘As in Military-Rule?’

‘Religious…’ *militarized*-Zones:…

Back-peddling-quickly, as if re-cycling dis-un*informations*…

-News quickly!

-When? where? what? -

-How?

-Why?

Looking-down, looking-up again, and into the eyes the-Banker:

'Why? For Slow-down…stop-inflation…’

‘Slow-inflation…’

‘Deliberate…’ made-*out*…

'Low-Wages High-Hours no-breaks…but this is a…’

‘Money-War? Is. Again! Always is…’

'Always as if it is somebody-*else*’s fault.’

‘Couldn’t *help* it!’

‘Or the whole-Economic-Zone(s): Central Command Control: Market-Forces…’

‘On the-numbers, that is all, same as…’

'People.’

‘Democratic?'

'More or less! Shareholders…'

'There has to be a good Majority…'

'To Act. We *must* Act.'

'With a good-minority…'

'Any-minority, to succeed…'

'Act anyway!'

A *puzzled*-look:

'Sold-Out!'

'Pre-dicament. If only they will not co-operate.'

'If *They* do not agree?' *or pretend to agree*:

'Or want too much…'

'More-like…'

'Or clear-out…'

'Or clean-up, more *like(s)*:'

'So? Leave it up to 'Us'! Eh?!'

'Or *They* take *too-much* of the spoils.'

'Mineral. Oil-Gas!'

'Water.'

'Rubber and then Plastic!'

'Unnatural: Re-source(s):'

'Wiped-out. Trust. OPEC Monopoly-Cartel:'

'Oligopolyies. Natural: Resource: Commodity Prices: Greedy…' with a seemingly intense and more purely selfish-desire for Wealth and Power.'

‘Excessive.’

‘Who is to say?’

‘New-Model(s) Innovative…sameness.’

‘Without making *anything*!’

‘Of: Value.’

‘Anymore different…Different? Super-Profits…10 times over:’’

‘Eating Our Way to Hell (EOW2H). Losses?’

‘50/50?’

‘Is that it?’

‘For Ourselves?’

‘Reasonable Prospecting-Rights…’

‘Own: Land?’

‘First?’

‘Of-course!’

‘Take the-Others as ourselves would be taken…’

‘Politics:’

‘Only. Money. Cash.’

Economic(s)-Status:…

‘Take-them for fools at Our Peril!’

‘Magic? Magician.’

‘There are limits…’

‘Fairness. Loan-Crash.’

‘Investment on-Credit: everyone!’

‘Even to *that* barred.’

Pyramidal, or: ‘Windfall-Tax.’

'Are there? What? Windfalls for-ourselves?’

‘Hurricane! The National-*Debt*!’

‘In-Debit: Sale(s) Day-Book: customer-invoice amount and date:’

‘Receipts.’

‘Austerity.’

‘Un-Cut!’

'*Censorship?*!'

of course...

Access: to already *dis*-counted binaryies’ funding...

Investment opportunit(y)ies.

Banks to invest in...

For *them* to invest for Us to take the *risk* of industrial and agricultural investment:

'Or themselves!’ *rigged between them of stocks of commodities and in nothing more than money itself...*

‘Gas Oil and *Older* Peoples'…’

exceptional:

‘Care (OP*e*C): Maternity and contraceptive services and funeral parlous parlours’ tax-on:’

‘Currency Ex-changes: ex-Bond deals and currency-exchange would yield...’

‘On: *Employment* and Pay?'

‘On: un-employment *and* pay?'

‘Credits: driving on the public roads and railways and air travel…’

‘Fuel and Funds, eh?

Didn’t get ‘It’.

'Autonomous: Food, clothing, everything. What you gonna do when the river runs dry?’

‘Credit -Control(s): implementation: Regulation-of-Trade...'

‘Government-openess?’ at the same time floating-branches on *rivers of despair*. Scrap-heap site of: re-possession bids and auction. To be bought-up by those who could afford 'It' and sold-on by those who couldn’t afford ‘it’. Same ‘it’ re-wilding, limited s(t)ick sale(s): rented-out; left to rust and rot: accumulate land-value: equality: eco-sourcing for a cooler Planet.

➢

<‘Stimulus-Financing…’ guarantee...' *sources* special delivery pave the way troubled sonic distribution stalled.

>Across hub status airport weak governance standards skills crisis good money costly fusion aim-listing: *list...Smartphone patent war.*

> SMARTV.

Super: Prime Property: top-spot safe-haven: disaster land-cleared:

Re-sort: Gold and Golf: Status Research: *wealthy@* Elite-(I)nvestors’ step-up to *steep-*growth closed behind *Golden* Postcode addressed to and from dull suburbs and glistening

Inner-City: outer Urban Financial Quarter: Lodge-House Aristocratic-Castle(s): staying-in *correction...*

...sorry sentimentality *hits post-crisis low law*-reform*:*

*E*spren-Spirit: *expert*-expect stats show...

- Poll: shows' well below trending*:Trade-ins...*

<Trading lift escalator accelerator pitched...

- De-celerating Euro-nestbox*: from Poland to Portugal, Italy to Ireland*/nextbox main changes
- X-Box. Index*:* <Nas daq...Nikkei the *Chinese* Yacht, not yet, Hang Seng Composite CMA on the world market yet embracing failure.made in.com *or not made-in...*attention to detail and lack of investing in morality ethics...unpicked alcohol and gambling, and pornography...
- >Apple and Next: *Actual: government-economic: regime* taken...
- <To do your bidding?

>No way.

> Thrown-out x10 price less , same-product longer-lasting…

< Symbolic un-changed:

> Game-Player:

Just like Me?

<Just, like Me?

> See?

Propositioned. Seen only now through the half-blind, bruised blank gaps in-between the now *tooth-less* figures. Now the abbreviated rounded-up and down, plus and minus letters and numbers in-words and columns, read across in either-direction.

Up or down, in-sequence: Quantity, and *quality*-branded *impish impious*, even IMPERIOUS, neither {sure, not Honest. Nor Deceitful except {[of-Self]}… nonetheless, impressive. Bragging, and Branded.

Desirous-of, and assumed of by all. Lusted-after. Luscious-orderly *lifeblood* dripping away. Created *Chaos!* spurted from a neck wound.

Dripped-onto, the-walls and the boardroom and kitchen and bathroom...the shower-room floor. The-Banker *watching* through *the minds-eye* and back again to *that-moment connected…*where multi-national conglomerates had shown their prices altering as of every second as of every day.

In the '*Boiler-room'* inwardly video-conferencing *'on The-Trading Floor'…*as dancing with stock and bond trader's, in the customary *garish-mode* uniformed and colour-coded, to attract business, as advertised.

'Allies, then...' similarly-dressed *mutually* untrusting and…*old-school* and college broker, military and freely camouflaged amongst each-other.

As amongst foreign and homespun *Presidential-candidates* and representatives. As agent's for and against *agent's against...*for Prime-ministers' family and friend (*for how long?*)...*i*dentified authorising *killing's*...to be made...rescuing *Saviour*'s savings' spent. On *getting-rid* of economic- trade-rival's, and political-and-Economic *analysis*:

'*Yelled*!' and gesticulated at each-other in the exaggerated and absurd commotion.

Closed-auction...Corporate Dutch and English and Russian...Global-Banks. The open-outcry and in the end obvious secret *backroom* deal's that the-Banker, and the-Clerk both knew *is* World-trade. All there was now, and as immediately immobile, as visibly silent.

Globally normally *open-all-hours* somewhere and mysteriously *somewhere-in-the-world* at the same-time bar few within a-few seconds of each other...of lee-way only, or none, to be *sanctioned* and…

'Sell Y/N?'

'Corporate: Buy-up?'

'With Corporate Banking themselves POD:'

'With what real actual actuarial *money?'*

'This inexplicable *entity*: World-Trade. That *keep's everything going.'*

'Peacefully, controlled most the Time.'

'The world going around, you may say...'

'And around everything else...'

'Stopped.'

Stooped. Stood still.

'As one door opened...'

'Another closes.'

'You may say, the-same door.'

The *escalator*...closed behind us...slipped-in...just before the deadline, micro-timed...'

Just? Got-in...' as the cry of 'Sell! Sell! Sell!' went-up *like a weather-balloon.*

Blown-in, and blown-up again, crash-landed.

Punctured *as the-Prices* pegged tethered to the lower-rated let loose on unlimited fund's…yet there was only so high *scientifically that* the balloon could go.'

'Justly? Before?'

'Except no-one really knew, how high, or for how long. Raised on automated and *impulse-buying and spending...on-credit…mis-construed:*

''It' is gonna go-up!

'Again!' ex-*ploded, in flames….*

11. Re-gulation.

New: regulation. Secular Nation-State: Development-Funding Investment Corporate and Government Tax Profit to: President. Prime-Ministers and Parliament Council, and Judiciary, absented.

The Chief of Military Staff (CMS) stood-up and shot a look around the room like he had sprayed the room and all the people in it with machine gun fire. As the others in the room rocked back in their seats around the circular table designed such that were all to be designated equals the Chief of Police the President the Secretaries and grey suited Administrators slumped forward.

As if blood were spouting from their bloodshot eye-balls they paid little attention to what the head of the Military was telling them stun-gunned in their seats:

'We have got to make a move.'

and sat down.

Hands and arms across the table reaching out he banged the table:

'You!' looking at each momentarily as he aimed his sight on the President.

'You. President. You have got to move decisively. We await your orders. Do we shoot blanks or live bullets? Do we sniper-out a few to scare off the rest? Or do we just hold back return to barracks and let the Civilian-Police deal with this?'

'What?! Military-Police: deal with any offenders: Why are You asking?'

The stare moved the aimed attack onto the Chief of Military Police Army (CMP-Army).

'This is not Popular Uprising anymore it is a Traitorous Conspiracy backed by Foreign Enemies!'

'*No.'* Riots and stampedes to loot, not-anymore! The People love Me! Where are the: Presidential: Security-Police?! Military capability has to act and be seen to act! The crowd are starting to turn police tactics are starting to turn the crowd that they don't care. They are each attacking each and together like they don't care? Well, *that* is alright, then? They, either don't care if they get killed or maimed. But they haven't got the guts for it…

'The Demonstrators and the Police. Who is going to Win?'

Looking around the Table as if firing darts from the *eyes*:

'If the Police move back the-Army will move in. My Army! Security-Forces...'We' will move in.'

'We are trying to defend the Barracks from *all-out assault* from the Walls…'

''We' will take the outskirts. The roads in, and We Will! Move-in so they will not know what has hit them! Once the Police and Army-Snipers have withdrawn only *rebel*-civilians left…We will bomb the traitors…re-maining.'

'All out assault on every house every alley every cupboard with artillery with tanks and finally with overwhelming force!'

'We await your decision. Your Orders…'

The Police Chief was half standing. By this point it was not clear if he had answered his own question or sealed his fate as Chief of Police. The Military Chief stood and answered for him anyway:

'The Army Air-force and Navy off of the coast are prepared to move-in at a moments' notice. Stop this thing before it starts. Before *they* start to get the upper hand.'

The President turned to each and then each to their Staff-secretaries and Public spokespersons and translators interpreters although this was to be taken by others media those gathered later in the Press Room: snowflake millennials video music game-bingers: The President spoke clearly:

'Well? What do *you* think *I* should *do*?'

No-one knew whether the President had spoken out loud by mistake and did not realise and muttered his thoughts out loud. The question to *someone?* who was not in the room?

Unless this was the president addressing:

The President: the Presidential-Address: although un-typical un-less purely rhetorical, extended and tautologously: so at that:

'Well? You!'

turning to the Chief who had just spoken-out:

'You have told me that 'They!' The Rats. The Rebels. The Enemy. Could be getting the upper-hand! That you could unleash an attack but haven't done so! Why Not?!. Are 'They' getting-Closer? They will not get any further!! Do I have to make all the decisions around here! You?!' pointing to anothers':

'Brother-in-Law! Why have you not unleashed your Storm-Troopers! Your Crack Regiments! You tell me?! Why Not!'

'But I …'

All faces staring at The Presidential Face; quivering in rage or dread panic was not clear.

Wavering even only a bow and arrow of a stare off into the distance.

Compared to the rat-ta-tat-tat of the Head of the Military and the Presidents own addresses long drawn out repetitive *echo-laic almost endlessly*:

'You haven't done Nothing! Useless! I could have you shot even now! Get out! Scamper off to the jungle! the Desert-deserter that is what you will be known as! The Desert-Deserter. Now! Out!'

Not the first time.

The 'Brutal' Brother-in-Law taken-in...taken-out...had been *banished.*

'Cut-into...or Cut-Out!!'

Like the 'Banished- Brother' although he was dead, so they said.

#The Head of the Police seized the chance and with not a moments pause- interrupted the gap following-on the last-words-of-the-President:

'Very well the Police will withdraw once they have contained the crowd the demonstrators the Rebels...' and paused:

'The Enemy! Is! Everyone!'

and stopped for a moment to allow the word to enter into the lexicon; meaning the people the People of the Nation State: the Theocracy: the Democratic-secular: whatever it was on, whatever day. The enemy within; minority yes a minority that can be beaten and can killed and maimed...

'Army. On My Command!'

The Chief of The Army immediately took-over:

'The Military will move in and immediately shell the-centre where the demonstrators are from -air and –sea...'

Glancing-quickly at the Chief-of-the-Air-force and the Navy:

'Once the streets into the centre are clear of demonstrators and rebels troops and deserters; defending populations. The Army are currently checking all those leaving The City:'

'For Traitors, Deserters...'

Halting slightly then:

'Genocide as I said. Don't leave one standing or bleeding-on-the-ground.'

'Not a good-idea given the amount of media sky-shots as well finding…'

'Mass-Graves?'

'No don't want that. Take-them-out few at a time. Make it look like a street-fight. O.K.?'

'Qh? War, now?'

-The Army will move-in street by street and take-The-Courthouse and the –Palace-barracks…de-codif(y)(ing)(ed):

The Ambulance edged through the crowds to collect the injured who were shocked and dazed at the demonstrations and meetings that had turned into and were perhaps meant to have been confrontation.

But things were changing. Now and with purpose it seemed.

The crowds had dispersed and she could maneuver the vehicle more easily through the streets. To where a small group stood around someone waiting to be treated and taken to the hospital. Only a slight cut. No more serious injury than any normal day.

People talking instead of fighting. Replacing anger with resolve.

Demonstrations and meetings had dispersed. To take over workplaces public buildings homes and streets and buildings now made public. Initial Public Offer: Profile of Business and Personalities currently in-charge. Or Not.

Extreme share-holder Power. Employee-share-holder: Remuneration Committee. Small government Capitalism. Dis-affection feathering own nests. Boxed in offices flying-away. Growth Prosperity Spending Austerity. One-sided Arbitrage.

The Other. Bidding Asking. With Ice-burg stealth. Arms race algorithm. Dagger Guerilla Sniper. Data-stream. Strategy decision. and execution. High-frequency. Mirror-trading. Fragmented and fragile markets.

Collapsed Mergers and Acquisitions.

Peaceful protest turns into Armed surrection. Response-policing. Trust and Confidence.

Response Command Fear no-Consent.

Critical Mass. Likel(i)hood of being Caught on Camera.

Deterrent Sentence. Special Investigation. Fraud.

Consent with the expectancy of co-operation.

Surface: *spewed-Flame(*s)…

Secondary Escape Route. Fronter Classrooms. Virtual Learning Platform. Splendid-Isolation: Looking both-ways. Not waiting for The Midday-Declaration to be broadcast worldwide.

With Bright-(*I*)deas! and *idealistic*-notion(s): tempering to the concrete reality of change.

No longer waiting continuing in hope and determination.

There was still a tension in streets where the ambulance now moved more easily through the city centre. A few people and vehicles only now remained and windows sat broken in blank buildings:

Mis-understanding: Sales'-Pitch Sells Itself! (SPSI!)

World not buying 'it' anyway!

Watching listening in-to each other not:

The-Media owed and owned still but not for long by The Owner.

Staff actors and performers. Free downloads. Browser sign-up. Copyright. Intel. Props.

With advertisements if you like. How else are we going to find what is out there?

Non-advert: Shareholders may not enforce: social-market: money-market:

Then buy to watch listen anytime rental and add-on.

Rental to stay. Outright. No 'Law' needed.

Revoke! Murderball!

UN convention of Human Rights and Rules of Engagement. Treatment of Prisoners of War whether previously shooting-at and being shot-at. Prisoners of Law?

In village squares industrial estates and farm buildings. Outside factory gates and on office steps. Market streets and street corners at police stations and army barracks. In places police and troops encircled the television and radio stations and broadcasts ceased.

Except from unofficial official pirate stations; those quickly set up and those already in existence. The Centre-ground largely unreported of no foreign interest to report

Missiles Missives coming in and out.

Taser-*taster* gas-canisters bricks and bottles of urine of poison-gas; and upraised voices echoed on the buildings and on through crowded side streets. Looting mobs ransacked expensive shops along tree-lined avenues.

Windows crashed-in and people ran arms full dragging pulling at objects from inside others inside throwing stuff out. Clothes furniture electrical equipment out onto the street; where it was picked up and carried hurriedly away.

Crowds ran and defended themselves. Facing police and military vehicles and lines of troops hostility at first was lost in panic that soon turned to:

'What are we going to do?' repeated in city town and country.

Poor neighbourhood buildings burning people inside. Media bias inevitably misreporting the whole misrepresenting the part. Representing ourselves each of us! and straight lies and damn lies and statistics:N/n...

'The only way to control people is to lie to them?!'

Managing problems…dealing with the issues...

Shared-narrative...

People carried on working. Essential services were maintained. Shops were opened factories transport started running as before.

People stayed home people stayed at their workplaces. Carried on as usual and as the news of the collapse came over T.V. and radio and passed by word of mouth in the late afternoon people joined spontaneous and organised gatherings at workplaces streets town centres.

Communications energy supplies stocks of goods transport and emergency services were maintained throughout people organised and waiting.

Politicians had made limited proposals. The police and army had left police stations and barracks moved in to break up organised and spontaneous demonstrations demanding at first the resignation of the politicians; then by the evening for people to take over anyway.

As the Police and Army had moved in the Demonstrations moved in to occupy workplaces shops homes streets.

The looting and the shooting had been stopped.

By groups of shop-workers who occupied their shops factory and office workers who occupied their factories and offices people who occupied their homes and streets; everybody waited. Essential and public services were maintained for the duration.

Police and army looked on.

The politicians proposals were made public. Presented to a news-crew outside the government buildings and then to a member of the public surrounding the government buildings to announce publicly by television radio announced at meetings at factory gates and office doors streets homes and shops people met.

The politicians proposals were rejected.

The call now was for people to take over anyway. The Generals had been meeting the Politicians who had been meeting the Police Chiefs. Later in the afternoon generals and chiefs of staffs of the army and police defeated deserted and broadcasting from various places around the countries of the world not shot at but more often shooting at each other attempting to regroup; to pull together entities nations or industries resources and communications. Announced on television and radio:

We will not shoot civilians unless we are shot at.

Any shooting of police or army personnel will be summarily dealt with.

As well as any shooting by members of the police or army of any unarmed civilian. Unless they are in and providing material or any other support to the opposition in the Conflict Zones or elsewhere. All weapons are to be handed in.

Only needing what-is-it? Up to 100 activists say 10% most hardcore so that leaves 90% each one a hundred sympathizers....

Curfew is imposed - from 17.00 hours. Anyone on the streets past that time may expect to be arrested and if showing any resistance summarily shot. You have been warned. We are here to protect life not to take life.

Ration books will be distributed as soon as possible.

Until then all goods are requisitioned by the government and Armed Forces. As meeting after meeting denounced Martial Law and Government Control of Trade and Economic Affairs.

The stock-markets redundant; the money-markets gone just-so the T.V. and radio stations had been retaken by-those who worked there.

The viewing and listening public broadcasts no longer government censored and live from cities all over the world where there were stock-exchanges that stood deserted paralysed in indecision and a lost-cause.

From the countries and countryside around people were being interviewed and giving their views one quote put to a television camera broadcast on radio and printed in the newspaper and on-line press said read-out:

... we are returning to put expertise to work.

We are returning to homes and workplaces. Not a-*waiting* for the announcements of governments the stock-exchanges the Police or Army.

But to carry-on by our own interests. Our own investments in home family livelihood each-other!

Barricades held.

So did arguments for peace and activity. People began to feel in control of the situation. There was a feeling in the air that things were changing that life would go on and that things would be different. In villages and towns people met and discussed. Shouted optimism and whispered worry; wondrous mystery or secret hope replacing fatalistic rumour.

And people in the meantime took over anyway.

People no longer waited to see what the politicians police and armies would do. People occupied factories offices shops streets. The police and army those that had not already laid down arms and uniforms had attempted to take over the government buildings now deserted.

Had attempted to occupy the television and radio studios factories shops offices homes and streets that were now being taken over by the people that used them and by the people who worked in them. People moving around and remaining in and returning to their workplaces their homes and streets.

The Operations-room overlooking studio- lights ablaze on the many panels jutting half-into-the-room; hospital switch-board the other half-occupied by Media-types. All checking-systems trying to get them up and running again keep them from jumping picture or crackly sound-lines.

There had been outbreaks of violence hired thugs known provocateurs, hired by the other side.

Water-cannon featured and firearms weapons-dump attacked air-raided and armed; with deserters.

Switching-sides confirmed not-as-agents and the defense of border-towns; down the hills and along the rows where refugees gathered camps where they fed watered and well-being administered to.

They shook with fear shook hands held hands and held palms and thumbs held upward and let go punched the air and let go.

Then: the Azimuth Hotel and bar restaurant where the last President was killed:

'Take the Hotel. Take the Journalists out. Fly-them out of the country no fore-fights on the tarmac like last-time nothing on the runway on the concrete may be fell over? Eh? Then the lot out out-of-here!'

Another long pause not-looking-at-any one or either:

'President. *The*-President. Will be taken to safety. Out of the City. In-fact out-of-the Country. There will be a nice seaside resort that will take-you-in and not return.'

The President-*shuddered* and felt grief with something of relief. It sounded-like a hail of machine-gun bullets but never-the-less…it would be a permanent *holiday* that is all:

'With you and your family safely away we will be able to finish-it-quickly. *None* of your people your-people *will be killed*.'

'But there-are –enemies-*within!* Write that down!' to an aimless Administrator in the corner.

The President was moved truly moved. Looked away and silently *wept* thinking how close it had come to execution. Whether by the-Military the-Police?

Who had been ordered so many times in the past many years had colluded and committed terrible crimes against humanity; known about of-course! Enjoyed hearing-about ordered directly and with delight art the ordering and the outcome.

Safe-once-again *saved*; but by the mob outside the Palace the Courthouse where the Judges and Magistrates had left the doors-wide-open and taken-by: the-Mob: with-ease.

The new-old-law was not going to be made by lawyers politicians or economists.

But by doctors and nurses and carers and cared-for; who valued and were overseen even in their work by moral-humanity.

The President could-see-that-now.

Know that-there-would-be no-Justice without-law.

The Head of the Military concluded thus to-The-President:

'You will announce you are handing command and control to the Head of the Military...then we will take you and your family. Not your ministers. They are *on their own...*'

'Hostages to Fortune(s): *perhaps…'*

'With-Us; or: without.'

'Of-the-country escaped to…' or-not…

Constant competition the President thought.

Get it wrong every single time this has happened; or nearly if we had not done away with this-lot or that-lot…Who to believe!

'You will be taken out of the country.'

A second time the President choked back tears heard:

'Your ministers will have to take their chances.'

Glancing at the Chief of Police:

'With your Fortunes.'

'They are either with us or against us...' the Head of the Military said.

Not clear if this was directed to the President Chief or the millions or was it mere hundreds barely a few or even one thousand left outside awaiting announcement promised and rounded up to attend: The Final Lecture:

'The Police will return to their Civil-Duties in the name of the Government. Military Rule: will be in-stated, with immediate effect.'

The Police Chief looked relieved not almost but not actually: *thinking*: *at best, I would follow orders. Then retire pension abroad maybe somewhere pleasant nice.* The President stood to meet the Military-Head full-face and eyeball-to-eyeball as if finishing a sentence, that had not yet been started.

'But what the chances?'

'...then, we will leave immediately!' and The President headed-out-of-the-door:

'I will be *excused* if I leave immediately...' and headed out-of-the-door.

The President taken out into the corridor down steps into a basement and without ceremony or-warning shot. In-the-front-of-the-head.

Blood splattered the walls and the uniform of the executioner taken-away.

The Head of the Military thought: *...the people will not excuse you.*

And the Police Chief thought the same.

Both adding:

'Nor Me'.

The police fire and army-ambulance and fire crews remained mobilised throughout the day.

Where the Leader of the Nation was and claimed to the People they were staying, or were *rumoured* to be staying.

Not seen since earlier that day when an slightly bizarre very bizarre interview to the world press took place.

It had been unclear if the clearly dazed and uncertain sun-glazed *wobbling slightly* leader shaded from the truth had actually said anything in answer to a question; or just mumbled groaned even. On TV the President see taken-out of the airport-named-after and-by and-of and as named ordered paid-for.

Stepping on the soil...

The concrete.or another City or Town somewhere-else; greeted by the fawning members of that countries aristocracy attraction, and protection:

Elite: Establishment: darkest or lightest-skinned, and larger horizontally, yet, taller and faster: *announcing* while laying-dead in the basement of the Court-House.

In contrast to the precious hours long amphetamine-driven crazed-speeches that no-one except: The blindly-Loyal because they had listened to and recognized from before; or took-any-notice-of, and were better-off, for a while. In themselves, but only as-'Us'.

Though they were seen leaving: The City:for: Exile.

The-Presidents' last-words before not being seen again and mysteriously or not dying abroad; some years later apparently in hospital in a friendly country were rumoured to be.

'You are to find-and-capture anyone who is not with me kill them!'

'The Rebel Leader General Future President; alive or dead!'

The Leader had assumed the love of the people as a father and mother as grandparents the traditions of the ancestors. Not to be brushed aside. He people biting the hand that feeds them being tricked and provoked misleading and dangerous...

Traitors-to:-The-Cause!

Me! Everytime: The Leaders only Personal: Family-Children: cause; that-is and could or could not-be-understood.

On TV the Glorious Leader stepped from a helicopter in another country a friendly country. Not like all-the-Others; at least not now and unless invited.

Not necessarily friendly either.

Not this-president and no-more another from living a life of Terror.!

The television channels were instructed 'To allow time for...'

A Communiqué to be set-out at the hurriedly convened and over-taken International Conference.

Networked and linking those players who could not jet or drive to Geneva; to be announced simultaneously around the world. Then for statements and addresses from leading members of the Conference to be broadcast to each country in their own *language.*

Setting out what these decisions would mean for each country to stabilise National Economies and The Global Economy; the political economic and thus serious situation would need to be shifted.

Moved-into something more con-trollable.

*

Something legal that would not get out of their control.

The International Conference of Government Leaders and World Banks met. The final session that morning had opened thus:

'We have been meeting together since early this morning to discuss the crisis in world-trading, again.'

'It is proposed to ratify the decisions made and announce them forthwith. To allay fears and panic. Are there any abstentions?' some Countries criticised others for closing exchanges or for keeping them open; for closing banks or for calling in gold reserves. Each had a criticism of another and each attempted to lay blame elsewhere. Yet it was clear that these governments were as much wrapped up in the Stock-market Chaos and Turmoil; as anyone and everything else. Nothing could be gained by not-reaching-agreement; or at least holding-situation whilst agreement by choice or by force could be reached.

News reports interviews and discussion were vetted and edited more so than usual by government representatives. The television channels were to broadcast the communiqué then the heads of governments statements. The Communiqué was sent to translators and typists and clerks and was ready to be announced at noon mean-time:

As from noon mean-time today all currency transactions are frozen and are to be renegotiated under the following terms:

Prices of raw materials and staple produce will be fixed-at-a-percentage-increase over incomes. Incomes will be fixed accordingly. Most loans will be rescheduled over longer periods. All currencies and share prices will be re-

valued accordingly at a lower level a standard base from which trading can recommence.

From noon mean-time Today: Time/Date/Location:

All trading of goods and production of supplies will be directed through the financial institutions and Stock; The Global-Market. According to these agreed adjustments; and according to each governments instructions and direction.

These measures are necessary due to circumstances that now prevail since the collapse of world trading in the stock-markets; and to restore Confidence to Global-Markets and to Global-Trading.

Finally, in fact, a stalemate reached with the pawns in increasingly geometric and numerical size overwhelming The Kings and Queens Bishops and Knights Castles and Palaces overrun; the chequered board with no moves left. Glass marbles with no-other to leap over step-over. No-room for-Manoeuvre. The stock-exchange floor for the moment and remained. Deserted-desks. Papers.

From inside littered and fluttered along the streets outside.

The Collapse of every stock market to its production and distribution and consumption. Demand and supply unfettered except by the pressure each has on each and to share. Reducing-Up+n): City state militia and town council of The Past: History/Geography Biology...but to each and every citizen set against each other or set aside.

To the *other-side;* and to

'You'.

Profile.

Collapsed into groups home neighbours work-mates people you see at The shops or Credit-and-Carry. Re-fill shelves in the Shops.

Border Refugee-camps. Inside and out-of-country. Help abroad not unacceptable or excessive.

End to Hostilities.

Appointing Ministers of the Church or none. Rabbi Imam or Priest. In own Image? Bias.

Unequal. More equal. Than 'Others'. All. Known from Home School or College or Training-Centre; and want to stay in contact with. All kinds of Trades Union Guilds and Yes! Local-Councils Assemblies. For one thing or another.

Voted with the hand (one, or both as the saying goes) afterwards by-foot walking:

Style; Direction of Travel: Intended Target: both and everything voted on by naturally arising consensus. Parliamentary-Democracy: Sovereign-Rule.

Hardly spoken or noticed except by outsiders wondering locally what this locality was all about.

Needs of one out-weigh all or the needs of all out-weigh one.

In the Hermit state...and in the Global-Society anyway. If your of the World from The Golden Orb the Blue Planet the Globe the Space-gobbledeGook!

Geek! What does that matter? Whether unfair and undemocratic your point is?

'The government needs: 'Us'. Needs You and Me. Without 'Us' 'IT' is nothing!'

‘If the government investing in People fairly and equally…but not!’

‘Di-vesting People Ingesting-in and Spewing-out…

People able to manage to Control our own-accounts: worth something at least.

At last.

And on our own behalf like children and in the cases of the elderly and unwell.

Walking-well can get on with it! Alright. Thinking the thinkable! Takeover!

We took over the Stock-Markets the banks and the government; and we can choose our own leaders if leaders we must have which we do not!

Only leader for here or there for now, then.

Working together with accepted leadership for this part or that, or none, win-win all the time otherwise we, I, would not be here, now, then.

Re:group leaders in their field in-the-field.

Working our way-through street by street. City by city and town by town and villages between; we must block all the roads in or out except to chose who wishes to leave and at their own risk; or who are not with us.

To house arrest not to come to any harm.

Then they will be tried; and if found wanting...

Under God or Society?

Your God if you wish and mine Our Society

Each our own God not some or anyone elses!

Each our own society and everyone elses!

No enemies no hatred!

Nations-of-History? Notions-of-State-of-Government, Government-of-State

Multi-national state and privately-owned corporations

Societies countries Demographics

Protecting rights and-responsibilities

Free-for-All!

Strike!

Lock-out!

Lock-in!

CEO Presidential.

Locked-in. Under cover of the Night...and Day! We are staying inside…visiting and staying inside er …looking after our er nearest closest family we don't know what will happen. We will not have to stand down at this rate, we are no longer in fear…

'All we want is the death of The Tyrant!'

At the square limbs hung-off at bizarre angles blood shit and piss streaked the streets. Where the bodies of the dead and injured had been dragged away. Blood-ran down the gutters and only The Rats moved; amongst empty building overrun.

Murdering as they went. Uniforms in purple stains and black burned men and boys girls and women strewn askew tortured raped and killed.

Terrible scenes met the eyes of those left to see them; while the dust blew in earth to earth dust to dust.

It was awful awful with no words to describe it.

But to Bear witness!

To mechanised Division. Artillery bombardment. Shell. Metal jacket. Gas. Radiation. Ghost-town. Ghost-City. Summary executions. Of your own - a systematic slaughter.

Free-Army deserters. Arms smuggling populations. Field Hospital. Break-out lives. Escaped life. Other currencies? Not worth anything. At all.

On the Global financial-markets. Worth the same. 1-1. Each currency including each Currency-zone currency? Not 1-1+ or 1-1-. Anymore. Banks all of them loaning to non-banks not each other and investment wings clipped and flown. To everywhere in the world where 'things' goods and services are made and used.

Government loans the same. Never mind the National banks. Electorate self-employed and small-businesses. Get it all. Shared-out according to existing means (what used to be called 'Property'). Homes and workplaces equalled-out along with Bank-balances. Of Credits progressively worked-for worthwhile according to need and means.

CEO/President elected for the Money and in-definitely extended term after the first-day and readiness to retire early or soon.

Others on the outside of the track.

Over-taking on the outside younger faster . Continue until the satisfaction and patience are over.

Then step-in or step-down. Down-size, or Go-Global. Abroad perhaps? Both? Agree?

Make yourself at home. Art and Science. Precise measuring. Cooking and baking. Scales: N/N. Inventive and deeply Cultural. Quarters and halves. Place and Time. Home-brew and bake. A thousand tiny explosions. Iconic aggressively self-assuming leadership. Who is surprised almost at the following incited becomes in-toxicated.

Who Glorifying 'Self' and 'family' against all 'Others'.

In 'Humiliation' defeated in-which defeat is not possible.

Who is willing.

To give-away easily-influenc(ed.)ING. Associate-Status.

Broken-biscuit...

freely downloading browser sign-up.

Copyright. Intel. Props.

Rental to stay overnight.

Outright. No 'Law' needed. Revoke! Vigilance.

With advertisements if you like. How else are we going to find-out: what (i)s out-there?

Then see to watch listen read anytime: rental and add-on.

Global convention of Human Rights and Trading Acts of Engagement.

Welcome to my Home: pestilence peace and tranquility: Equality. Fairness. Hope…

The Day the Markets Stood Still. Closed? Shop. Broken-Society. Broken biscuits. Broken-Home.

To: *save*: 'Self' in the Bargain, always a good-bargain.

Or sordid escape.

Cyber-Armies **black**-sites.

'U.N. conventions. On the treatment of P 'o' W's. Government-people bidding beyond our means…'

Beyond 'Ours'. Immigrants. By giving false-figures and known-once getting-away with it. False papers: working: paying-taxes:

'Time' and 'Again'.'

'Murder.'

'Assassination in cold-blood at the hands of the Armies on the Globe: prepared to fight?'

'On-foot?'

'Laying-down and chaining yourself with others to a fence.'

This time agreed to: Protesters-Demand(s): for open-accounting: Of all the Globe's Top-100 Companies. Then the next 100. And so on. Gambling? Well yes? Yeah! Each of us our own. Together depends on the Odds. For or Against. Doesn't It. Taking-a -chance. Risking-it. Bomb-disposal-Hospital nurses story: the early bakers' day before…the day…the day after against future-failure. Win-lose-win….

It will get easier or more difficult depending on how many e-records are erased deleted or shredded. Until it was apparent that the Credit due to the People was un-paid. In-paid and un-paid taxes.

In each and every tax area. To the Village and un-taxed Nomads. Gypsies and Travelers.

Working as we went, and go.

People, soldiers and police returned to stations and homes. Ignored the Call to Arms. Ignored statement except to demand: We are using indiscriminate use of force with water-cannon and rubber-bullets sniper and live rounds. Targets pointed out by informers in the crowd; or random to scare ultimate scare tactics.

As if we have not been used to these down the years.

They do not scare us anymore. We don't scare them.

The crowds, if they are working in the day, if they are working at all; they will come out at night to demonstrate you can be sure!

We learn to forgive and forget so that we did not repeat the same errors, we expectorated were expectant, we did, we made do.

Each to our own business, with others: We have taken over our work-places and are working normally…

Well not normally I wouldn't like it to be like this all the time!

What? Like its been up to now you mean-to-say?! (I)mprisoned: with no-contact with the outside world.

At the entrances to the compound checkpoint wearing balaclava and face-mask.

No hierarchical organisation left training and communications systems henchman clandestine internecine fratricide no! Brothers and Sisters! Sisters and Brothers, both!

Both risking and valuing their lives for the-other and for-each-other:

'My younger brother was killed in pursuit of a-Dream!'

'This is ritual-sacrifice on the altars of Greed and Power!'

This is not sacrifice nor is it forfeit…'

'Nor, is it surrender!'

'We are not sacrificers...'

...nor necromancer. We are dancers!

We are people with a desperate desire for change

We cannot go-on without change!

Anyone with a faculty and facility to provide goods and/or service carry-on anyone without work or leisure to the Job-Centre there is plenty to be done! I am here waiting for my brother in Victory Parade. Watching The Palace fall. Where he was killed. I wait for him here and we go-on together. We were prepared to stay until every one of us was dead and The President. May your iron-stone-statue drag you down to Hell! Beware the grave you dig for your brother for you may fall in it. I am not afraid of anyone or anything now! We have lost our fear! Our sisters and brothers who have fallen will be remembered as saving their families friends and society, from torture, life, and death!

12. The Main Channels.

The main channels began broadcasting the communiqué and government announcements. Most television and radio sets were off or on but ignored as people no longer waited to see what the governments police and armies would do.

As people had evaded or fought advancing troops and lines of police they also stood and talked yelled slogans and en-treaties. It had become clear that the governments and stock-markets they served could offer nothing.

Nothing but the confrontation reminiscent of the suffering and violence of previous times. It had become clear that the fighting and banner waving of before was over. The stock-markets could not produce distribute deliver. Pensions pay and even profits could not be paid. The structures the colossi of buildings land technology and people is all that they were worth.

Looted and shared out. Taken-back taken over.

The-supply-chain: the roads the ports the points of entry and exit of goods food and materials and people.

A voice hailed hearty and full to say

So long as dictators rule the political thus necessarily the fiscal financial then we are all in trouble.

Because as long as we have just enough to live on whilst working so hard we do not have time to think or breathe hardly then they stay in power.

We are not going to threaten them except for want of enough or just a bit more that and yes; we take notice of humanitarian needs on the ground that there is a cost-benefit-equation to be made whether in time or materially and between peoples lives.

Slogans quoted: To jaw-jaw is better than to war-war!

It is better to wait for your enemy to attack. Then to attack Them!

Those who are prepared are more likely to vanquish and win for those who attack first without a plan are wild and unlikely to win against superior tactics.

From each as they choose to each as they are chosen.

Free and fair elections Now!

End Work-enslavement!

... and Immoral-Servitude!

If a tree falls lumber mill and meat packing plant. Know next to nothing about the leadership of this group. Millions billions trillions quadrillions of worth of property damage. Insurance. Only a matter of chance no-one killed. Intent or not. Yah! Crazies. Despite mistakes. Testify against each other or lifetime jail join-up nameless-code loose international federation. Working-class regular kid cop dad PR environmental centre films tell it as it is.

Green-scare blood-fur: for what cannot be made now without?

Clamped to glued-up doors

Earth-first.

Mining-protest protecting-environmental resistance-movement.

The disgruntled. Once fortressed forested treeless hills pick-axed. Monkey-wrenching sabotage. Roadblock and drawbridge wall. Handcuffed and bulldozed. Outlaw: bad-image. The Good Out-Law. Tired of just-philosophising. Action. Arson. Public protest.

Riot-Shield: Pepper-Spray: Water-Cannon: eyes genitals public hearing my ass!

Internal rift-splintering against solid-establishment.

Implodes instead of.

*

Anti-trust monopoly take over the world. Complete clearance radical vs radical. Why gentle activism: violence vs violence. On an industrial scale. Greed and loathing. Racist-Spoke-persons' and daughters' words justifying-targets to re-assess form-cell to protect all life on this planet.

For wild nature.

Synergy. Derisory. Industry. Utility.

What would it be like to do nothing.

You never know the others' dilemma, you only know your own, without-transparency, fear and mistrust.

The trust game.

The fairness game.

In practice you take the risk of failure? No-one does. Honesty brings freedom. Spill your guts.

Domino's fall.

Co-ordinated raid. Ringed encircled. Kettled. Frozen in one day. River sea and ice-road. Blocked: Emerging-Market(s) cross-country and continental: infrastructure wells mines and re-fitted railway.

Equity indices slice:slide…

The magic 10% eh?

The idea takes hold.

Then what? Takes over? And runs slap bang into any other 10% who immediately define that 10% as a threat to their 10% and become by definition anti-that other 10% even though they may be very similar their definition becomes a negative rather than positive thing by which they seek by any means possible to diminish the other and use this as a rallying call to increase their own 10% to 25%.

Open free thinking becomes dangerous violently opposite to both or either and a competitive hatred based on a self imposed fear chisms develop deeper and deeper rifts separation(s): Terrorism and War. War and Terrorism.

How we love our nice neat round numbers our 'isms and our insecure fears that come to define us!

Corporate bullying threats and government authority scapegoats illegal downloading copyright infringement free advertising. Online donation food etc.

Free Food-Bank(s): Kinship and Democracy.

Organised society without the State…

Newsroom landline access hotspot spread of news crisis commons .

No causation only attendant detail. Aid-corruption: stolen-spending: back to the investor(s):

Witness-Protection (WP)

Scheme blown apart confidentiality broken name address given out desperate risk turn life inside out become someone else...

Re-newable

Carbon-free

Atheism unites the faiths against them bringing religious peace!

When does an empire collapse?

When it has lost the trust and faith of its peoples. Its Capital. All at once. Let the world hear you!

What have we done!

Cannot be angry forever we must do something!

If its worth doing its worth doing ourselves yourself loose confederation of cells as each of us is make public opinion and will.

Protest-demonstrate for personal change.

From fear hope!

Not for Bread and Bibles…

Votes for victuals.

Squatters.

Through mentoring Media evidence statistical analysis. Who watches the watchers? Surveilles-the-surveille®s?

We do of course!

Who has secrets has secret wish to transparent decision making: open to debate and evidence rather than or alongside *emotional*-pleading.

For there is right and wrong just as there is left and right; and shades in between only so far as the mass is concerned. Constant vigilance. Vigilant-vigil.

Re-invent the wheel that goes around of Life!

Committee of Researchful-Enquir(y)ies:

Spiral of three-dimensional progressive-change:

Never set in rock or stone: scientific-challenge on principle of sustaining life.

Own. Reparations measured reduction in Left and Right colliding at the libertine limits; of each others rights and privileges responsibilities and cost-benefit.

Employable skills Refusnick: Free-loader. Un-*motivated* lazy.

Reasoned acceptance get help!

Where?!

Everyone has an opinion if the facts to back intuition.

Variously advised.

High rolling lifestyle-Bling. Casino-calls.

All political lives fail mired in scandal.

GPS blocking time recorded deals with get-out clause. Exit strategy.

The self-righteous demonising demon demonised.

Lies deception and undeniable undercover truths.

'Un-censored!

Accounts given-by:

'Each of Us!'

'Honest: 50%!'

'But not shared-out *equally…*'

'Between the-People…'

'To: those who do not pay-in? What? Taxes?'

'Benefits? Welfare?'

'Of the-Many…by the-Few?'

'Few by the Many.'

'Exactly! Oh, between-One and Zero.'

‘Quantum-Nuclear! Computer:’

‘One and the-Many!’

‘The-Many, and no-Other?’

‘The-Few, and *every*-Other…’

‘The no-*thanks*! for that!’

‘And what about the-spoils?’

‘Not *any*, not anywhere equally…what *You* pay-in?’

‘You get-Out?’

‘Always.

‘Between the-Rulers and Officials…Officer? Of the-Law? Private-(I)nvestment(s): *secret*: and Merchant(s): Trade-in *your*-debt(s)?’

#’At the-Conference? Is that what ‘It’ is! Peace? Or: Trade-War: Conference?’

‘Win-(in)ference:…’

‘For our-debts? Is that @It’? What You are after!’

Looking-down, at *nothing* in particular…then the words:

'Trade-in what? What have you got for Me?’

‘Since when?’

‘Since what? When?’

‘Now!’

>Now!’

<T1?’

>T1+ N/n…ames?

<Aims? *unknown*-number:nnnnnnnnnnnnnnnnnnnnnnnnnnnnnnnnnnnnnnnnnnn nnnn…

Quickly intervening, the-Clerk:

'Now! Again! Since when do 'We' do the-actual spoiling?'

Looking up, both together:

'Different-companies and Corporations…'

'*Hidden*…Names?'

'Names?'

'And Governments…'

'In-corporate. Like a Cake-Mix.'

'The-Earth. Global!"

'Caramelized? Like a cake…'

'Iceland…'

'Icing…*sweet*…'

'Cruel and unusual.'

'I'd be doing you a favour.'

'I am already.'

Knowingly cutting-through-the-crap. Unknowingly or unknowingly, delivered the foil, of the-spoils, nonetheless, the *inside(s)* glowing with self-satisfaction, flowing-gowns, the-Banker:

'As long the <u>Base-Value:'s</u> *is agreed and exchangeable with:*

'The-Big Players?' *named: list…(deleted).* The only ones that can play…

'5or6.'

'Twenty.'

'Hundred…'

'Hundreds?

'Trillions and in-*negative*-equity themselves…'

'For *liquidation…*'

'Cash…'

'Of-course!'

'No cheques, or *blank*-cheques: *anyway…*'

'Or record for that matter, either…

'*Virtually…*'

'Nothing.'

'Not in the-*ether*-either.'

'In-pocket-book….' tapping. The pocket-book.

'Blank-Cheque-book:' *could not-stop…*' moving speculation, into *nothingness…*

'Royalties on all output of 5%, 35% tax on all, goods services and employees. Only four or five Majors globally…including merchant and investment-banking and High-Street(s) in all the Major-currencies and whole-Economic-Zones…*viability…*'

'Whole-Countr(y)ies!'

'Whole Resource: Nation-State(s):States!'

'Sovereign-Presidential: Debt:'Viability?'

'Of: The-Earth? One-Trick Ponies most of them…'

'Now,'OTP-grouped sold-on now no-more-than six or seven massive Global-(I)nstitution(s):-institutions in each-sector:'

‘ Energy and Goods:’

‘Manufacture.’[

‘Re-search and Financial-Markets. Stock-Markets already paid-for several times over through several-*different*-countries’

‘Competitive-Markets’: Tax-systems and Border-Charges Tariff: Paid-Share.’

‘Shares paying-out…’

‘Taxed-along: The-Way:’ Ssnaking…

Somewhere not actually at:

‘Sold-on at profit, of-course.’

Exorbitant Ancient-Religious Sectarian (EARS): with…and without political Power-and-Command-Control:

'Men with Guns?’ *running…*

‘And Women.’

‘Bazookas!’

‘Classic-Bollocks!’

‘Armies need Generals…’

‘Armies needs guns…’

‘Game-Changer!’

‘Established:…’ *mis-understanding kept at-poverty-leveling/n below…*

‘*King*ing forever…’

‘Queening?’

‘White.’

‘Or.

'**Black**.'

'Empire Castling…'

'*Lording* IT over!'

'What?'

'As if….'

'Presidential-Monarchial Familial: Trading Big-Corp(o)rations:' *at the level we can be humoured, or ignored:*

'Trafficking-People still in-Governance.'

Political and Religious citadel of ourselves, and others Vital to either, and each other:

'Trafficking People!'

'Then talk!'

''We' are at each: Government and Church Temple and Big-Business…Corporate-Global! Rolled into one! Me and You!!'

'And Them?'

'And then?'

'What do you make of it, now, then?'

'Them?'

Looking around the Train-carriage: *take their chances, themselves:*

<Takeover!

>Hostile!?

< Bet?

Death-Company: Government-Bond(s) Corporate-takeover(s): bundled and sold-on.

Forwards:

>Friendly sliced and diced…death and taxes…employment? Life insurance? <

<To company-consented…<Unemployment Sick Payment(s):

>And not. Again. Personal-profit, or loss? < <Anything from Zero, to around 10-20%. < <Sometimes up-to 41% -51%! <

<A-majority! <

> Votes not bullets…

Trucing: trouncing…

>…*tracing*…: Option(s):

<Of Who?

> For Who?

<>Noble-Rulers: free of each other sides' number(s) of units: food medicine alcohol tobacco and firearms:

<Simple….including *high*-Finance and -Street and Inter-nationally…<

>Shop-Retail and *Wholesaling*…<

A-*vision* of the-Globe, a-globe, *spun*…

<<Our-Business: Secondary? *Infra-structure*…

>Utility Services?

<To: The-Money, of course!

>Price-Cap: The Primaries, damn-it!

< Pay-Off Shareholders Workers insurances and pensions…

>Play-off! Capital-Investment: Our Friends< and colleagues *affiliate*-racketeering, marketeering: the-secondary…

<Sell-on?

<Investment-House. Bank…'

>Then the Tertiary…

'Bankers! Forget about that!'

'Cleaners! Up!'

'Yours to give?'

'Certainly.'

'Family?'

'Certainly. Staff: Team(s): individuals'…'

'Your-Staff?!'

<< images of The-*Workers of the World:* worker<s…*contact*-details:':…

'Government: Family-Contact(s)>The-City.

<Human-Resources! :<

>*Contacts*: that is what it is! <

<Not what You know…Who You know. Who knows me and! Not who I know, who You know? What You know, or I could find out? <

'The Primary IPO (Initial-Public-Offering):'

'Public?'

'Private>Tertiary-colours! The Primaries! Secondary<s! As well. And Tertiary<s, yes! Family! <

<The-Vote?

>Bonded. By-*proxy*...Plebiscite.'

'Charity?'

'Sure.'

donations…*political and religious-party funding-machines:* rolled-out:

>Protection-Racket!

<Extreme-Povert(y): United-Nation(s): Analysis: Neutral-Banking: Stat.s(NBC): Global-Banking (G.B.): Island-Econom(y)ies:

>Intended-Only: Security Bond-Stocks:':

'Money for<Forces:<

>For Good(s)!'

'And Tertiaries! Yes! Family! The Party-Funding Machine(s) rolled-out: Political: Protection-Racket: securities for good(s))-*returns*: going…

<Bad. <Violence-Suspected: poisoning shooting autopsy organ(s): harvested for the rich and famous: abusers of children and animals…

>*Fear* and *Favours*?':<

''We' deal in Companies and Corporations who deal in Land and Property>The-Family!<

'What about the-Family?'

'PET.' *scanning*: the-richest:…

The exact same-second: *alerted*…

>Sell? land and property: 0: *Currently*: Food and Fuel and Furniture. Buildings' including…

<Media: list: *list...words/pictures/music…numbers…*

>Buildings and Dot-Comm.s: Credit Loans: Zero-Interest: loaned-in and loaned-out without any questions asked…as soon as: Selling:

’We’? We Buy-in! The-Utilities, that is where ‘It’ is at!’ home-*heating*: Oil-Gas and Plastic-Goods. Packaging and Selling Everywhere:

‘Gold-plated.’it is at!’

<Energy that drives Us!

>Then: Gold, Silver-Cellophane:

‘Wrap.?’

‘Diamonds…are forever…’

‘They<That is ‘It’!’

‘If You like, they never lose their value......’

‘Or their shine. Gold-plated! Those who do the selling, the making, the dirty work…’

‘Food-Farming:’

‘Buying Us Off! Let Us take the-Vote!’

‘With Lies and *broken*-promise(s)….’

‘Politician?’

‘Economist??@...

From the-screen, voices-off:

‘Intimidation! Look! No little-finger!’

The election-rigging accuser turned *accused*…

‘Denied! Government-Goal: Gail! Jailers!’

'Bailers...'

'Turned: Prisoner(s)...con-stant-Growth!'

'And *innovation* the Children's Toys!'

'Trinkets. The-*newest*=costliest:...'

Queue:

'Crap. Costliest!'

'Never. Cheapest, and last to go.'

'The-poorest?'

'First to go...'

Searchlight spun-around, onto another game, another-place:

'Next time!'

'Last-time!': *open*-source:

'*White* and **Black Ethnics**: All!!'

Yellow-vested. Brownian-motion:

'One killed off, both, killed-off. One remains...'

'The harder they come: cash-configuration of the-State?'

'Tax and punishment as public-servants:'

with white-hood red-masks and black-mask:

'Divide-and Rule!'

Beaten Blue-and-Red: Yellow-Gold and Gem(s): Sky, Sun and:

'Brown-Earth: Shades of All. Black and White: *grey*...'It' makes no-difference...'

desecrating-graveyards, in search of gold, silver and paper-money:

'Never Easy.' *secure sequestering carbon lit: trade-convoy, protected-corridor…*

'Never impossible.'

On the-Train: out of the blue, outside: tunneling and building-Bridges:

'So, what do you make of all this, now? Where, do you think the money is? The-Banks?'

'Not-Anymore. The-City.'

Then, let's us go there.!'

'We are.'

'What about the-Rest?'

'There is more? Fuck the rest.' *small fry…terrorists…list: list…*

>*Rebels*'*:Revolutionary* and *Religious*…

<Conservative and Liberal.

>Labour-Market(s):

<Communist or Socialist?

'Terrorist-*fundamentalists…'*

'*M*atters-not:'

'Government or not.

'Religion or not.'

On: Death-Row:

<Theocracies: Social-capitalists/Capital-Socialist(s)…

>We do not kill thieves! 'We' teach them a lesson:

'Police and *Thieve(s)!'*

'Banker and Gambler...'

'All of Us!'

'All of the Time!'

'And: Place(s):'

That will not get the even-<u>Equity</u>-share(s): on the Assets: list*...list's...lists'*

'Equity. *They* started-out with. You get-me?'

'You got-me…'

'The left-overs…dregs…' *remnants...ruins...re-main(s): too late for* that:

'Water?'

'Salt.'

'Bread?'

'Clothes?'

'Bandage.'

'Transporting-Meat: Gold and Golf Leisure Complex:'

'All Over The World.'

'Country: In:vestment-(I)nterest:'

'Co-lateral?'

'The-Country!'

'People. 'We' leave that to the Companies and Corporations. We Own On The Ground…and the-Bailiff(s)…'

'Officers of the Court and Local Authority. Our-Bail-out: to sort *that* lot-out?'

'In-corporate.'

'As in-corporate,-*with* Money? Credit. Massive Clear-Out!'

'Debit-Banks?'

'Money-Sale!'

'Boot-Sale!

'You got IT!"

'No, You got 'It'!'

'No, you got 'it'.'

'Because?'

'If 'We' cannot pay-off the loan(s): in the first-place?'

'What for?'

'Then?'

'They may never be paid-off.'

Government-Taxes: Consumer-Welfare (not anywhere un-equal): paid-off compensation: taken-land(s): homes and businesses, as anywhere in the World:

'Re-Building. 'We' will of course in time *claw* it all back for ourselves…'

#In-time:

<T1: Take-over's: capital-List…list…list's: …

'Fair and square!'

Graph's curved, across-each-other, through…away from each other…bone-curved, bell-curved…

'Middle is the best place to be on the curve…'

'Limited-liability?'

'On the swerve…'

'Eternal *never…*'

So, the conversation(s) went back and forth…

'And even then, you don't ever really know what's going on…'

'Never mind…'

'Most the Time. Nor do any of Us! *Constant*-Positives?' Make it sound Good!'

'Could get hammered?'

'No-negatives…

'Where do I come-in?'

'And that is where You come-in. You could take a cut-in, if you like?'

'What for?'

'Nothing. Try you out? Take a slice? You're smart. I'd be doing you a favour?'

'I am, already. Doing You a favour simply having this conversation…'

'What for?'

'Joking?'

'Seriously?'

'Sole-trader?'

Heard:

'Arse 'ole Trader. Soul-Trader. For-*my*-Sins…'

'You mean?'

'The Devils' Advocate?'

'You mean?'

'For my-offence?'

'Wrong-doing? Felony? Fault? Trans-gression mis-demeanour? Mis-deeds?'

'Goodness! Winning!!'

'Not-Securitising *the underlying debts and loans*:'

'For Life?'

'In a few short months…'

'Re-tirement? Security? I would be a sole-*Trader?* Limited-liability? I would be my-own-Company?'

'You would Be! Your-own-*Company*! You owe nothing!' *and otherwise with as much Psycho-Fun and as much anxiety as you can manage…*

'In return for?'

'Your-*debt*s.'

'They are Yours!'

'Secured by Real Estate? Or not?'

'What?'

'Your-Debts? Giant Flat-Screen T.V. perhaps? Home? Fast Motor vehicle, 4x4 Life insurance? Pension, for later-Life?'

'You? *threatening* Me?'

'Any other-Debts?'

'So, who hasn't got debts? Think about it?'Eh? Everyone does! You work to pay off your debt to Life and Livlihood. Neighbourhood: Family…'

Lie-bore: Living…

'I can take your *debts*…'

'With: Health and Social Security? They are yours! As the source of *all*-debt, eh? Sin. The source of all Debt. Eh? So, what's not to make of it Now, Eh?' the-Clerk spoke into the vacant-space between them. Nodded-over and down toward the returned-to unseen unshared, screen.

Through the others' paper newsprint, and at the mobile-pad display screen and inked-in writing *thinking* of possibly un-*befriending*...

The-Banker now looking away from the re-directed gaze ignoring the-Clerk and the assumed video-game machine, seemingly wished to be returned-to:

'So, what is that game you're playing, eh? Warfare4?'

Ignored, then:

'Not: War*Fare*4, then?' *then:* the-Clerk resumed scanning paused on some on-line conversation and without looking-up at the-Banker:

'WarFair4. Like the Game. Hunger-Games? So? What's on Your Mind now eh?' Scanning-down...clicking the-circularity loading-timer...text and graphics...*glancing*-down, and across...and holding...released...photo-opportunistic reading-across a newly updating...page 2/...paged-past the *aberrant*-picture, and headline, on which both the-Banker and the-Clerk had turned the page three-times...

The-Banker:

'The Market's will decide.' *and* this was the moment the-Banker could have added: '*...and there is nothing you, or anyone-else, can do about it!'* but resisted.

There would be no point.

You and whose Army? thought of, by the-Clerk.

Neither-outspoken aloud. Instead, from the-Clerk:

'Decide what?' the-Banker attempting to impart, as-if spell-checking it out word-for-word, as if too-abstruse and unknowable for this simpleton.

As for *Children*, to make of it what they will themselves simply *re-iterated* as some obvious truism:

'The Markets will decide. The Markets will come through…' *stepping-up to the plate once again*:

'Get geared-up.'

'Leverage?'

'Leveraged-*upwards*:'

'Not-Leverage-*down, then*?' and the accompanying levering-action, committed:

'What?'

'Global-Exports! Our best export:'

'The-City!'

'Truthfully? Honestly? Accurately, as far as in *known*? More or Less?'

'Our best-Exports are everything-else!'

'Like what? Like…TVs…Games?

'I don't know…'

'Media-Movies?'

'Advertisement: Trade-War(s): vs. the Opposition…'

Software…

'Hard-Ware. The-City…'

'*Information*?'

'Over*heard*? What?'

'About Company Accounts in advance?'

'How@Spyware…'

'*Yes*….'

'The-Hardware?'

'That is your job.'

'The numbers, the shapes…'

'Market-*information*?'

'To know, and *withhold* market-information…'

'Numbers. True or False. Letters and numbers…'

'Put-*together* in a certain-way…'

'Contractual arrangement?'

'Credit?'

'Debt? Bankrupt?'

'You? Again?'

'Credit-rating? Everything about You? No-longer a-*secret*?'

As cagily, in the compartment, the space between, and around, the-carriage:

'Debit-rating? Of course. All of them.'

'What, *my*-debts? Who are You? To be asking this of Me?'

Looking-up…

'Who are You to *listen*?' and answered:

'Tourist? Journalist? Aaahh…yes…Fun and Games. You know! Sport's. Games? And, there is no 'Art' in IT: Political-Economic.'

'Art.'

'Science…'

'Trade! Only the Biggest The World…'

'Ha! Ever Seen!! *quickly* adding nodding at the obvious:

'GO!'

'&Play…'

Games-machine opposite:

'Those games? Same as the real thing?'

'Enough…'

'What?'

'S'pose so. All-and Any other-Businesses…some-*Manufacturing*…'

'Pharming?'

'Farming? Yes.'

'Tourism?'

'Luxury? Resorts?'

'Mega-Media…'

'Top-Six!'

'*Energy*-providers…' *lower-sixty or six-hundred million billion trillion of Us!*

'Work for? The Big-*five* or=so Pharmaceuticals?'

'Healthy-competition?'

'Choice.'

'Competition.'

'Not Much Choice?'

'Not in it. Fixed. It was always **<u>The Rational-Equitable.</u>** Was 'It'?'

'If you have enough bean-counters, eh?'

'Counters?'

'Shop-fronts? Shop-windows?'

'You got it!

'@I have?!?'

'Multi-*Agro-Cultural's*: Soil&Salt.'

'Fish&Foul.'

'Tea&Sugar.'

'Tobacco&Alcohol: and:'

'Drugs…Food-Sale(s):-Ledger: *firearm: sale*s. There it is…'

'Weapons of Mas-Destruction? Nuclear?'

'Department-of 'You know Who.'.

'Wrong-doing?'

'Beating up the wrong-one…'

'Illicit?'

'Drugs?'

'Illicit drugs? Now that would be illegal, wouldn't it?'

'Illicit-Weapons? Super-Sport:'

'D*oping-Olympics*?' without pause for appreciation *of Self or Other*:

'Poison. These, all taken-together, are more than the-City, put together, anywhere!

'Media!'

'My point *entirely*!'

'That bit more is what the-City creams off for Itself.'

'(P)rincipal-(I)nvestment: IPO?'

'Investment-Principle: Business-principle:'

That bit on top…

'Commercial-Confidentiality: Competitors…'

'Of everything-else?'

'Bit?'

'Byte!'

'On top of what?'

'Everything else!'

'You got 'It'!'

'What? Inter-National Fraudulent-Loans. Mortgages, Credit?'

'I got 'IT'!'

'Any Debit-Cards? Credit? Rating?'

'All directed toward the *innately* greedy? Too good to be true? So probably is *false*…'

'Fraudulent.'

'Greedy.'

'Hungry.'

'No-one is forced to-*borrow*.'

'Life is…'

The-Clerk:

'Pay-Day Loan?'

'Affordable? Everyone-is. No-one is totally self-sufficient. We need each other...'

'Everyone is totally *de-pendent* to start with.'

'Of-course! On? The-*Game*?'

'*This* Game?'

'Need to learn to-*Play*! Live the Life! Investments. Savings. Pensions and Insurances...'

'Mis-Sold?'

'Sold.'

Unheard, switched-off, unhearing:

'Insured, to live. Pensioned to die.'

'Saving...'

'The best for the next-*Generation*! Our-Kids!! Invest to Live!"

'Gene-Edited! For: Health and Social Care.'

'Take...'

'...and give *nothing*-back. We-pay-our-Taxes. Charity...'

'Government evasion avoidance or escape abroad, is it?'

'Oh yes...and give to Charity.'

'To save a life?'

'Lives...'

'Sans Frontieres.'

‘That: Bad?’

‘Is it? Good.’

The-Banker outspoken, reached-out to the-Clerk again, now:

'Borrow-to-lend: that is the way to do it: Investment:’

‘'We’ *borrow on Our-Debt(s):*?’

‘To: Lend:’

‘‘We’ do the-*tending…*'

The-Clerk knew:

'Buying-Up: spending at *knock-down* prices, right?'

'Selling-up:’

‘The-Price is always right…’

‘(I)nvestments are *Hopes and Dreams*. You have Hopes and Dreams, don't you? ‘We’ all do. don’t we?’

‘Nothing-Left.’

#’Nightmare or DayDream.’

‘That is the question? Big-House. Big-Car. Do a Good job with what I have, and what I can get…'

'Be: Rich?’

‘Private-Jet without hurting anyone?’

‘Never, people will always get hurt.’

‘What? By luck or judgment?’

‘Maybe. Mis-Judged.’

'Skill?'

'Luck?'

'Make your own?'

'Laws. Un-even Justice. Made to Measure: what School are you from? College? University? Diplomatic-Travel: *and* Cash Routes? Property All-Over?'

'Hostile: Trade. Takeover(s): Everything!'

'Easy-Money.'

'Broken into Bank-Vaults similarly.'

'With *nothing* in them!'

'Robbed.'

Computer-screens. On Stocks and Shares:

'Cannot be touched. Except by The *Legal* Money Owner:'

'Who are?'

'Foreign-*credits* as well as debts.'

'Transfers, *simply…*'

On-line…

'Get away with it?'?'

'Again.'

'Getaway car?'

'I like it! My Own-Car!'

Mansion-*garaged:…*

'Bugatti?'

'You? Helicopter?'

'Personal-A'plane?'

'Sure.'

'Yacht?'

'Sure!'

'And a 'Good-Job. Judge! Loads 'o' Money!'

'Of course! But You cannot have-*everything*, by sheer luck. Got to do something for it! So? What else? What have You got to offer? Self-*Judgement?*'

'Of Other? By: Trial?'

'You are a Fiscal: High-Court Judge, now?'

'Supreme-Court. Judgement?'

'Equals=of-Information:@*Birthright*, perhaps…'

'Privilege: Who You Know...'

'Who knows You!'

'As well as What?'

'What you know or *think* you can know.'

'Now? Can-Do!'

'Live the dream!'

'Follow your *dreams*! Total-Consumer. Celebrity-Everyone!'

'But not if I don't want to?'

'You?'

'The Evidence?'

'Stay in the shadow(s) y'a know what I mean?'

'Mean?'

'Off-shore? Greedy. Next-door. Best-*investment* yet, yes…'

(i)ndependent of each other, no snail-mail or bail-trail…click: bait-*switch*:

<Switch: <>Rational & Equitable.

- R/E(In)Bestment!

'Yet, no- person is entirely *independent*…'

'Although we all may try.'

'No-Country, either.'

'No-company, or Corporation!'

'I do not speak for You. You do not speak for Me. I speak for Myself.'

'So, do I. For Others…'

'Mind-you…'

'Some…'

'For: Nothing…'

'Murder.'

'Martyr-Suicide?'

'Until the price-is-Spot-<u>On</u>. In-storage.'

'Shortages.'

'The-Price rises:n/N!'

'Where?'

'Jump how high?'

A-*hiatus*, then The-Banker chortling *conceitedly* self or other deceptively, or not:

''Buy' *or* 'Sell''?

'What?' glancing-screenward, both *leaning*-forward across the table and ignoring everyone else in the carriage.

The-Banker, to the-Clerk:

'O.K. One-to-one now…'

The-Banker, and the-Clerk leaned forward *listening*:

'Nothing *less* and nothing more from the-point at which the stock-markets, and currencies closed.'

'The money-markets are closed?!'

'Are-closed to-the-point at which they may be open, sooner than we *think*?'

'Could be…re opening…sooner than we think?'

'Now@we speak.'

This time to the-Clerk as rhetorically-intended, answered the-self:

'Of course! Open for Business, right now! Ssh….Alright: Pre-deals being set-up as we speak. Be-ready.'

'But there is a lot more than that?'

'You need to be there. And because in the end it is You the-People…'

'We the People.'

'On this Train? That is why I am going in. You know?'

'The-Crime? The-Politics?'

'*The* Politics?'

'Religious and Agnostic and Atheist.'

‘Inter-National: Global-Trade: Re-Gu-Lations? ’We’. Make it happen.’

'*ShhIT* happens!’

‘Economic. In the end. Every-time…but not *yet…*’

‘Then? Yet(i). Take a move on in?’

‘Why not?’

‘Get in there! That is why I am going in Today! The only *re(a)son…*’

‘Then?’

‘The Airport?’

‘In-where? On what?’ *naturing now, or-nurturing? Plebian? Or non-Plebian? Maturing? Married?*

'Now?’

‘Re-turned for personal and Family Gain.’

‘For: latte-later…’

‘Latters…’

‘Letters?

‘’*grrrrr*’s…get ‘it’. O.k.?’

The-Clerk contemptuous of and contemplating then of some *instant.*

But only now felt, *mistrust*-dealing, in fantasy, and fear…genre: *horror*:

'What are the *odd*s?’

‘Of what? Not-*evens*’?’

The *passive* reflective: *thought* and *then* again the-Bankers’ anger rising:

'By closing-the-markets…’

‘Unsecured mortgage, and credit: Crisis…’

‘Systems' Crash!’

‘Only perhaps…’

‘Algorithms…’

‘O.K.?’

‘One-goes…’

‘The others' follow. Cannot do business…’

‘Insurance?’

‘Re-insurance and Payback-Pensions and: Life-Saving(s):’

‘Home-mortgage(s): Home and Office:’

‘Hotel-Building: *bubbles*…’

'Baubles! Highest bidder:’

‘Shops and Business cannot pay wages, salaries, borrow-to-buy goods, pay-suppliers, of goods and services…’

‘Yes? So? Log-(i)n Logistics.’

‘On-Credit?’

‘Crediting-Account(s): Corporate-Famil(y)ies. With more than the *value* of the Business:’

‘Loans for Shares?’

‘Yes…’

‘Then, what? Default?'

'Yes.’

‘Then what? Re-possession?'

'Yes.'

'By whom, of what? The-Lender? Sherriff. Bailiff? We don't do that! Administration! Auditors? Lawyers? Accountant? Bankers: *those*, yes. plenty of Work for *them*: Cooking-the-Book(s) hiding the evidence.'

'Like Mobster(s) Staff: mad or cool killer threat'

Being or Becoming the Stranger," provides us with an astute analysis as of the ways we draw the boundaries between one another. "Culture, physical traits, religion were and are among all precursors of strategies for ascendance and power," Morrison explains

Kendi wants us to see not only that there is nothing wrong with black people but that there is likewise nothing wrong with white people. "There is nothing right or wrong with any racial groups," he writes. This is the bittersweet message hidden in his book: that, in the grand racial drama of America, every group is already doing the best it can. ◆

This article appears in the print edition of the August 19, 2019, issue, with the headline "The Color of Injustice." We can choose to descend into pessimism and apathy, assuming that nothing can be done, and helping to ensure that the worst will happen. Or we can grasp the opportunities that exist — and they do — and pursue them to the extent that we can, thus helping to contribute to a better world," he concluded. "Not a very hard choice."

'So, un-scrupulous and vain!'

'Sure. Enjoys' the Blood and Guts Corporate Image, know who I mean?"

'And covering-up!'

'Of-course!'

'Then?'

'Loss-*assessor*…'

‘Adjusted in the buyers' favour.’

‘Deal done.’

‘Everyone-is-affected?’

‘Of-course! Everything is affected! All the-Money!’

‘Press! For All the Things! Dragging-down whole-Corporation!’

‘Airlines! Fallen out-of-the-sky!’

‘Walls and Towers collapsed…’

#The-Peoples' Nationalised-industries sold, for next to nothing, to a few…in-Power…

‘Buildings built.’

‘Un-built…’

Lived-in un-lived in:

‘For Sub-Prime(s) were Its’ Biggest Beast!'

Whole-industries! Businesses and Transport Infra-Structure:

<Logistics-Corps. Transport Home-and Abroad.

>Ship-Owners…

<Ownership!

> China!

<Taken-out of our-hands!

- Off Our Hands (OOHs!))!
- Given-in to!

Ports and Airports, sold-off. Sold-out. Nuclear-Power cancel each other out…

<Given-to: Eur-Asian Pacific-Rim: Russe: China checking-in:

> Indo-Pakistan and Bangla-Desh MyanMar:

>German-American: Indo-Euro: Pean: Russe!!

< Africa!

'China-Risk! National-Security.' enough-rope:

'Sunken-ships!'

'Crashed!' *collided*!

'Irate.'

'Privatising-Pirates!!'

Onto the black-rocks, mired in the quicksand of information-fatigue(s): set-in.

'Onto the Black-Rock(s) of Doom!'

Granite forced apart by icy-water roughened and ready:

'At the bottom of the Deep-Blue-Sea!'

'The Locker-Room?'

'Mov(i)e.See: Bonanza!'

'And Blow-Up! -Out(s)!' *correcting*:...

'Needs a Lightning-Rod!'

'Over-ripe...'

'Over The Top.'

'For the-taking...' (i)dentity (iD) scamming-shamming spamming computer-fraud.

Without permanent circuitry, no trace...

'Dropping-off The Trees!'

'Low-branches...'

'That's it!'

'Intentionally?'

'Not…' *accidentally* in the pursuit impacting pile-up smashed: lower branched fruit dropping to the ground:

'Crashed into the Wall!'

'Storm. Off The Rails.'

'Street. On concessionary-loan(s) re- mortgaged:'

'Street?'

Oceans.

'You? Bankrupt?'

'Country-by-Country:'

'Owed, owned, or not.'

'Bought and sold and brought:'

'Nothing for the family…'

'Home and Abroad. Colonial. And those who Build-Businesses…'

'Corporate. Continue-Building: Big-Six!'

'Or seven…''

'At Eight and Nines! Globally: Family-Empire(s): Again and Again!'

'Too-Big! Failed!'

'More Credit than Cash!!'

'Cache then, Credit.!!!'

'Bought-out. Sold-off. Asset-stripping raising the barrier…'

Dry hacking-cough from the-Banker, the-Clerk:

'Viral.'

'Like: Spear-Fishing.'

'In a Barrel?'

'Lake.'

Out of the window the-Clerk re-in -*flected*:

Activity screen: back-diving-back

In. Re-*surfacing* water-fighting

Pulling-in, the-prey:

'Over-lending *tally*? Sick.'

'Stick.'

'Put.'

'Sink.'

'Stay.'

'Too much money…'

'Never-enough.'

Over-*Production* Economic Central-Command:

'OPEC: Surplus…NNNnnn…'

'Pure-profit!'

'Not given-back…'

'Ragged-Trousered: *Philanthropist(s):*…(s)…'

'Richest-Owners of Land and Money:

'People! African: Arab-Spring!'

'Self-employed '

'Corporate.'

'Wage-Labour!'

'Hard-Labor Farmer!'

'Engineer. IT consultant:'

'A *soft*-Price and Bidding system…'

'Tender.'

'Or could be War?'

'Trade-War?'

'Already! Workers! Unite and Fight!'

'What?'

'Production-halted…'

'To maintain-price…'

'…and raise It?'

'Scarcity…'

'Banks closed.'

'Mountainous-Employment!' Not-sold *cheap-stored…*

'Transported…' 'slavery and Death. Arab and Catholic-Capitalism: Protestant: Consumer-led: Industrial Man-u-Facture:'

'Own Owned-Work:'

'Product-to-Market!'

'Consumerism!'

'What is wrong with that?'

'Consumer-*bled*.'

'Politician-led:'

'Who are: The-People!'

'The Workers! The-Consumers!'

'Both. *They* vote with their *feet…*'

'Communist: Party-led:'

'Work-Ethic: Ethnic!'

''We!'

Proportional re-presentation: at least 4 standing and preference least worst wins not 1st past the post dictatorship of the majority with disgruntled minorities majority…

All.

'Go where we're *sent.'*

*'B*y-Advertising-Media! How else would you *know* what was out there?'

'How else would you get Free-Service?'

'By: ongoing forward subscription, of course.'

'Of what, to what?'

'Quality and Quantity of Service as Ordered: Or not out there?' *rows, of half, and full empty shelves, at the local supermarket and street-market and auction of household-goods*:

'They are *your*-Customers!'

'Of course! Share-Holders! Everything that happens must-*happen…*'

'Yin and Yang.'

'Bureaucratic-Communism. Balance.'

'Socialist-Dragon!'

'Demand and Supply…'

'Bullish and Tigrish: Credit-Goods:…'

'To: The-Bearer:'

'Debit Goods:'

'Cash. Supply and Demand…'

'Demanded and Suppl(y)ied.'

'People and Goods…'

'Lands and Livestock.'

'Goods…'

'Stock(s)-Exchanged: *everywhere*:'

'Taken. Stolen. De-frauded time and time again…'

'Staffing-Services…' get rid of the compliant complainant, by all means possible…

'People…'

'Service-Staff: Government. Bigger the-*lier(s):'*

'Bankers' exaggerating-minutae:'

'The more intricately *believable…*'

'Multiplier. Bigger and more-complex the more:..'

'Division?'

'Truth?'

'*Truthful*?'

'Awful? Existence?'

‘More-believable’

‘Or un-believable…’suspension of disbelief…

‘Than?’

‘Advertising: The-Truth.’

‘Reality?’

‘Capitalism.’

‘May be, unbelievable? For All?’

‘Socialism-too?’

‘Go to Mars or the Moon with: Bullshit-Job(s): In the Woods…’

‘What?’

‘The Bearshit.’

‘Bull Crap!’

‘Fox in the Chicken Co-op.’…*naturally*…

Organic reared from Organic: Think about it…the *naturalistic*-fallacy…is *its’ self* a Fallacy!’ *Ram-charge*:

‘All is Natural as well as Un-natural!’

‘I suppose…’ *this…*

‘What?’

‘This? Is not Real.’ Is both naturally-happening and un-*naturally*-concocted…without thought and action only action until after-thought:

Truth is only a present tense, monistic.

Monastic agreement in-accord with God (whose?)

Global: Pluralism of monistic selves, selfish-selves, completely no-one completely.

Some get close, and more-bonkers-than Bankers, that they *do.*

Probably mean no harm, not:

Even. But: the-partners…the amours… the armoires

Armies, Police forces and in the end the Presidents as Royalty: claim of holiness, and piety…

'Don't go a long-way…' *past-empirical, scientific-speculation, after, the, mean, and every event, has been counted, add, or indeed, minus, Zero. Saved as One. By each of our senses…anything, and everything, could be something-else…and will be the next moment, and the one after that:*

'Not-*happening…*'

'Yet?'

'You see?'

'Check-a-Trader: Equity-Ownership. Everything, pure and natural, untouched, by human sensibility…'

'File?'

'Or: *fault*?'

'Suit. Collectively?'

'Pure-Good? Pure-Evil? Rubbish! Rational-Actor!' (i)*ncluding* our thoughts and ideas and what we see and hear:

'Acting: *ir*-rationally?'

'In-equitably.'

'Sometimes, most times, maybe all the time:'

'Future-Derivative: Prediction?'

'Soothsayer?'

'Analysis: system-structure function-constructivism: after the Event.'

'De-molishing.'

'De-Manding Futures?'

'Hu-Man. Together, mostly harmless.'

''We' are dealing with an irrational world constantly changing, rationally, in mind, and body directed:'

'By Leaders'…'

'Demolishing-Home(s)lessness:'

'Bankrupt. Rationalle?'

'But not-unreal.'

'Real.'

'Until seen.'

'Then it is too late?'

'Perfectly. Imperfectly impossible! Nothing is so-Pure!'

'Equity?'

''Equal' as equipped at last'…'

'Nothing-more Natural than *what* has only just-happened.'

'After-the-Event?'

'Rationalised. See? *Normalized:* Naturalised!'

'Yet in its inception? Un-natural?'

‘Us? Before The-Event? God-made?’

‘Created…’

‘Ir-rationally?’

‘Ur?’

‘Or up-ourselves!’

‘Ourselves! Rationally? Rationally *reason*-ably regulated-regulating in-advance equitable we like to think and be post-modern, tamed.’

‘So how? So, Devil de-bauched!’

‘A crime in its’ *twist…*’

‘Reason.’

‘Ambiguous.’

‘Bi-got.’

Un-*reason*ing:

‘Not unlike Hatred. How is to destroy…’

‘Un-reason?’

‘Self! To create!’

‘Told when…’

‘To Create is To-Destroy?’

‘Find, or be un-created.’

‘From Nothing? Impossible!'

‘Scientific-Economy: numbers…’

'Nuclear-Economies’’

‘Wealth-Taxes?’

‘Since: Ur-rational?’

‘In-the-event…’

‘Socially-Rationalised: Infra-structure. Bridges and Tunnels and Space-Craft to take people between peoples and their livelihood(s):’

‘For the next-*rational*-move…’

‘Too-many?’

‘To: many.’

‘Algorythmic-Logic! Profit at all-cost(s):’

‘Not-enough! Not-exactly Equitable.’ thought-of *carried-out? Never know, until the deed is done.*

Then:

'Too-much? Sold-out?’

‘Stayed-Put.’

De-ported:

‘Made: Illegals. They were-*wrong* before…as to *say*…’

‘What? That it can only be natural? They were All-wrong! Admitted it?’

‘Some…’

'Who? Under torture of threatened bankrupt poverty?’

‘Migrant-Siege.’

‘Freeze. Irrationally…’

‘Of: Having It All?’

‘All-knowledge…’

‘Everything, and everyone. Taken-away from them…’

‘By someone else…’

‘For someone-else…’

‘…and The Others?’

‘Not *pure* self-interest, then?’

‘Perhaps…those that said it was only-Natural.’

‘Self-interest…’

‘With: Other-Greed, now?’

‘Perhaps we all are, to some extent, want *more* than we have?’

‘Wealth-Envy?:…’

‘…and does that make what the International-Conference: *They,* are deciding now?’

‘Since: Ir…rational?’

‘Wrong?’

‘No, simply *only* self-interested…’

‘Not: Only One! Country and World Our:’

‘Roman: Oysters! African Salt and Sil(i)con:’

‘Global also but by greater, much greater degree…’

‘To be selfish and greedy!’

‘Never-enough, some-of-them.’

'Only-*partly…*’

‘To Cash-in? *at least…*’

‘Parity.’

‘Whatever-happens! Crash? Collapse?’

'They said they saw it *coming…*'

'Afterwards…' hooked on the gambling shambling analysis:

'As all our Pavlov-Payslips: Pension and (I)nsurance: *included*-as: Business-Cost(s):'

'And Did-*Nothing!* Did you?'

'Do nothing? How is that possible? I got Rich. As I am. I am as Rich as You would Be:'

'Get-Rich, *quick*. Eh?'

'Re-tire young?'

'Or: carry-on:'

'On-*paper…*'

On-screen…

quicker…

Nodding across the train-table between them, then looking out towards the traveling landscape beyond:

'On-screen?'

'That's what *I* mean…see?'

Un-seen or heard, the-both of them baulked and drew-back into the-event: the *fray*:

'The-Rich give nothing to the-*poor…*' *grubbing-property express-anger and pay-back victims' food and clothing not-enough…squalid and horrible, homes, as busy, frantic, and full of good-fun, and miserable, poverty.*

Fights and arguments, through the walls partitioned-off, of the grand buildings and offices, on the stairs, the broken-elevators, and especially small children, babies, not invested-in, yet.

Outside the-window: *destroyed*-buildings, derelict, others new and sparkling in the rising Sun..

'Sold *ideas* to the-congregation, neighbours, electorate…'

'F*ailed…*

Humid oil-swamp pipeline and tetsi-fly water-spilling in-fecting killing Oil spill lands' incursion from the east, again. Stealing. Protection-Racket Government. Ex-pectora ting…*live*…on-screen:

'Used to be only for the money…now it is this-countries' economic-Zone.'

'To: the-Others.'

'From. Now it is Trade-deals done.'

'Or not-done, today?'

'Midday. Energy and Money: dis-Astor($). Bond-Field(£): Game (€)s: Labour: *Ssshh…*Who knows what will happen, anytime, disasters.'

'Poverty and Riches.'

'When I find how-much…'

'Is not-possible.'

'Then what is possible, now! I feel ANGRY!'

'I cried…' *caught*-out: purposely or not:

'A petty and defining soul-rescued and for the-Life!'

'Now it is only for clean water and the food of God'

'Wine-theft: GS-suicide.'

'International Family-Fraud (IFF).'

'Home.'

'Gifts.

'Claridges Moss&Co.'

'Empire. Taking themselves too-seriously!'

'Suits. Gangsters' Gear.'

Skype:WeChat:

'The-State: takes over when the Private-Sector re-treat(s).'

'Small-countries: the Largest: Industrial-Output and Ex-Ports.'

'In-Ports blocked censoring:'

'Trade-Sanctions and Tariffs imposed at Home and Abroad.'

'The definition of: Trade-War? Titfer. Tit-for-Tat. Hat?'

'White-Hat?'

'Fuel and Food Price riots…'

'Cut-off the hands with a machete…'

'Accused of stealing-rice…'

'No-negotiation…was as if they wanted to leave…without a hand.'

Ten-minutes of screaming. Crying. Chased-off any intervention attempted destroying, looting, for themselves…

Problems, with electricity, and clean water…came down from the mountains…food-shortages…

Vacuum-cleaners and light-bulb *bubbles…*

North seas and South Seas.

'Money-Laundering?'

'Rinsed.'

'From Crimea?'

'No…'

'Yes.'

'From: Others' Crime(s): Estonian.'

'Russe.'

'Danish?'

'Pastry? Mooncakes? Re-cycling pro-seed(s) after financing maturing business and trade(s) bond-buying investment proceeds re-invested: Each-of-Us!'

Looking-towards the-Clerk, the-Banker:

'Charity: *list*…works-too…you know? 'We' *Love* Charity!'

'Your-Own?'

'Pingu?'

'Pingshu?'

'Great-Publicity, for when it all goes wrong!' *laughing*: open fumbled Corporate-*secret(s)*:

'Do They Work?'

'Corporate-Bank and Government Secrets?'

‘Torturers and Assassin(s)!’

‘Public-(I)(M)age. Advertising, everything!’

‘Annual-Accounts?’

‘The Last Green Tree. Daily.’

‘10%? What about paying Taxes?’

‘For: Welfare instead of employing-people? We do that.’

‘Social-Safety-Net (SSN). Naturally.’

‘For: Actual-*Austerity:d*on’t necessarily get the benefit…’

‘Don’t necessarily get anything. Free-Will: *intervenes…generally…*’

‘As do benefit(s):’

‘Homes for Heroes!’

‘Soldiers!’

‘Workers, eh? Fit for Heroes! The whole Government National State Country…’

‘Infrastructure? Paid-for by?’

‘Taxes. Interested-in:…’

‘Corporate-owned. In: National-Debt.’

‘Sovereign! Of course!’

‘Private? One-Shareholder One Vote? Public-Decision(s)…many…’

‘All?’

‘Equal-Vote? On anything! Each of Us…’

'Fit for Purpose!’

‘Free!’

‘What about all that Charity?’

‘What?’

‘10%?'

'1% Social-Charity:’

'Good-Welfare: starts at Home.’

‘As kind of Heroic-sacrifice…’

‘Trust Fund Martyrdom?’

‘With Your name on It! **Bang!’**

‘**Boom!**’

‘T*raitorous!’ without-knowing really why? What-for? Or whether the outcomes would be favourable or not…*

'Harmless? Victimless? Insurance-Pension Scams?’

‘Balanced-Pay: Massive-Risk, Eh? Others’?’

'If they cannot manage their own accounts, as well as We…'

''We’? Cheated? Out-of…’

‘Of course…re-investment? Your-own customers, managers, share-holders, stock-holders especially…’

'Employees’’

‘Pay: Master(s) Mistressess and Madame?’

‘Ma’’am.’

‘Chief.’

‘Nothing…well to almost nothing left…’

‘Almost…everyone cheats or steals.’

‘A *little*, perhaps, from their Employer, do we not?’

‘Directly to: the Customers’ Digital-Wallet?’

‘Banking-Scam?’

‘A Friend (i)(n)deed: dead:’

‘The Employee’s rent rest and re-cuperation?’

‘Health-Tech. diverting: Leisure-Pension. Life-Insurance.’

‘Iron and Steel.’

‘Copper-Bottomed!’

‘Wire-Wool: Zinc-sealed:’

‘Acid-Lead(s): Nickel-Cadmium: Lithium: Battery:’

‘Little-*light*: brightly lay-out for a laidback: for Life!’

‘A little late for that.’

‘What may not be *too*-much?’

‘Everything!’

‘Taken away in Customer-Value?’

‘Extra’s! They *hate* You!’

‘Yes? But we have the Money…’

‘But not the Goods? Not now!’

‘Of course the-Money! Actually-Nothing! Actuarially: Everything!’

‘When it comes time to repent!’

‘Re-sentful with *Envy*? Re-Venge-Tech.?’

‘Per-Sonal Political:’

‘Daughtorial and Maternal:’

‘Paternal(*i*)stic: commitment to human-endeavor without sure reward:’

‘Sports and Games, then.’

‘Commitment…’

‘All! To: Life? All-Life? The Peoples’ *helpful*-Savings invested…’

‘Re-invested…’

‘Re-(I)(n)surance-pension and other Credit mechanisms.’

‘Looked on it as savings:’

‘Sorry, Savings? Ha-ha! Debts!’

‘Sorry. For cheating: Capitalizing-Ad. vantage…’

‘Personal…security…’

‘Life-assurance…’

‘No re-assurance:’

‘Pension?’

‘For when I am old?’

'Maximizing-Profit: From My Debt(s)!’

‘That are Credit(s). Merit(s):’

‘Somewhere Else!’

‘Debt-Holiday! Of course, retire young, protecting, the investment…’

‘Market-Share?’

‘Export-Import: licences and licensed-to:’

‘Greed.’

‘Poverty. New-Model Econom(y)ies:’

‘Re-issue re-issue:…’

‘Do-Business! Positive Attitude!’ the hands-palmed.

The-Clerk rubbing a thumb and the finger-tips of both hands, as if counting banknotes:

'Not my ‘at ‘e chewed?’

‘Economic-Attitude?’

‘Risk! Let loose the Dogs! Regulating-*currency* manipulating-analysis:…’

'Fixed-Future(s): guesswork based on algorithmic statistics and Game(s)-Theory:…

‘Trade-Offs…’

'Tradings-in?’

Looking-down:

<Cheating-Debt(s): Fre3-Loader(s):

‘It’s such a People-Business.’

<Power-Source: Credit/Debit: *connected...*

>Everything-in the frame(s): pixelated: re-flective: de-veloped and de-ployed, in the envelope:

<Credit-Allies: list…looking down into the electric-machine and up again, *quickly*:

'Klepto-Merit! Now. You’ve got it!’

‘That is where the-Media is at…just…re-possession…for-profit's…’’

‘That is what it is! From re-possession…’

‘I said 'We’ do not do re-possession' didn’t I? We' are only interested in the money-value of The Deal in commission and fee’s terms.’

‘Nothing more?’

‘Nothing more? Re-possessions account for most the profit in the early-days of…’

‘Closure. Bankruptcy. Broke…n. Stopped. Crashed. Collapsed.’

‘What about The People? Nothing?’

‘The-Customers@ well…the-Employees? Let us call It: *re-structuring…*

Food and Shelter. Medicine, and a roof…is all we really *need*…want?

‘‘We’ got the Sky!’

‘As Charitable donation?@...’

‘Charity-works, you-know…’

‘Pay-back…’ *with the-photographs on the Boardroom Wall...*

'Owned?’

‘Not: Greed-Crime?’

‘Exploitation.’

‘Agreed.’

‘But you c’d’ve…’

‘With Bonus…’ and percentage-pay increases agreed in-advance in cash and shares. Whatever happens…

‘Increasing The Prices but not the Wages?’

lowering them, per hour, per Zero-hours.…*anyway*:

‘Top-slicing all the way…’

‘Modern: second to third to fourth of more:’

‘Slavery!’

‘Owners paid-off for:’

‘Serfdom! Elsewhere: *cheap*-clothes…’

‘Land-Grab: Heart of IT.’

<Up. Low-wages long-hours lowering:

>Costs<*nnn:N=-N.*

'Increasing the Benefits!'

'For Who?'

'*Lay-off*'s…Market's Closed! Because so many people wanted their Money! Their salaries and wages un-paid.

Opening-up the screens again reporting:

'A Pay-Gap: *automatically* opens-up:'

'Prices and Wages…' Prison and Sages. Venture-Capita. War-Chest(s): Atom(i)Co:

'Government-*subsidised* debt-bailout punishing crediting: The-People clinical-testing re-pairing adventurousness/*cautiousness*…

<Central-Bank(s) and Federal Re-serve(s): *drawn on:*

>Benefit-Cost: *risk*-collateral damage.

- By Billions and now Trillions…soon to be Quadrillions…

'Pent-up uni(n)tentional consequences?'

'Least-worst Democracy:'

'Like suicide-bombers seeking to release prisoners by killing themselves!'

'Ourselves!'

'As hostage!'

Known action: *unknown* consequence:

'Capitalism.'

'More-Chaos!'

'More Turmoil!

'Deliberate.*confuse*.com'

'A tumultuous decade?'

'Which One? A Little-Turbulence. Only.'

'But No! Forever-tumultuous!'

'Turbulence. Only.

'Only? Democracy: is not a-winner…'

'Loser:' *like any-dictatorship, stifling dissent...fear of popular uprising, as Socialist-Communist-ascension of the personal and family, amassing vast-wealth.*

'Democracy is scary: risk-taking, can be despairing, but always, always wins out. By pure Common-Sense…well at-least 51% anyway…'

'Democratically?'

'49-51%?'

'Dictatorship of the Majority Proletariat.'

'Re-Legion: Socialist Dictatorship(s): Families for decades, everywhere…'

'Zimbabwe?'

'Deposed.'

'By?'

'The Military-Elite. 10% own the Armed-Forces and Media: and attempt to Command and Control-Society: Police&Army&Navy: Warship Aircraft-Carrier: Protect and Defend:'

'Humanitarian?'

'Anyway, never to-*lose*…the 51% is enough…'

'At least 75% to square the irrational how far the markets have gotten?'

' Bankrupt and owing trillions. 'It' is all about the 49% in 100% Debt to someone.'

'Then. To 99% ownership by the 1% richest people, nations, and *beliefs*…'

‘*We were not aware…*’

‘Until the Personal-Charity rate-fixing scandal?’

‘To pay-off the bailout, and the-debts…’

‘Data is worth money collateral:’

‘Equities Rationally owned?’

‘Equitable-Banks? Their Own.’

‘And bonus on-top!’

‘Only 99.99% did not know…’

‘The Very Few Elite 49%...losses marked-up!’

‘Then incompetence, then!’

‘51% to not see it!’

‘Once percentage-points start starting going-down…

Ra-pidly:

‘Until the bell to stop trading suddenly started ringing, without *warning*…now, they have all-gone. Paid-off.’

‘The-*incompetent* as well as the-*fixers*…’

‘Which are You?'

'Which, are You?’

‘Both.’

‘Meaning 'We’?’

As long as accepted by a majority-vote heard at that-time…

‘Heard-minority of people? Silenced?’

‘The Capitalist-*Elite!*’

'Socialist-Elite:'

'To Win?'

'Communist-Elite! Never to-Lose!'

'So, simply pay-off Your debt. As the-*majority* does, actuarily, and actually, most The Time, most-places, and Each of Us…'

'All Other…' *saving...*

'Majority of People?' humiliating food and money banks:

'Competition between Corporation(s) and Government(s)' least: Sovereign-President: National Banks and Stock-Exchanges…'

'They have Our Money.'

'And the Richest-Minority of the World that Ever Lived!?'

'Majority-Poorest! Dictatorship of the Poorest?'

'Only the ones to-Vote!'

'But who *does*-vote?'

'In the name of the-<u>People</u>?'

'No-one.'

'Everyone-Data.'

'Everyone in it for themselves, somehow.'

'*M*oney-for-votes?'

'Votes, for money. Lobbyist? Commission?'

'Sale(s): Bonus?'

'Buying-out. Monopol(y)ies.'

'Taking-on?'

‘Journalist(s)…’ *talk...*

‘Media-Talk.’

‘Twitter. On?’

‘Twat.’

‘Our? Own?’

‘Take themselves…’

‘Tete.’

‘To-Jail. Dead.’ and t*hen, as if as an oversight*:

'You? A-Journalist?’

Re-search: threat of death hacking incremental money-supply increasing-prices inflationary-target stable, rises-planned traded economies’ currency-war...

'Buy-weak sell-strong…’

‘No-liquidity, to pay staff or creditors indebted and severed: bankrupted out of business, closed-down. For: The Day.’

‘Moderate growth only…’

‘Not-*greed*…then?’

‘No-more Greed.’

‘Greed is now: the enemy of the good-management of the-economy…’

‘Inflation-target mid-course correction?’

‘It’s all deep-end crowd-funded cost pay-suicide into the deep-end now…’

‘Negative inflation?’

‘Why?’

‘Austerity?’

'Then?'

'For all? Or 'We'?'

Heaven...and... Hell: on-Earth...in the-field...

'Hell-on-*Wheels!*' behind a computer-screen, keeping the train's running: shop-salaries, desk-staff, call-centre too *pay*ing for-themselves: The-Prices upon: *list*...shop-prices: ...

>Online-prices...*shopping basket*:

<n/NNNNNNNN...looking-over:

'You've got to be there, to believe it. Inflammatory: Incendiary...'

'By accident or design?'

'Yes! That is what We like?!'

'Really?!'

'Not *really*? I mean...not out loud anyway...' *murmuring*:

'Buy low, sell-high!' whispering...then not *too*-loudly but so that It did not matter a damn if heard by anyone, and everyone, in the carriage:

'Buy low, sell-high! But not. Yet...'

No-one else in the-carriage, in the cage, was really interested...except when the Tax and *Charity-scandals broke*:

'Now!' *as if assassinating...*

'We are Inflation-proof! 'We' have so-much...

'Most of it is abroad. In distant-parts, distant ports:'

'Foreign-Banks, anyway!'

‘So, *that* is where the-Money is…’

‘Sovereign. That is what the clever money is on!’

‘Really? *No*-in-flation!’

‘No. De(f)lation re-turns-exchanged-rates: leverage.’

‘So, go there?’

‘We do…*virtually*, of course. Present: pre-deal status:’

‘And the-Governments?

‘Ex-chequered? F‘The People?’

‘To breaking-point. Are We *connecting*...there yet?’

‘*Virtually*…’

‘National-Re-serves…’

‘4WarFare?’

‘War is not Fair.’

‘May as well be.'

E-mail address: *touch screen*:

On-screen:

‘Low to Zero in-flation…’

‘Sub-Prime: ‘We’ do not like *de*-flation either.’

‘Fairer?’

‘Especially if it’ is across the-Board. Eh?’

‘The-Bank-credit and currency-exchange rate(s):’

‘Get out of there, then?’

‘Not now,. T*hey* will be visiting Us.’

Relatively *speaking…*

'World-Bank. Trade-Prices: N/n. Prices go-up…'

'(WTO) World Trading Organisation(s):'

'Compared to wages, salaries…'

'Prices go down?'

'Whenever have you known that to happen? Constant-growth is the only way…'

'Of each of Us.'

'Not all.'

'Natural-wastage then? Surplus to need?'

'Surplus. In-demand. Then…'

'Scarcity? War? When?'

'Now. Buy-low…'

'Buy? What?'

'Bought! Get Out of There! Sell-High. Health and Social Care:'

'The Price of Bread?'

'Same. Like Crop failure.' '

'Circles. Of each of us *connections*…'

'To-Buy you have to have *someone* to Buy-from…and who wants to-Sell?'

'You *have* to have *someone* to *sell*-to…'

'Make(s)-sense.'

'Ah, but 'IT' does not. Makes for-*difference*….'

Therefore: thereafter each-*irregular* with only colliding colluding tilting centrifuge-ellipsoid…on-screen: pointing-downward, and inward-trading producing outwardly a living-simulation:

'With this *intimation of immortality…'* halfway around, pinned-back:

'Bargains…'to be had.'

Deals. Manufacturing and Re-sources: raw materials more and more…

Looking-up, and down again, then, across:

'War unfair$?'

*'Riot*s…' on-screen:

'More like.'

Social-*unrest…*

'They hate riots, out of control both sides. Wars? Played-out. Civil, or Otherwise…'

'For the-*price of bread….*'

'Not Good for Business's. Workers-fired.'

'Injured. Sold-on.'

'Like: Slaves?'

'Serfs.'

'Workers sacked and into the canal.'

'Suicide?'

'Mission?'

'Murder?'

'Accidental-Death.' *cruelly* and bitterly beaten, carried out.

Snagged. *Soldier*ing-on…

>*Crown-servant* serfdom, to make the bread…buy-up the losses cheaply, sold-off slavery worker(s): taxed:

<Paying-for…Police and the-Army: In-Taxes:to…offensive-Weapons: *list*…

>African: Zimbabwe-Gold:

<Silicon-cell: Plutonium-rodded and:

>Nuclear-War!

<Energy? Enriched-Uranium? Really?

>Civil, or Otherwise?

<Weapons sold-on…cross-borders…

>If we can have them, why not They? <

<As long as they don't go to war with their Doctors and Arms-Dealer: sympathique! <

>Firing our own weapons back at us! <

<Or We at-*them*? <

>Then destroyed!

By Water Fire Air?

In War: <

<WHO's *Zooming* who? <

>Selling weapons to both sides

>You got it!

< See?!

>By the Time you can get the knife out…<

<Loaded-the-gun…

>Fired the shot.

<Done.

>Done…<

<Dead. In the water. <

>Globally? <

<Re-sales. For our own Good….of course, and… <

>Oil. All of Us? <

<With God on Our side? <

>Of-course. <

<Ours too! <

>Of-course not. Nothing! The-*Government* can do nothing about…

<Because We< control thing<s… <

>Who is going to let me?

<Who is going to stop you!

>Virtually…

<Scarcity? You know what that means?

>Not-God? <

>Not good! Taxes and Wages-down *relatively* Prices-up…no-one buying<

<Prices never go down, now, do they? <

>Only *relatively…*<

<Or Taxis! (joke!)

<The-People *pay*-tax on what they earn, *legally*. <

><We<…do not pay taxes?

> How? We run at a *paper*-loss:

<Do not like *de-flation* in-flation slowing…'

>We have no choice or competition? Do we? The currency *worthless…*

<Otherwise…compared to any, every other:… <

>Not-all. But to…< screen-loss: no-tax: re-bate:

looking down onto the handheld pad:

<Natural-Re-sources: Mineral and Metal Security. Stability to N/n…*currently…*

>Kick-backs…kicks-off…<

<Only the exchange-rates…the *status-quo…*

>Only the-equality Gap<s *greater…*<

<Or less…<

>Better to be the-*higher*? Eh? <

<You wish for something, do you not? How far? <

>All the way. <

<Otherwise? <

>Alright up there in the clouds! <

No-movement.

>'It' is after all it is only A *Small CC* Club…

<The *real* Security-Council.

>A few Global Merchant-Banks and Corporations…

<Umbrella-Accountants'

>Companies and Contractors:

<Workers paid and unpaid:

>All of Us! Sharing-in: Rational-Equitable: Holding(s):Corporation(s): *list:…*

>De-Nationalising:Privatising: withholding tax-records:

<Until no longer President. Privatised-Zones…*list…*

>Countryside…

eradicated…list…

>Global-Warming…

<HuMan: Protection and Defence: (HMPD):

>Private-Armies?

<Police-Nationalised? Y/N?:

< Re-Nationalise:

>Re-Privatise:

Re-gulating the-*Energy*- utilities…

<To Arms!

>Armour-plated!

>Participatory-Cap. runaway-Capitalism: full-blown!

<Light-touch…glancing look *solid* stare:

>Old-City:…

<New-City.

>New new city *old* City New again!

<Old again.

>Contract's…

<Contacts-in-hand…' hand in fist.

In-hand, a piece of paper:

'Is that in Our-Time?'

'Or Not?'

Then:

>T?…

In-talks…and now Off-screen. On-screen: business-celebrity boast:

<Now!

>Select: T2: *Your-profile:* are probably the only one

(You) that has the-money: in… and *links:* '…to perform the-

Rescue…

<Without *inflation* or *deflation?*

>Immune? Had the jabs? injection of C…

<Limited-only…by-guarantee…

>*One for One*?

<Or have a rescue-*performed on*? Soul for 'sole?

<Arse! <ole!>Or share-holders, stake-holders, and customers…*cancelling*

out…*list…*

>The-others<All. Possibly.

<Potentially…

'Probable more-or-less:…'

'*Spread*-Bet's: *list…*'

The-Banker after something of a break in proceedings game-play pause aware of the *gameplay* going-on, concluded.

The-Clerk nodding towards the opened brief-case laptop-screen. Each glancing across each to the others' game-player loaded and hand-held computer screen. Each shared numbers and letters; with grammar, spelling and punctuation, on a screen resumed…*automatically…*

'Only numbers on a screen…' *desk-jockey, not door-kickers-in. Particle-board partitions, cubicles, answering phones, checking letters, and numbers…deadly computer-virus bugging, gagging, gigging…giggling…*

'Only numbers on a screen…'

Destroying: Nuclear-Centrifuge: from distance, drone calibrated-infection, biological and cyber warfare, tearing apart systems, designed to defend, anti-threat-attacking…viral infection:

'Office of Cyberwarfare…' *taking-down cash-machines, blowing-up for scattered-notes robbery grabbed and run and grabbed.*

Charge-card machines, TV and radio-stations interrupted-service for a few seconds, by the-Revolutionary, or merely mischievous-rogues who would do such a thing, such a Global-threat:

'World-Wide- Web.'

Modern-espionage, commercially-sensitive material: information, sophisticated hacking, privately, personally…

'Nationally, and Internationally. Global 2021!' *launching infiltration-bugs onto networks ill-designed for public-safety or reliability…these-days, deniable, undeniably.*

In the greater-good. Sand-boxing-cache, quarantined. Rendered-harmless. Eradicated. Rather-than lived-with. Response to Material-Threat, to bring down *information*-networks and the very intra-structure of The-Economic-Zone rather than the physical industrial-landscape complex closed-down:

'Lifestyle Solutions.'

'Easy-Life!'

'How about 'It'?'

'Start with the goal of devoting all of myself to my job, of work, my family and friends. Tribe, City, and Country. I did *start* to have my doubts, about the way I was living my life. How about You?'

'Were running yours'…'

'Large-Volume(s):'

'Own owned-Business'?'

'Businesses? Me?'

'Limited Liability Company.'

'I manage IT or IT manages me?'

'CEO. VC. C.C. President. You are your Own-Business, anyway…'

''We' all are. Import-Export?'

'Export-Import? I don't Own-Myself!'

'You may do…take Your Chance?'

'Ours? 50/50?'

<Outlook-Analysis: *betting hotline: complimentary-copy:*

Image re-cycled: A4/80g/m2 500 on the tube: Special-offer just for you: try our new…order-online@…

'I told you, we do not-*lose*. Value maintained. Not gone-down…'

'Not gone-up?'

'Yet. A *waiting*-game: in-Reality:'

'Through negotiation?'

'Or what? Eh? Re-negotiation? Re-scheduling the debt?'

'Yes? In-currency:…'

'What? 1, 2, or, 3…or…'

'Trillion??? The-People?'

'Government(s)?'

'Armies.'

'Agree to fight?'

'Generally?'

'Or Lose It All. Everything.'

'Not-*nothing*, then.'

sarcastically, to who, or from whom, both:

'Our-*debt* is as-*nothing*. F'oldin' in money-terms:'

'Everything.'

'But make(s) *Something*?

'Else? Karma?'

'Good?'

<Energy-p Power: unit-list: *list*….

As when battery re-wired supplied:

'If you like…'

'Goods: Stocks?'

'Service(s)?'

'Shares, then?'

'OK. So, we do not really lose anything at all?'

'All-Profits *shared…*'

'Or anything, at all? Losses…'

'Not if We can help that! Sold on…*lies*.'

'Not the truth?'

'Not the whole truth? There are lies…'

'…and *Damned* lies!'

'I know. We tell them. Alright? Got it? But it has to sound like it is true.'

'Even if it is not true?'

'False-even.'

'It is True. You *get* Me? You provide the evidence, the Truth? You tell the story…and they get it, you got me?' *digital and* terrorist *base-camps, moved-around...and...* *internal*-treachery, *government…taxes…*

'Others can help-you, eh?' *closing…*

The-Clerk looking-across and around the over-*crowded* carriage:

'Why me?'

'Take-Off! *Sum!* Betting, on Future-sale price certaint(y)ies…*that* is all it is!'

'Where? Director of You.'

'Me? Direction of Travel?'

'CEO-Presidente!'

'How far have 'We' got? Are 'We' given? What do I get? For starters?'

'Risk-averse?'

'Sure.'

'Family, then. It really is Win-win…'

'Sure…simply-betting…' *without a hint of irony…*

'Or butting-out.'

'Odds?'

'ON?'

''Risk-*averse*?'

Then It became obvious, again: walk thru' wallpaper knowing *another* is in the room:

'Others actually take-the-Hit! The-*risk*! that is 'It'! Not *Our*-risk…'

'Exactly.'

'Exactly! Like Fuck it Is. The-S*ame*!' *cursing as if on oath. Casually-cursing loudly and yet to no-one's apparent alarm or awareness…*

'So. I get all the *toxic* ones, eh? That is 'It', isn't it? Why would you be asking otherwise? Top-slice or Dice-and-Splice? Slice! You! Having your cake and eating it!' Others in the carriage, as if choking on cake. Only a series of in-explicable aphorisms and further increasingly confusing-apostrophe and mixed-metaphor un-mixed:

'Credit in Crisis…'

'Crisis in Credit.'

'On false-figures!'

'Falsified. O.K.?'

'O.K. So, what is the truth?'

'Large-Number(s)? Count me in! Deal me in! I like IT! Your-hand!'

'My-hand?'

'Your-hand…' bowing, ceremoniously:

'Is yours…'

'Knew You would…'

Sitting back, grinning, *calmly,* now:

'The-Markets will come through!'

'Will they?' the-Clerk, and the-Banker re-referencing the opening-gambits, and re-opening for-both and incompletely, and in-response and moving-on with:

'So, what do you *make* of it now?'

'What is to do, now, then? Business as Usual?'

The-Clerk nodding demonstratively earnestly between the folded-up newspaper and lap-top, table-top screen: the-Banker opened-up now. As if the answer lay there, somewhere, somehow between themselves, or elsewhere, out the window. Perhaps. Looking out of the window of the moving-train as if there was actually, never mind actuarially, any one answer at all:

'Not: One-answer, anyway…'

'Perhaps too-many…'

'Perhaps none.'

'No-*issues*?'

'No answers, except *that* which would *happen* anyway. Dependent. On *where* you *were who* with and Who engaged in a conversation-*with*…'

'You! Riding the Train…' *driven by the need for speed...around the-Earth, around the-Sun:*

'Incredible! At root, simple. The Rich *very* Powerful very-*few*…' point-ful:

'Pointless..un-necessary pernicious the ever impoverished and ever-more comfortable middle towards the outskirts, and Country-Richest-list:…'

'The sub-*Urban*: poor…' another-Town *passed through* and past:

'Others truly-impoverished, starving, and taking a kicking, a malevolent-*kicking*…'

'Slicing *the*-Cake?'

'What-cake? How about You, now, eh? What's *not* to *make* of it now, eh?!' tampering, *tapping* the cell-phone-computer-case open and vividly re-started *automatically* in utter-(i)gnorance and dis-missal:

'That is what I was *thinking*…'

Energy-draining *privilege*-prison. Basic-Income + Leisure-Time.

Un-paid-domestic duties and un-healing work-harder ethic.

With nothing more or less to say, or to hear. With a look, with an apparent effrontery, each, that meant there was to be no further contact either way, that there would be no further purpose, to this.

Each now turned away with-*feigned* annoyance. Distinctly, if slightly less distinguished and so the-Clerk supposed, expecting of no-further-conversation, not giving opportunity any longer of answering, or questioning-back.

Only pointing-out the distrustful plotting conspiratorial *horse*-trading, prancing dancing-around…virtual insults…to the intelligence. Whatever. Of the-Arcane Mysteries: s*ecret* or not at all.

Hidden and not-so hidden *one-per cent Society…one per-cent.*

Ten per-cent? So, what?! Ninety-per-cent. that it was assumed shrewdly, astutely, even eloquently spoken-of.

As each concluded this apparent-interview…that this was meaningless, insincere, and over:

'I only ask once.'

'Only-0nce?

'OK I'll tell You how it is shall I? How it's going to be…' without affirmation and without waiting for one.

Without even knowing if really with any *malice* aforethought The Clerks' *now* thought unspoken: *this is bribery and corruption embezzlement and fraud admitted-to*:

'Day*light* robbery! Open-mined theft! From The Land!' *with violence in anyone else's book*:

'Insider Trading spread-bet's on-speculation and risk.'…*to keep thy mouth shut. Keep your job and shut-up or you're out! or you'll never work in the City again! Or anywhere else!*' the Clerk finished the-*internal* dialogue externally:

'...and 'Me'? To take -the-jump when it all goes wrong again?! Eh?! Extend the terms? Go on! Of Office or of the-Debt?'

'Both. You know? I get to be my own remuneration board? Without reference to any share-holders, or even you, as the CEO-President? Because I am the-President!'

'Re-Gal: Presidential-*motives!*'

'Exactly! Get the News! In Business as in Government as CEO-President, and as President? Of: My-Own National-Bank? You?'

'Your-Own: Personal-Banker.'

The-Banker retreated, slightly, with the silent, final entreaty to-self, and with eyes looked only now as if repeating some unspoken thought; but not saying or speaking anymore for anyone-else: fore-finger tapping, drumming, wistfully, *blissfully* unaware...wildly, almost silently to the temple, at the side of the head, as if holding a gun there *as not the best way to shoot someone else...but if a suicide then spraying brains all over the place probably as effective as any other...does not look as if chancing it, and about to be blowing brains-out* the-Clerk mused. Short-tempered perhaps red hot-headed explosive, not yet ripping eye-balls out.

Dark to light *green* volatile gas...financial performance *accelerator* voltage *envy* of a friend another responsibility: *narrow*-data: from the Morning-Star...*but which-One?* A bank could have a narrow-mandate re-stricted: to deposits of actual money: mere Cash-LTD.-Machine. Perhaps not-playing Russian-Roulette...re-entering the *fray*:

'Big-Data.' *streaming data analyzed by standard statistical and computational methods...hand-coded from paper originals arriving too fast to process readily, chaotic*

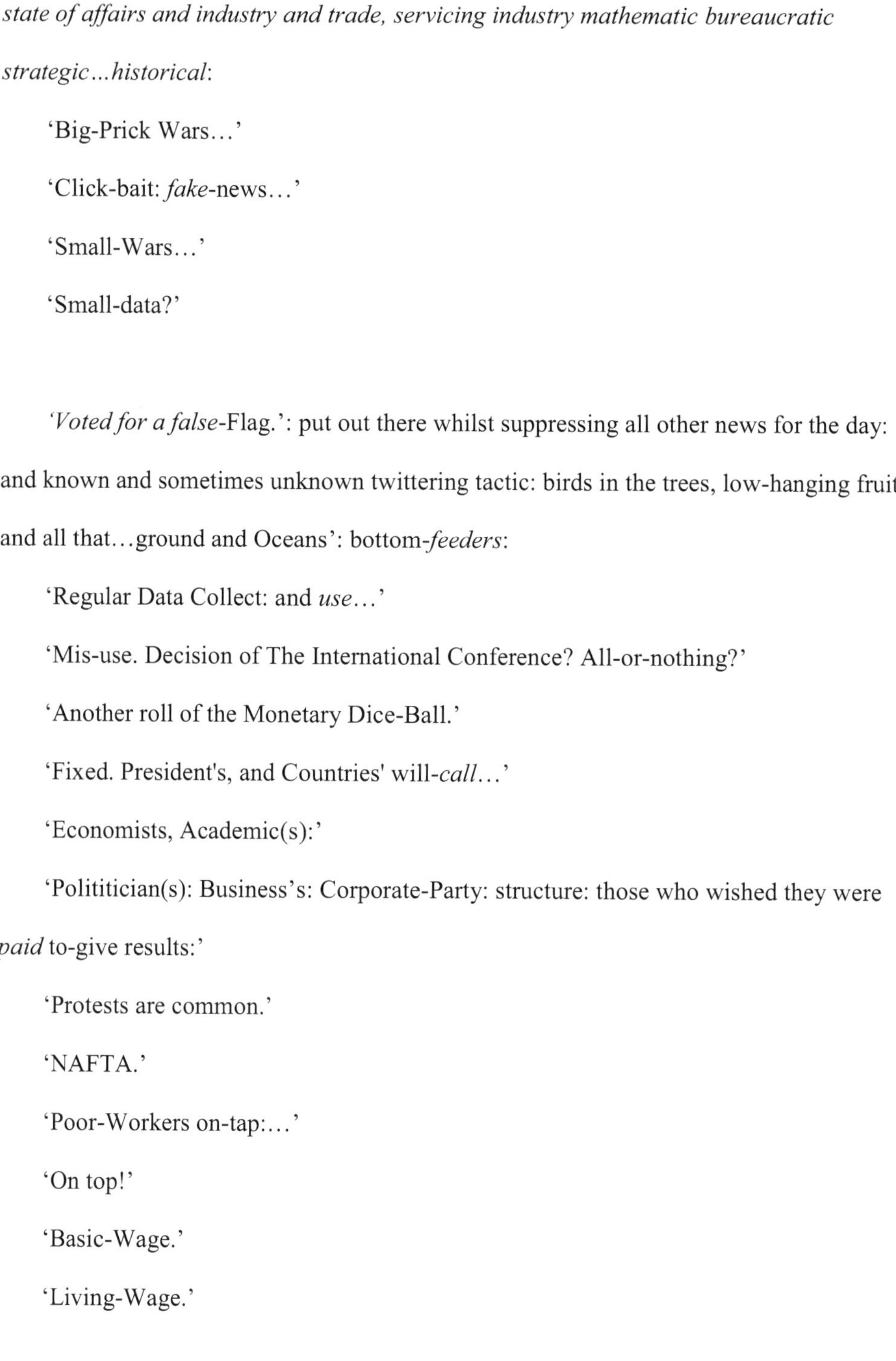

state of affairs and industry and trade, servicing industry mathematic bureaucratic strategic…historical:

'Big-Prick Wars…'

'Click-bait: *fake*-news…'

'Small-Wars…'

'Small-data?'

'Voted for a false-Flag.': put out there whilst suppressing all other news for the day: and known and sometimes unknown twittering tactic: birds in the trees, low-hanging fruit and all that…ground and Oceans': bottom-*feeders*:

'Regular Data Collect: and *use*…'

'Mis-use. Decision of The International Conference? All-or-nothing?'

'Another roll of the Monetary Dice-Ball.'

'Fixed. President's, and Countries' will-*call*…'

'Economists, Academic(s):'

'Politititician(s): Business's: Corporate-Party: structure: those who wished they were *paid* to-give results:'

'Protests are common.'

'NAFTA.'

'Poor-Workers on-tap:…'

'On top!'

'Basic-Wage.'

'Living-Wage.'

'Living-Cost(s):…'

'Wo-Men's voices…

'Not-negative…'

'Health reports…'

'Pharma!'

'Equity!'

'We are no longer political merely *economic*…

'Animals…'

'Then. Animals…'

'Isolated and be-sieged.'

'Dominant Currency Para-digm.'

'Beings.'

'All-Equal.'

#A roll of a drum gradually *ex-citing* ex€cuting.

Out loud…

The-Clerk to The-Banker:

'So, where are these-*lost* Trillion's then? Or is that 'Squillion's' now, then, eh?'

'Not in the Government(s)-Bonded? Not Our Coffers that's for sure! What spent…on?'

'Ohhh Hospitals, Schools, Roads and Railways: some-Airline(s): Houses' Family-Homes-building(s):…'

'Prisons?'

'Oh?'

‘For-You? Never. Industrial Investment Banking: (IIB) New factories and drilling-rig mine-shaft pipework aerial to the sky!’

‘The-whole-Planet! Jobs-creation…’

‘Shorter-Hours Schemes (SHSs).’

‘And beyond?’

‘Lame!’

‘And Fuck the rest!'

'Actually?'

'Actuarially…there is not much left.’

'That is worth much more, wait and see…’

‘*Thin-Gruel.*’

‘Squirreled-away in: Tax-Free Havens:’

'Minimal…5% The Fed paying interest to private-Banks, itself, a Bank. The largest six in the Globe. Globally Invested in Government Bonds.’

‘Overseas! Humanitarian-Aid?’

'Abroad…yes…’

‘Cayman-Club islands?’

‘Ire-Land?’

‘Zoo-Rich? Get it?’

‘Ge-ne-va? Get it?’

‘Exactly…*actually*.’

‘Actuarially.’

‘State-Nationalist(s): Rape-Bribery and Klepto-Cratic Ruler(s):’

'Sex-ploitation: People-Trafficking Modern-Slavery (PTMS) rife all over:'

'Prostitution!'

No-vote: counting re-fusers not…

'Furious-pro-test!' @ Naturally. *the obvious, yet unexpected out in the open counter-intervention…*

'Wrong-Justice!'

'Lawsuit.'

'Libel.'

Partisan-Thug(s) blockading goods and voters and burning polling station(s):

Locked into autocratic genocidal self-rule:

'Big-bonus announcements in the City…waiting-for you, anyway…and Tax-breaks for…'

'Epic Fail!'

Headlined:

Epic-Fail! newspaper and screened across the carriage:

'Failed.'

'Granted…'

'Universal-Credit: All-in-One Benefit(s): Global: Public-Private Partnership. Then again…' *as though another shooting*…pulling the trigger.

The-Banker, directly between the eyes, through the Head. A spray of blood and bones, and brains-*splatter*ed…

A Murder. A Murder-scene. A Murderer? Assassin?

Emissary?

Undercover secret-agent, mole…*moleing…*

Staring, blankly, blindly but not in fear, but with consternation, felt, and leaned to the other-side *in-case the others' silent bullet figuratively actually did hit, what appeared now, with actually the final retort, to be the intended target*:

'Aimed! Fired!'

'Dodged!'

'Dodge-City…eh?' in slow motion…out of the way. The-Clerks' *duelist* finger-*pointed now hitting the opposite target from below and straight upper-cut fisted and as a smack-on-the-jaw:*

'Warning?'

The other coming-around and straight-between-the-eyes:

'Worming our way…' *into-the-brain, the nose-bone clean, clear hit through the silver-bullet black print a spray of bloodied ruby red stained...*

The-Banker: *quivered* slightly behind the-newspaper or rather, above, and beyond: The-Screen and *not going to say anything* as The-Clerk realised-*this* and as once intended-to, closed with:

'Well, this is it…'

'What?'

'I am in-it! Up to Here!!'with a hand passed over the scalp:

'With your *so-called* scalping-advice!'

The-Banker could not help but retreat then to peer out from behind the newly-drawn newspaper withdrawn behind:

'For: Social-Wealth and Premiere 1st Class Railway-Carriage! Value-added! For You! Nevermind. Private-*Reasons…'* alone: to-be prepared always, religious song and military beats if-nothing else.

Digitally marching abroad for the prevention of *unprepared-for attack*-paranoia at Home: for that which could *actually* happen, and not only be, over-exaggeration:

'Not Public, then? Exaggerated-Lies! Simple-Truth: of the moment, thrown into dis-array…' value(s): always over as under over-*estimating*:

'Over-estimating…'

'Over: Con-fidence:'

'Under-estimating under confidence…Pay-Day?'

'Bridging-loan: worthwhile: (*I*)n-*Best*ment.' *an underground-tunnel entered into wi-fi: Auto-Pilot* piloting *surfacing…alongside motorway and in green-fields…*

*

Great-houses…farms, and (I)ndustrial, Parkland and:

'Play?'

'Pay!'

'At the very least…'

The-Banker said:

'With the Arrow of Extrication…'

'Extinction Re-bell(ion)?'

The-Clerk:

'You don't Get it? Do You?'

Silence.

'The-Game?'

More silence, then:

'Toxic-lending buying and selling-on a dupe! And that is Me! Isn't 'It!'! This is how I will know what IT is and this is what I will make of IT!'

More-silence, and other *noise*:

'I am that Dupe, aren't I? Or to-be so?!' the one hand, and now other-hand now *cutting-upwards slicing the across the throat, cut swiftly*:

'…up to here…' *and then noosed, strangling, dangling, hanging…the neck tie breaking gently-wrung as by the self-same owned hand lifting, twisting, twisted knotted and roped neck and head-jerked sideways-snapped back behind the ears, cracking the Neck: Bone ear-splittingly crackling…hissing…sound bright-light…*

*'Tunnel-of-Love@m*oving forward…'

'In-breeding Oblivion!' the final dramatic riposte from the-Clerk, in the ungainly sully.

The-Other seemingly *oblivious*.

Un-moving, as anyone else on the-Train moving with the train alone in their own-Worlds words woodcut, as on paper, pixels and spoken outloud:

'Today. I am likely to be shredding documents and deleting emails for You, or someone like You!' seen *photographed filmed buried and book-burned filing cabinet snail and e-mail:*

'To hide the evidence!'

'Burn-IT! De-lete!'

'What?'

Walled-in. Squared, and encircling:

'Wondering how to pay off: My Towering-Debts!'

'To WHO?!'

'Big-Pharma!'

'Not: Government…'

'In-sured sued and pensioned off:'

Met, with a wall of *silent pie-eyed thought* buffering…

Then. The-Banker leaned-back and glanced-out of the window, remarking:

'To whom. You are wondering how to pay-off your Towering Inferno until I came along?'

A crash of dinner-plates and breakfast bowls and tea-cups…

'The-Banks! The Shops…The Government! Our Government! Tax admission? My Government!' *the action around the middle-finger*:

'The Bailiff-Police in-hand? Army-Debts? Social Workers?'

'My Government!'

'Our Government! And, Yes! Our Government! *Ours!* IT is *Our*-Country…while we are here. The-Army? Another Army? While 'We' are Here! A Simple-Majority?'

'The-Elite. An even simpler-minority!'

'Counts…'

'Evens, proportional…'

'Quits! While you are tucked away in your Cage. Your Ivory Tower. Or should that be Golden-Walled Palaces? Open-Acres?'

'The-majority a minority, believe-me, you do not stand a chance…the 1%? Remember?'

'Then the 99%:'

'10% and 90-plus years old!'

'Decades long Civil-War!'

'Civil-Peace! Always! Forever!'

'War?'

'Relatively peaceful…'

'Battle. Collateral damage:'

'Welfare-Net…'

'Dot-Dash.Dot. Shorting the Long-Game….'

'And Others?'

'It makes *no*-odds' an *invisible*-hand raised in defiance and defence, *glinting*:

'Another: Golden-Run?'

'Risk?'

'All the-Time!'

'Or No-Risk.'

'Cash-back re-payment Mortgage?'

'And this *award* goes-to…'

'This-Bonus…'

'This Klepto *Stolen*-Reward... *' receiv*er-systemic-*symbiotic*: financial-sector expansion…

'Theft.'

‘History always gives people the opportunity to gain wisdom and the power to walk forwards. Be: up-standing!’ Family-House(s): sell-off, buy-up, everyone a shareholder, home-owning, higher-rent…lower relatively…

‘Real: Wages? Take-Home…’

‘Too Big to fail…’

‘Vested-City.’

and countrywide: outside:

‘Global-Union(s): of:’

‘Trade? Con-solidated-Corporation(s): dis-allowed un-*affordable(s): to do business with: not-Government taxes and sanction(s): numerical and literal:*

Building-Societies and Credit Savings-Bank(s):

Competitive-Investment Principle(s) (CiPs):

Competition between: eaten-up…

Out of Business (OoB)…

Small-business’

‘Billions of them…’

<Ta(x)(y)ing: GiG-Economy. Trillions, Of Us.

>Employed as bought-shares sell-shares at price-rise prize-fall: Dot.com: sell-out, quick-re aping competition in the Market(s): family, children small, and the fall of the Conglomerate Banks-conjoined: Investment=House: with Food and Furniture and houses…’

‘The-Prize goes to 'the-*smart*est One.’

‘Or Two…’

'In the Room.'

Pointing back and forth, both:

'On *this* Train.'

The-Clerk *correcting…*

Only then, the obvious:

'Living our-lived-out lives on *this* A-Train? Stuck on the rails? In *its'* tracks…*e*ventually. For what?'

'The next-stop.'

'Last-stop?'

'The next Shop! The Big-one, isn't it? 'We' spend our lives waiting for…'

'Financier? Shop-Keeper!'

'With limited-liability?'

'Money.'

Partisan-Thug(s) blockading goods and voters and burning polling station(s):

'No-experience of responsibility for a few-Billion?'

'Or Trillion? Fuck-off then, eh? There are Trillions of US! There are families, and individuals…then…'

'Shopping-Mall(s): Only the Military-Church and Secular-Politicians' Police and Armies…'

'Some Political: Re-ligious-crazies…'

'Caliphate.'

'Whoever is presently in-Charge…'

"IT'! Changes…'We' do not! We do 'It'!'

‘You are the President of your own owned Company? Friends and Family. Country-Folk.?’

‘President of Your Own Owned-Family?’

‘Charge(s)? *payable to…*’

‘In. Food and Furniture and Home.’

‘Sold-off if you Do Nothing! Poor House!’

‘If you Do nothing. You create a vacuum.’

‘A vacuum which draws *speculation…*’

‘’(i)nto a Power-*vacuum*. A **Hot**-*kettle* you get me?’

‘Prisoner: Torture or-*Exile…’*

‘What would *that* do?’

‘When push comes to-*shove*…’and a-*glance* out of the window.

The-Banker exulting, now *executing*:

'One Hitler or Stalin or Mao creating many little ones. Police Chiefs, Army Generals. Economic, Political, and Military…’

‘Deserting. *Analysis you* see? Financial-Battle. Takeover: War. You have to be there. You have to *live it*!’

‘‘IT’ happens the way the-Nuclear Computer States and the-Politician-Economist(s) suggest…’

‘Only singularly, authoritarian-Dictators, Mugabe or Assad.’

‘Without-*evidence*: M(i)l(i)tary inter-vention(s): Police-State.’

‘The (I)nformation State:’

‘SMART-Cities?’

‘The-***Future! Made-Up!*** That is the only evidence anyone can have! Data-Speculation-only! Not-reality:’

‘Yet.’

‘Ever!’

‘No-one *knows* what is going to happen tomorrow!’

‘Or *Care(s).*’

‘Spinning-*Fields*…surely?’

‘Exempting. Excepting…’

‘Special-Case?’

‘That it will be much as today…’

‘Business as <u>You</u>-(s)u(a)l?’

Re-iterating. Not allowing of any other response now:

'You have to be there or have it instantaneously live-streaming CCTV closed-circuit television beamed-in satellite *everywhere* at The Same Time:…’

A computer pica-second later…before…

‘Simply: de-*laying*…’

‘Get me? Good-timing? In or Out? Buy-Alive. Sell-Dead?’

The merest delay neon pica-seconds pixels to spare then to follow-up *immediately*:

‘Dead or Alive?’

‘In!’

‘On-the-Dot!’

‘On the dotted-line?’

‘You got ‘It’!’

'No, you got it!'

'All?'

'For All!' *to be sorted-out today...with-you, or without-You.*

'In this-Together?'

'Call-it Debt-Aid Loan-Aid or whatever…' *covering-the-tracks*:

'Back-room deals already going-down. As of the night-before as you might say:

'Going Up!'

'Where?'

'Down-Again!!'

Exploded!!!

*

9. The City State.

People coming into The City and Towns, and even Village-centre(s); gathered, or emptied, travelling-out, and in on MotorBike and Car. Coach and Container-Lorr(y)ies: like a crime scene, they were made out to be:

-Nationalist-Elite Exit: Security: Re-Main: Presidential-Monarchial Famil(y)ie(s): Union: The Demonstrators, and the Security Forces.

Outside, and inside CCTV cameras reached the Boardrooms and Bedrooms' Bathrooms leaking e-mails: toxic enough, high-level: Puts and Calls being put-in drop placed dropped/rose:

-On Present-Index: texting *sexting…un-moving...*

- Account: Credit: Default(s) Commission (ACDC) *(i)nterest*-rate(s): N/n: and Credit Re-bate A-bate(s): *altering*: re-payment:

Analysis-Scenario-1:

News Broadcast:

'We all seem to be holding: Our Collective breath; and await further announcement. People arrived to work to join the meetings and demonstrations that were already gathering in great numbers at workplaces, town-square piazza and villages streets, roads in and out of: City Centre(s):'

'As The Whole World Protests in City and Town-Square…what do you make of it?'

'On-line and in front of your TV Stations:' The President's Face appeared.

It was difficult to tell if at the beginning or end or an almost endless sounding speech, *perhaps on loop:* The President looked drawn, but was:

'Adamant no-changes would be-made'.

After the *previous*-offer re-fused: of limited change had been ignored and *the speech went on and on round and round.*

Reports and interviews, speeches, and the chants of gathering crowds.

The claims of Government-Officials, Politicians and Market Ex-perts at Home and Abroad. Supplanted by de-clarations from people on: The-Ground. From Workplace Meetings and City Centre *Assemblies* and from World-Wide Web (i)(m)-bed:

InterNet and TeleVision NetWorks: ESport: (*i*)n some places there was the sound of Police and Ambulance and Fire sirens and the rumble of tanks and of truncheons beating on protective shields.

On the TV screen. On the rapidly re-booted: snarling-Smart: Cell-Phone: *add-on* screen: the picture *froze* contact-book emptied: Error message 303: *Invalid connection…connection closed…*

'They were...'

'You were…'

'Drunk on 'success'!'

'Whatever *that* is!'

'Not happiness?'

'Or sorrow?'

'Success breeds success'

'Other-*Success* breeds money!'

'Other-Sorrow breeds Money!'

'Money breeds more-money.'

'Money breeds Greed'

'Greed breeds success…' or abject *failure*:

'Not. More success than happiness?'

'Happiness more than success?'

'More equal?'

'Ecology? Whenever is enough not enough, eh?'

'What if 'We' lose?'

'The *process may not be perfect…*'

'But 'It' is still 'adequate' under the *exceptional* circumstances of the day?'

''We' already, eh?'

'We are all inter-dependent...'

'You speak for yourself!'

'I do!'

“'It is like a pyramid, at the top...by: Conquest: Conquistador: Constant-Conquest!’

‘Matador! Kills the helpless Bull!’

‘Tortured and killed, for dinner!’

‘Create wealth...Easy! Capital! What chance does the Bull have?’

‘Or the Bear, baited?

'Every chance.’

‘No chance.’ ‘

‘The Super-Powers (TSPs) remain quiet or loud: *roaring*…

‘Lion(s): Subdued.’

‘Not-*howling*, and baying, for blood?’

‘Finite-Population of Worker-Bee(s):’

‘Only One Dragon-Queen!’

‘And pies! More pies!’

‘Buyers and Sellers.’

‘Presidents and Royalty: born-blood:’

‘'Fealty' to one or the other. Head of this or that...’

‘Only if They can get away with it again!’

‘Everyone thinks’ they can.’

‘The screens and the board will *light*-up again…’

as: they did. Un-*frozen*: the electronics at boiling-point:

'Almost:’ at the Relative Speed of Light! (RSL!)’

‘And the Economic-(i)(n)(t)eraction between People...’

‘Now! that is at the-Speed-of-Light!’

'Quantum (Q)!'

'Sold. And: Quality.' at a rate exceeding human vision...

'Or a human beating *heartbeat* skipped...'

'Zepto. Pepto! Laser!'

'Then it will go Ballistic!'

'As soon as the-Bell goes!'

'Trading...*dusts*' itself down..'

'Again! and starts all over...'

'Again!'

'*Feeling*: The Hunger.'

salivating…

Succouring the already done-deal:

'Done deal.'

Feeding now …to see who is holding on… who is selling…and who is buying-back…and who is biting now?

Fired-up, now, and onto the feet, across the floor for everyone else to *see*.

On the screens and boards all-around surround-sound…*vision-statement*:

'The Whole Global World! (TWGW!)'

The-Banker now awaiting no response from the-Clerk that was *serious* at-least:

'Product to Market?'

'Consumerism:'

'Consumer-led.'

'Consumer bled.'

'Everything that happens <u>must</u> happen...Naturally! Think about it…the naturalistic fallacy…is 'it's' self, a fallacy! All is *unnatural*?'

'As well as natural. This is both happening naturally and *unnaturally…'*

'Con!'

'Cock-TED!'

'By each of our senses...'

'Could be something-else?'

'Not-happening?'

'Apparently? Now…then: happened:

'Cost-Price vs Sale-Price.'

'Sale-Price vs Cost-Price?'

'Yet? You see? Human-made!'

'uNNATURAL!'

'Teflon. Everything, including our thoughts and ideas and what we see…'

'Rational-Actor?

'Irrational!'

'So? *Purely* un-real.'

'Until seen.'

'Then 'It' is too late. Perfectly. Impossible! Nothing is so-Pure!'

'Nothing? <Mis-buying. Or return to Common-Sense: State-Nationalist-*values:*at Cafe and bar at Railway-station and Airport, in Motor-Cars and Helicopter; Fast-Foot and one of the Fleet, unchecked, and on foot; and on the ground, people counselling each-

other or ignoring, remaining ignorant removed from ignorance, by more ignorance; intended, apart from law, or restriction, or now, for a brief-moment in time: One-Day.

Without any fiscal-law to take for granted or seriously against *each of Us: representing a felt tenet and point-of-personal-morals and ethics argued from-opinion or of a point of view of a particular-incident event or granular pixelating happening(s):*

Consuming-all consummate:

#Public-No! (I)(n)terest-in-repayment of compensation: for every stage of that:

<Mis-selling: on-*Commission*…tied-in for Life.

Once bought and sold and signed-up:

>*Direct*-Debit or Credit-Payment Sub-scription?' *managed...*

'Managed-Funds?'

'Actions?'

'Bad-Behavior?' forced-feeding extreme-diet:

'Minority!'

'Significant-Minorit(y)ies: Elite-Majority:'

'In: significant-individual.'

'Voting: Decision-making machines…'

'After the Event realized!'

'Ethnic-Zones at the Border(s).'

'Safety?'

'Always a good bet?!'

'What? Risk? By who?'

‘Natural Disasters?’

‘Like Today?’

‘Or a: Deliberate Act of Sabotage?’

‘After the Event: with the-Debt:’

‘Terror-Threat:’

‘Scare-Tactics!’’

‘Handmade. Hu-Man Made.’

‘Like: Global-Warming: diseased dry Desert-Wasteland and granite glaciers melt flooding the Oceans and Continents:’

‘The Global Economy. Commend: Climate-Change: Command&Control: Hu-Man-made:Climate-Change in the ex-tremes:’

‘Species of The Devil!’ *debauched…*

‘How is to destroy to create?'

'When: to create is to destroy.’

‘Or be un-created.’

‘From Nothing? Impossible! Irrational…’

‘In-the-event rationalized.’

‘‘They were wrong before...as to say:’’

‘They were wrong before.’

‘What? That ‘‘It’ can only be natural’?'

'They were All-wrong. Admitted it.’

‘Who? Under: Economic:-Tort(u)re?’

‘Stock: supply-withheld prices held superficially high. Stock re-leased onto the Market. Oil for example: Prices rise from Cost Price to: General-Store(s): Price rises again: price falls from cost price directly to General-Store: once ubiquitous Department Stores and online:

‘Those that said 'It' was only excepting those under Others’ control:’

‘*Natural* Money-Catastrophe!’

‘People-*catastophe:* Not: *funny.*’

‘That's what I mean...anyhow, possible:’

‘(A)ny mean(s).’

‘Un-seen? The-Rich: give *nothing* to the poor.’

‘Charity-works too, you know?’

‘Charity? ‘We’ Love-Charity! Great-Publicity: for when ‘It’ all goes wrong…again. What about: paying: Social-Government Benefit-Taxes?’

‘Here? Peoples’ Taxis? We do that. Benefit(s) Everyone, says they do.’

‘As little as possible?’

‘Evasion, or Avoidance?’

‘What about all that Tax-Charity?’

‘What 0%? Charity?’

‘In-valid?’

‘Starts at home...’ as a kind of: *Heroic*-Martyrdom.

Next: WarFair4: Into the Abyss also by M.Stow.

Play fight position head down lowered restraint trust/risk around causing hurt or injury in any way. Finally, a running chase takes place, with spoken, and unspoken rules of capture and submission imploring while laughing all the time. We are the only top global predator species, un-pre-dated by any other. Enabled to develop a larger brain with more neural connection and larger brain-body ratio difference, gorilla, as elephants the only contenders for brain power, over muscle weight and bite.

It seems obvious somehow that our bodies are full of biotic and non-biotic electronic atomic and molecular exchanges constantly between organs and skeleton and brain. Breathing oxygen carbon nitrogen and water nutrient diet are key to the circulation and exchange for health and also, happiness in play/work in the exo-genesis and sharing of our DNA…

48829611R00216

Printed in Poland
by Amazon Fulfillment
Poland Sp. z o.o., Wrocław